Portage Lake

The University of Minnesota Press gratefully acknowledges assistance provided for the publication of this volume by the John K. and Elsie Lampert Fesler Fund

Portage Lake

Memories *of an* Ojibwe Childhood

MAUDE KEGG

EDITED AND
TRANSCRIBED BY
JOHN D. NICHOLS

 University of Minnesota Press • Minneapolis

First published in the United States 1993
by the University of Minnesota Press
111 Third Avenue South, Suite #290
Minneapolis, Minnesota 55401-2520
Printed on acid-free paper

First published in Canada 1991
by The University of Alberta Press
Athabasca Hall
Edmonton, Alberta
Canada T6G 2E8

Fourth printing, 2010

Library of Congress Cataloging-in-Publication Data

Kegg, Maude, 1904-
        Portage Lake: memories of an Ojibwe childhood / Maude Kegg;
edited and transcribed by John D. Nichols.
            p.   cm.
        English and Ojibwa.
        Originally published: Edmonton, Alberta: University of Alberta
Press, c1991.
        Includes bibliographical references.
        ISBN 978-0-8166-2415-7 (pb)
        1. Kegg, Maude, 1904- . 2. Ojibwa Indians—Biography. 3. Ojibwa
Indians—Social life and customs. 4. Portage Lake (Minn.)—Social life
and customs. 5. Ojibwa language—Texts. 6. Ojibwa language—
Glossaries, vocabularies, etc. I. Nichols, John (John D.) II. Title.
[E99.C6K445 1993]
977.6'86—dc20   93-14353

The University of Minnesota is an
equal-opportunity educator and employer.

CONTENTS

Introduction   ix

Editor's Notes   xv

ZIIGWANG / SPRING   1

Gii-ikwezensiwiyaan / When I Was a Little Girl   2/3
Iskigamiziganing / At the Sugar Camp   12/13
Ombigamizigewin / Sugaring Off   16/17
Naseyaawangwaan / The Sugaring Trough   20/21
Ingii'igoshim / I Fast   22/23
Ishkode-jiimaan / The Steamboat   26/27
Iskigamiziganaatigoon / The Sap Boiling
   Poles   30/31
Gii-paagijigewaad Animikiig / When the Lightning
   Struck   32/33

NIIBING / SUMMER   37

Gichigamiiwashkoon / Bulrushes   38/39
Jiimaan / Canoe   40/41
Gii-mawinzoyaang / When We Went Berry-
   Picking   42/43
Mikinaakoonsag / The Little Snapping Turtles   48/49
Bemezhising / What Leaves a Trail   52/53
Wese'an / Tornado   54/55
Gii-o-bapashkobijigeyaang I'iw Gitigaan / When We
   Went and Weeded a Garden   58/59
Egwanigaazod Odaabaan / Covered Wagon   62/63
Miskwaadesiwag / Mud Turtles   68/69
Minisiiwikwe / Lady of the Island   74/75

DAGWAAGING / FALL   79

Imbagida'waamin / We Set a Net   80/81
Naazhwashkak Baashkizigan Gii-madwezigeyaan /When
    I Shot Off the Double-Barrelled Gun   84/85
Mikinaakwag / Snapping Turtles   88/89
Indinigaaz, Indinigaaz Manidoominensag / I'm Poor,
    I'm Poor in Beads   92/93
Awiiya Imbiminizha'og / Something Chases Me (Ver-
    sion 1)   96/97
Awiiya Imbiminizha'og / Something Chases Me (Ver-
    sion 2)   102/103
"Ingitigaan" / "My Garden"   112/113
Gichi-jaagigaabaw   116/117
Manoominikeng / Ricing   122/123
Bootaaganikewin / Making a *Bootaagan*   128/129
Gichi-ingodobaneninj / A Big Handful   132/133
Biindaakwaan / Snuff   134/135
Memegwesiwag / The *Memegwesiwag*   140/141
Gii-nagishkawag A'aw Mooniyaawikwe / When I Met
    the *Mooniyaa*-Lady   142/143

BIBOONG / WINTER   147

Makwasaagimensag / The Little Bear-Paw Snow-
    shoes   148/149
Gego Onadinaakegon A'aw Goon / Don't Make Snow-
    men   150/151
Aazhawakiwenzhiinh   152/153
Gegoo Gii-madwesing Zaaga'iganiing / What Goes
    Clink in the Lake   156/157
Waawaashkeshiwayaan / A Deerhide   160/161
Gii-ningizowaad Miskwaadesiwag / When the Mud
    Turtles Thawed Out   164/165
Giiwenigewin / Return Mourning   168/169
Gii-maajaa'ind A'aw Makwa / The Bear's
    Funeral   172/173
Zhemaagiwebiniganag / The Snake Game
    Dice   176/177

Textual Notes 181

Glossary 187

USING THE GLOSSARY 187

FORWARD LIST OF ENDINGS 201

INVERSE LIST OF ENDINGS 209

MAIN GLOSSARY 217

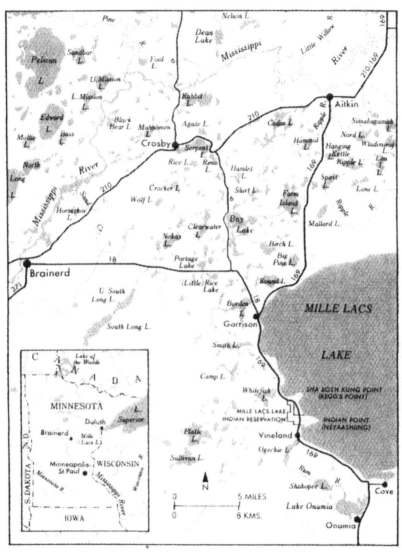

Map prepared by the Cartographic Section, Department of Geography,
University of Alberta.

INTRODUCTION

As MAUDE KEGG GUIDES visitors from around the world into the "Four Seasons" room of the Minnesota Historical Society's Mille Lacs Indian Museum, they step back into the past of the Woodland Indians. Surrounded by reconstructed bark and cattail mat lodges stuffed with birch bark baskets, woven yarn bags, and painted drums, she brings the static diorama to life for the visitors by telling them stories of her childhood of nearly ninety years ago. In this bilingual book some of her stories are presented of growing up at Portage Lake, to which the Anishinaabeg, the Ojibwe or Chippewa Indians, gave the name Gabekanaansing 'At the End of the Trail', and at Mille Lacs Lake, Misi-zaaga'igan, in central Minnesota.

While no written record of her stories can fully capture their charm, even on paper she becomes again through them the naughty little girl stealing the maple sugar trough to paddle around in or wandering off alone in her new bear-paw snowshoes. She becomes again the good little girl attending to the boiling sap with a fir bough in her hand to prevent it from boiling over or practicing sugar making by boiling off the leavings in the kettle-washing liquid.

In her recollections of childhood and of what her elders told her, we encounter many survivals from the rich traditional life of the Anishinaabeg: the ritual begging she is sent to do when she needs beads; the serious conduct of the women's gambling game with the snake-shaped game pieces; the honors accorded in the funeral of a slain bear; and the strict supervision by tribal officers of the gathering of wild rice, the dominant staple food supply of the past.

The Ojibwe language, Anishinaabemowin, is carried on in these stories as well, for they appear here in that language as they were told by Maude Kegg. While not in high formal style, the stories reveal the artful structure of everyday Ojibwe narrative and the internal patterns of Ojibwe words, wrapping up into their complex forms a people's unique analysis of the world. The Anishinaabeg—from Quebec to Saskatchewan, from urban communities in Chicago, Detroit, and Minneapolis to the Hudson Bay lowlands—are struggling to retain and promote their language. Authentic documents of the language such as these stories may be vital to the preservation of the living language.

Mrs. Kegg became my Ojibwe language teacher in 1970 when I started studying the language as spoken at Mille Lacs as part of my doctoral studies in linguistics. The stories here are selected from those she told me from 1971 to 1986. Twenty-five of them were published in 1978 in *Gabekanaansing / At the End of the Trail*. Sixteen stories appear here for the first time, along with the full glossary and revised transcriptions and translations of those previously published. We hope that this enlarged collection will be of interest to all students of the Ojibwe language and culture, especially speakers of Anishinaabemowin.

THE ANISHINAABEG OF MILLE LACS

The Anishinaabeg arrived at Mille Lacs sometime before the middle of the eighteenth century as part of a westward movement from the Great Lakes, replacing the Dakota, called Bwaanag. The people of Mille Lacs still tell about driving out the Bwaanag from earthen lodges. The land the Anishinaabeg entered was rich in resources. The mixed pine, basswood, oak, and maple forest provided them with wood for fuel and bark for building material and twine; a rich variety of native plants gave food and medicine; and the fish and game provided meat, hide, and other products for clothing as well as for other useful and ceremonial objects.

The history of the relations between the Anishinaabeg of Mille Lacs and the Europeans is a disturbing one, well told in Roger and Priscilla Buffalohead's *Against the Tide of American History: The Story of the Mille Lacs Anishinabe* (1985). The Mille Lacs band and the other neighboring Mississippi bands, despite their peaceful relations with the United States government, were forced again and again to cede land, and ultimately to be removed to a new reservation in northwestern Minnesota in a less hospitable environment. Although provision was made in various treaties for the people of Mille Lacs to remain on the reservation set aside for them at Mille Lacs Lake by treaty in 1855, the demands of land speculators, immigrant farmers, and lumbermen led to the attempted removal of the Mille Lacs band to the White Earth reservation in the late nineteenth century. Most of the band members relocated, but some families, as one agent wrote, "stubbornly and tenaciously" clung to their land and refused to move. Their homes were taken or burned, their homesites occupied by new settlers, and the trees stripped off the land, changing the environment forever. By 1911, only 284 Indians remained around Mille Lacs. Some, such as the family of Maude Kegg's mother, lived on scattered sites, while others collected together in small villages. As Maude records here in her memoirs, the Nonremoval Mille Lacs Band of Chippewa, as they became known, lived without much interference by government agents or missionaries, finding their own ways of accomodating their way of life and economy to the altered land and their new neighbors. They lived in cabins and shacks as well as seasonal bark wigwams; they drove horses and wagons as well as paddled birch bark canoes. They continued to make maple sugar, pick berries, harvest wild rice, fish, and hunt, but now sold some of their products to others to get cash for the European foods such as flour that had entered their diet and for other trade goods such as cloth which replaced their own manufactures. They continued to make objects of natural materials, but now sold some, often changed in form, as souvenirs to tourists. Others found wage labor, at first on farms and in lumber camps, later in resorts and commercial fishing. The Mille Lacs Anishinaabeg, essentially outlaws in their own land, made the accomodations necessary to survive, but still maintained a rich religious and community social life reinforcing their identity as Anishinaabeg, in which outlying families such as Maude Kegg's participated.

In 1926, allotments were granted to many at Mille Lacs and the process of recognition of their continued residence began. In 1934 and 1939 they were recognized as a reservation and government under the new Minnesota Chippewa Tribe established by the Indian Reorganization Act. In recent years, under a revised tribal government structure, the Mille Lacs Band of Ojibwe, sometimes referring to themselves as the Non-removable Band, has been regaining self-government.

MAUDE KEGG AND THE PINE FAMILY

Naawakamigookwe, Maude Kegg, was born in a wigwam at her family's wild rice camp at Manoominaganzhikaansing (Little Rice Lake) near Zezabegamaag (Bay Lake) in Crow Wing County, Minnesota in August of 1904, according to family tradition, although official records record a date in 1903. Her mother Agwadaashiins, Nancy Pine, died when Mrs. Kegg was young and her father Gwayoonh, Charlie Mitchell, remarried and lived at Gwiiwizensiwi-ziibi (Boy River) on the Leech Lake Reservation to the north. The *nimaamaa* 'my mother' of one of these stories is her step-mother Ogizhiijiwanookwe, Annie Mitchell. She was raised, however, by her maternal grandmother, Aakogwan, Margaret Pine, the *nookomis* 'my grandmother' and *mindimooyenh* 'old lady' of these stories. Maude's grandfather, Zhing-waak 'Pine' or Zhingwaakwakiwenzhiinh 'Old Man Pine', John Pine, died when she was young.

The Pines lived at Portage Lake, a few miles northwest of Misi-Zaaga'iganiing (Mille Lacs Lake), a major Minnesota Ojibwe settlement ninety miles north of Minneapolis. With them lived two young women, Mary and Sarah Pine, addressed by Maude Kegg as *ninoshenyag* 'my maternal aunts'. Nearby lived Misko-giizhig or Gichi-misko-giizhig, George Pine, the *inzhishenh* 'my maternal uncle' of these stories, with his wife Dookisin and their little daughter. Maude's grandmother's brother Aazhawakiwenzhiinh, known as "Chinaman," also stayed at Portage Lake.

Although the Pine family lived in a house in the winter and kept some farm animals, they otherwise followed much of the traditional seasonal cycle of the Minnesota Anishinaabeg. In the spring they moved to the sugar bush, Iskigamiziganing at Mille Lacs, for maple sugar-making and fishing. They returned home to plant a garden and then went berry-picking at Gichi-ziibiing, the Mississippi River. After returning again to the garden, they set up a wild rice camp at a nearby lake in the late summer. At various times of the year, they went to Mille Lacs for Midewiwin (Grand Medicine Lodge) ceremonies and for other community events. In their travels, they walked, rode horseback, drove a team and wagon, and paddled a birch bark canoe.

Mrs. Kegg learned English from her aunts and from white neighbors and so was bilingual from an early age. Today she likes to tell people that she did not really learn Ojibwe well until she went to live on the reservation after leaving the Pine household. It was, however, the only language her grandmother used with her. She attended the Esdon school where she finished the eighth grade.

In 1920, she married Martin Kegg of Mille Lacs. They lived near Gabekanaansing until 1942 when they moved with their children to a log house at Iskigamiziganing on Shah-bush-kung Point (Kegg's Point) on Mille Lacs. In the late 1960s they moved to a new house just inland from this point. Martin Kegg died in 1968; in that year, Mrs. Kegg went to work as a guide at the Trading Post and Museum, now part of the Minnesota Historical Society. Here many visitors have come to know her as an interpreter of the history and culture of her people, the Anishinaabeg.

Interviews with her have been published in *Circle of Life: Cultural Continuity in Ojibwe Crafts* (Garte 1984) and *Against the Tide of American History: The Story of the Mille Lacs Lake Anishinabe* (Buffalohead and Buffalohead 1985). Her skill as an artist in traditional Ojibwe crafts has been recognized by the inclusion of her work in several major exhibitions including *Circle of Life* at the Depot St. Louis County Heritage and Arts Center in Duluth and *Lost and Found Directions: Native American Art 1965–1985*, a travelling exhibition. In 1990 she received a National Heritage Fellowship from the National Endowment for the Arts in recognition of her achievements as a folk artist and her role as a cultural interpreter.

PUBLICATIONS OF MAUDE KEGG

Buffalohead, Roger, and Priscilla Buffalohead. *Against the Tide of American History: The Story of the Mille Lacs Anishinabe.* Cass Lake, Minnesota: Minnesota Chippewa Tribe, 1985. (Photograph of Maude Kegg, p. 23; photographs of Martin Kegg, pp. 33, 93; and reminiscences by Maude Kegg, pp. 136–39.)

Coe, Ralph T. *Lost and Found Traditions: Native American Art 1965–1985.* Seattle: University of Washington Press in association with The American Federation of Arts, 1986. (Photograph of Maude Kegg, p. 28; photographs and discussion of Maude Kegg's work pp. 90–91, 96, 119; one of the color postcards sold at the exhibition featured the bandolier bag by Maude Kegg illustrated on p. 119).

Garte, Edna. *Circle of Life: Cultural Continuity in Ojibwe Crafts.* Duluth: St. Louis County Historical Museum, Chisholm Museum, and Duluth Art Institute, 1984. (A belt by Maude Kegg is illustrated on p. 73; the dolls illustrated on p. 48 attributed to Maude Kegg are not by her; quotations from interviews with Maude Kegg on pp. 8–11.)

Izatt, Margaret A. "A Gift from Nookomis". In *A Gift from Nookomis and Other Stories,* pp. 10–13. Story Circle Three. A Let's Read Book. Toronto: Fitzhenry and Whiteside, 1988. (This includes an extract from a text of Maude Kegg, with illustrations.)

Kegg, Maude. *Gii-ikwezensiwiyaan / When I Was a Little Girl.* John D. Nichols, ed. Onamia, Minnesota, 1976. (Privately printed collection of seven of the Ojibwe texts included in the present book.)

———. *Gabekanaansing / At the End of the Trail: Memories of Chippewa Childhood in Minnesota With Texts in Ojibwe and English.* John D. Nichols, ed. Occasional Publications in Anthropology, Linguistic Series 4, Museum of Anthropology, University of Northern Colorado, 1978. Greeley, Colorado. (Contains 25 of the Ojibwe texts included in the present book and a short glossary of cultural terms used in the texts.)

———. "The Little Turtle". In *Signs of Spring,* pp. 84–88. A Let's Read Book. Toronto: Fitzhenry and Whitside, 1988. (Adaptation of a text for children, with photograph of Maude Kegg and illustration.)

———. *Nookomis Gaa-inaajimotawid / What My Grandmother Told Me.* John D. Nichols, ed. Second, revised edition. Special issue of *Oshkaabewis Native Journal* 1:2. Bemidji, Minnesota: American Indian Studies, Bemidji State University, 1990. (Contains 33 Ojibwe historical texts and stories told by Maude Kegg and a full glossary of words and prefixes occurring in the texts.)

Miller, Caroline et al. *Mille Lacs County.* Princeton, Minnesota: Mille Lacs County Historical Society, 1989. (This county history contains a biography of Maude Kegg, pp. 145–46, and photos of her on pp. 76 and 146.)

Nichols, John D. Ojibwe Morphology. Ph.D. Thesis, Department of Linguistics, Harvard University, 1980. (Language data analyzed here supplied by Maude Kegg.)

Nichols, John D., and Earl Nyholm, eds. *Ojibwewi-ikidowinan: An Ojibwe Word Resource Book.* Occasional Publications in Minnesota Anthropology 11. St. Paul: Minnesota Archaeological Society, 1979. (Maude Kegg was a major word contributor to this student dictionary.)

EDITOR'S NOTES

RECORDING AND TRANSCRIBING THE STORIES

THE STORIES WERE TOLD to me in Ojibwe by Mrs. Kegg and recorded on tape. We usually recorded four or five stories at a time. Mrs. Kegg usually chose the stories, although we often discussed which ones might be good for recording. Some stories were prompted by something that had recently happened or by my asking about a feature of Ojibwe traditional life.

After a group of stories were recorded, we listened to them and Mrs. Kegg dictated the Ojibwe text to me phrase by phrase as I wrote it down. Between visits to Mille Lacs, I checked my transcriptions against the tape recordings and marked difficult passages to check with Mrs. Kegg by phone or on my next visit. In most cases these problems involved missing particles, changes in word order, false starts, repetitions, and the transcription of unfamiliar words. Ultimately we came to an agreement about the form of the text. Mrs. Kegg occasionally made word substitutions during the redictation or checking and usually eliminated false starts. The substituted words have been incorporated into the final text, but the material originally recorded is given in the notes following the texts. A few texts were dictated and were not recorded.

TRANSLATION

After the rough transcription was made, we listened to each recorded story again and Mrs. Kegg dictated an English translation. Sometimes this was recorded on a second tape recorder. Occasionally a free English version of the story was recorded before or after the Ojibwe version. For the dictated texts which were not recorded, Mrs. Kegg gave me a translation as I read them back to her. I then took whatever translations I had and analyzed the text, returning to Mrs. Kegg for checks on new vocabulary or grammatical constructions. I worked on the translations for English style and parallelism with the Ojibwe text. The result is quite a compromise as I wanted to be fairly literal in the translation without being too awkward in English. As there are many points of Ojibwe structure and style difficult for the nonspeaker to understand fully and still more difficult, once grasped, to express in the translation, there are no doubt passages where the meaning has been misinterpreted. Preservation of the Ojibwe texts makes future improvement of the translation possible.

SENTENCES, PARAGRAPHS, AND PUNCTUATION

The division into sentences and paragraphs in the Ojibwe texts is quite tentative as I do not yet understand well the structure of Ojibwe narrative. Punctuation and capitalization conventions are mostly English ones. I use periods to mark off sentencelike grammatical units. Where such units are run together phonologically I often use a semicolon. Clauses of naming and doubt are often set off by dashes. I use question marks and exclamation marks although neither is really needed in writing in Ojibwe since the grammatical marking is clear. Within sentences, commas mark off major phonological units (not just breathing pauses) or grammatical ones.

PRESENTATION

The Ojibwe transcription is given on the left-hand page and the parallel English on the facing page. The paragraphs are individually numbered and aligned for easy comparison of the Ojibwe transcription to the English translation. The titles in most cases were made up during the translation process and are simply convenient references. The texts are grouped into four sections by season, but this is not to be taken as a traditional Ojibwe classification. When a story has been recorded twice, both versions are given. Comments on substitutions and other editorial notes are given in the notes after the text section.

WRITING SYSTEM

The writing system used in the Ojibwe transcription is a practical orthography based on one devised by C.E. Fiero. A brief description follows, but for more details and examples, see J. Nichols and E. Nyholm, editors, *Ojibwewi-Ikidowinan: An Ojibwe Word Resource Book*, pages 250–53.

Basic Vowel Sounds

LONG VOWELS		SHORT VOWELS	
ii	oo	i	o
e	aa		a

The long vowels which are paired with short vowels are written as double vowels and are alphabetized after the paired short ones. The vowel *e* is also long but has no paired short vowel.

Nasalized Vowels

Nasalized vowels can appear in front of the sibilants *s*, *z*, and *zh*, in front of ' and *y*, and word-finally. Before the sibilants, ', and *y*, an *n* indicates the nasalization of the preceding vowel. At the end of a word, *nh* indicates nasalization of the preceding vowel. A hook or line under a vowel indicated nasalization in some earlier versions of this orthography.

Consonants

The consonants and other sounds are written:

STOPS				
weak:	b	d	j	g
strong:	p	t	ch	k

SIBILANTS		
weak:	z	zh
strong:	s	sh

NASALS	
m	n

GLIDES			
w		y	h
			' (glottal stop)

The weak consonants, which are usually voiced between vowels and after nasal consonants, are paired with strong consonants, which are always unvoiced. The strong consonants do not begin words other than some enclitics and exclamations. The apostrophe stands for a glottal stop.

Consonant Clusters

NASAL-STOP CLUSTERS			
mb	nd	nj	ng
	nz	nzh	
	ns		

SIBILANT-STOP CLUSTERS		
		sk
shp	sht	shk

In addition to these, a single consonant (except *y*) or cluster may be followed by *w* except at the end of a word. For *ns, nz,* and *nzh* see Nasalized Vowels.

Other Symbols

The hyphen is used to separate a prefix (except a personal prefix) or the initial member of a compound word from what follows. It is also used at the end of an abstract stem and at the beginning of a dependent stem. A trailing equal sign is used to indicate a word fragment is being quoted.

SPELLING CONVENTIONS

We generally replace the normal rapid speech forms with careful speech forms. This reflects traditional Indian and missionary writing practice. The following note most of the places where the written form deviates markedly from the spoken or where our writing practice has changed from previously published texts.

1. The first person prefix is now written as heard; forms previously written as *nin*, *nind*, and *nim* are here written as *in*, *ind*, and *im*. These could also be written without the initial vowel. Particles and prefixes previously written with initial *nin* are now written as heard without the initial *n*: *ingoding*, *ingoji*, *ingodwaak*, *ingodwaaswi*, *ingodwaaching*, *ingodoninj*, *ingodwewaan*, *ingo-*, etc.

2. Word-initial *g* plus short vowel before *k* or *ch* is written on noun and verb stems even though what is normally heard is the *k* or *ch* (or a velar fricative followed by *k* or *ch*). The initial syllable reappears when a personal prefix is added. Examples: *gichi-mookomaan* (heard as *chimookomaan*); *gikendam* (heard as *kendam*). Compare prefixed forms showing presence of underlying /gi-/: *ingichi-mookomaan, ingikendaan*.

   A few particles that in other dialects may begin with *g* are here written without it, as the *g* is not recoverable: *akina, akeyaa*.

3. The following are given in full form as dictated:

baanimaa	for *baamaa*
maagizhaa	for *maazhaa*
gaye	for *ge*
azhigwa	for *zhigwa, zhigo*

4. The reduced form of *dash* 'but, and' is written as *-sh* added to a word, except for the combination *miish*.

5. Other than in *miish,* the predicative particle *mii* is written as a separate word, although in normal rapid speech it often merges with a following particle or preverb. Note especially:

   mii iidog for *miidog*
   mii eta   for *meta*
   mii ezhi- for *mezhi-*

6. Full rather than reduced forms of the demonstratives are used. For example, the animate singular demonstrative written *a'aw* may be heard as *a'aw, 'aw, aw, a'a, 'a,* or *a.*

7. Initial short vowels of prefixes and stems are written after prefixes ending in long vowels even when lost in normal rapid speech. For example, *niwii-ani-maajaa* is written for what may be heard as *niwii-ni-maajaa.*

8. Compounds are a troubled area and no consistent practice has been observed here. Generally where a vowel is replaced by ' at a compound boundary, the glottal stop and a hyphen are written: *wiij'-anokiim.*

9. I remain uncertain of the length of the middle vowel of *awiiya.* I have some difficulty in determining the length of *i* in certain locatives (such as *neyaashiing, neyaashing; ayi'iing, ayi'ing*). The prefixes *ani-, ini-* seem to be the same, but have perhaps been inconsistently recorded.

10. The strengthening of weak consonants after the tense prefixes *gii-* (changed form *gaa-*) and *wii-* (changed form *waa-*) is written. How to interpret this and the extent of its distribution in other Ojibwe dialects remain unclear.

ZIIGWANG

SPRING

Gii-ikwezensiwiyaan

[1]   Mewinzha gii-ikwezensiwiyaan, gaa-nibonid iniw onaabeman a'aw nookomis. Miish eta go inzhishenh gaa-ayaad miinawaa wiiwan, miinawaa niizh ikwewag iko imaa gii-ayaawag, oshkiniigikweg. Mii eta go gaa-tashiyaang imaa, miinawaa bezhig a'aw ninoshenh. Mii eta go gaa-tashiyaang.

[2]   Mii azhigwa ini-ziigwaninig, ini-ziigwaninig, "Oo, yay," ikido, "mii waabang ji-maajaayaang," ikido. Waa, niminwendam, niminwendam. Agaawaa go ingikendaan. Niminwendam, niminwendam megwayaak ji-bi-daayaang, megwayaak ji-bi-daayaang. Geyaabi goonikaa.

[3]   "Onapizh ingiw bebezhigooganzhiig," odinaan iniw ikwewan. Aanish, mii go apane gii-wiiji'iweyaan apane ganawaabiyaan aaniin ezhichigeng. Azhigwa wayaabang, azhigwa gigizheb goshkozi, akina gegoo gii-onapidood, waabooyaanan miinawaa ge-bi-miijiyaang, mangaanibaajigan gaye gii-ayaamagad i'iw apii. Akina gaa-izhi-boozitood imaa gii-pi-maajidaabii'iweyaang gigizheb.

[4]   Ingoji go nayaawakweg, mii imaa gii-pagamidaabii'iweyaang imaa neyaashiing, iskigamiziganing izhi-wiindemagad. Mii imaa endagoninig o'o odasanjigoowigamig. Biskitenaaganan imaa niibowa atewan, miinawaa ingiw akikoog anaamayi'ii ingii-ningwa'waanaanig. Gaawiin wiikaa awiiya ogii-pabaamenimaasiin iniw akikoon.

When I Was a Little Girl

[1]   Long ago, when I was a little girl,
my grandmother's husband died. Then there was
only my uncle and his wife, and there were two
women, young women. That's just how many of
us there were, along with one aunt of mine.
That's just how many of us there were.

[2]   Along toward spring, she, my grandmother,
said, "Oh, goodness, we'll leave tomorrow." My, I
was really happy. I barely remember it. I was
really happy that we were coming to live in the
woods. There was still a lot of snow.

[3]   "Harness the horses," she told the women. Well
I always tagged along watching how things were
done. It was at dawn that morning when she got
up and tied everything on: blankets, things to eat,
and even a shovel that time. When she loaded all
of it up, we drove off in the morning.

[4]   About noon we arrived at the point called
Iskigamiziganing 'The Sap Boiling Place'. That's
where her storage lodge was located. There were
lots of sap buckets there and we had buried the
kettles there underneath. Nobody ever bothered
the kettles.

[5]   "Oo, yay, wewiibitaag," ikido. Wiigiwaamaak gaye ganabaj imaa gii-ayaa. Agaawaa go ingikendaan. Mii eta go badakibidood, babaa-mamaashkawapidood wiigiwaamaak. Mii go imaa iniw apakweshkwayan gii-ayaag[1], miinawaa go wiigwaasabakwayan.[2] "Wewiibitaag," ikido. "Mangaanibaadamok," ikido. Mangaanibaajigewaad ingiw ikwewag, gaawiin inini gii-ayaasiin, mangaanibaadamowaad. Mii azhigwa gegaa onaagoshig gichi-boodawewaad gaye ningizod a'aw goon.

[6]   Miish azhigwa onaagoshig, azhigwa, miish i'iw akina gii-atoowaad gii-apakwaadamowaad i'iw wiigiwaam. Miish miinawaa azhigwa gii-wenda-ginzhizhawizid a'aw mindimooyenh, miinawaa azhigwa gaa-izhi-desa'oniked. Mitigoon ogii-aabajitoonan imaa. Miish imaa azhigwa debikak, mii imaa gii-nibaayaang. Nisaabaawe i'iw aki.

[7]   Gegizhebaawagak azhigwa miinawaa, "Mii jibwaa-onjigaag iniw mitigoon," ikido, bawinang iniw obiskitenaaganan, akina gegoo gii-pawinang, miinawaa akikoog, giziibiiginaawaad iniw akikoon. Mii sa go ozhiitaawaad igo. Ingoding igo azhigwa, apane endaso-giizhig igo waabamaad iniw mitigoon. Ingoding igo azhigwa, "Way, yay, wewiib enda-gizhigaawan iniw ininaatigoon," ikido. Mii go gaye giizhaa gaa-izhi-manisewaad ingiw ikwewag. Giishkiboojigan ogii-ayaanaawaa. Neniibowa ogii-okosidoonaawaan iniw misan.

[8]   Gii-michaa-sh[3] i'iw wiigiwaam. Agaamindesiing mii iwidi gii-ayaawaad a'aw inzhishenh iniw wiiwan miinawaa bezhig ikwezens. Gii-agaashiinyi. Baanimaa gaa-ozhigeyaang, gii-pi-dagoshinoog. Gaye wiinawaa gii-pi-bagamidaabii'iwewag, ingiw bebezhigooganzhiig, mashkosiwan imaa gii-piidood ashamaawaad bebezhigooganzhiin.

[5]   "Oh, hurry up!" she said. I think there was a wigwam frame there. I barely remember it. She only had to pull the wigwam frame upright and tie it tight all around. There were cattail mats there and birch bark roofing rolls. "Hurry up," she said. "Shovel it out," she said and the women shovelled—there wasn't any man around, so they shovelled it out. When it was nearly evening, they built a big fire and the snow melted.

[6]   Then it was evening and they put everything in place, covering the wigwam with mats. The old lady really was industrious and made sleeping platforms. She used sticks. When it got dark, we slept there on them. The ground was wet.

[7]   When it was morning again, she said, "The trees aren't running yet," and shook out the sap buckets, shook everything out and washed the kettles. They were getting ready. The time came that she was looking at the trees every day. Then it was time: "Goodness gracious, hurry, the maples are running just fast," she said. The women had cut wood beforehand. They had a saw. They had piled up a whole lot of firewood.

[8]   The wigwam was big. On the other side of the fire were my uncle, his wife, and one little girl. She was small. They arrived sometime after we had done the building. They too drove a team and brought hay to feed the horses.

[9] "Oo, yay," ikido, "azhigwa onjigaawan iniw mitigoon. Babaa-wiijiiwishin, Naawakamigook," indig. "Bi-dakonan iniw biskitenaaganan," ikido. Miish i'iw ezhichiged, mii bezhig iniw mitigoon ezhi-naazikawaad, ezhi-ozhitood i'iw ayi'ii, iniw ayi'iin negwaakwaanan, ezhi-bimoondang iko, gichi-ginwegambizod⁴ ganawaabamag iko, gichi-nisaabaawed, gichi-gagaanwegadinig iniw ogoodaasiwaan gichi-nisaabaawed, ganawaabamag iko babaa-ozhiga'iged, gaye niin ezhi-bimiwidooyaan midaaso-okwapidewan biskitenaaganan.

[10] Mii go ezhi-waabandamaang ji-onjigaasinog mii onjigaag, bigiw imaa ezhi-agokanangid. "Weweni atoon," indig. "Gego ganage ziigwebinangen," ikido. "Mewinzha giiwenh gaawiin ogii-siigwebinanziinaawaa ziinzibaakwadwaaboo. Gego ziigwebinangen," indig, "i'iw ayi'ii ziinzibaakwadwaaboo." Miish azhigwa, gichi-niibowa azhigwa gii-ayaang i'iw ziinzibaakwadwaaboo.⁵

[11] Mii gaye iniw makakosagoon atoobaanan iidog izhi-wiindewan. Azhigwa onaagoshig, mii go azhigwa mooshkinebiig iniw ayi'iin biskitenaaganan, azhigwa naadoobiiwaad ingiw ikwewag imaa ziiginamowaad, ayi'ii bagiwayaanish imaa ziikoobiiginamowaad i'iw ziinzibaakwadwaaboo. Mii azhigwa niswi go mooshkinebiig iniw makakoon waabaninig, ezhi-onakinaawaad. Biindig igaye dash iskigamizigewag, gaawiin agwajiing, iskigamizigewaad, atoowaad.

[12] Miish i'iw enanokiiyaan niin, mii ezhi-niibawiyaan jiigishkode ganawaabandamaan gegoo iwidi ziigigamidesinog, ezhi-dakonag zhingobaandag, ikwewag boodawewaad. Mii go imaa ziigigamideg, mii imaa o-gondaabiiginag zhingobaandag⁶ akikong. Mii eta go enanokiiyaan, mii go gabe-giizhig.

[13] Bezhig azhigwa a'aw akik, mii imaa ani-ziiginamowaad i'iw azhigwa ayaamowaad, giizhigamizigewaad. Bezhig a'aw akik miinawaa dibikak, mii a'aw eshkwegoojing, bezhig iwidi akik eta

[9] "Oh, my," she said, "those trees are running now. Come around with me, Naawakamigook!" she said to me. "Carry those sap buckets!" she said. This is what she did: when she went up to a tree, she carried on her back the taps she had made—she had a long skirt on—I was watching her and she got wet—their skirts were so long then—she got really wet, and as I watched her, she went around tapping trees; as for me, I carried along the bundles of sap buckets, ten to a bundle.

[10] We looked to make sure they wouldn't leak and if they did, we stuck pitch on them. "Place them carefully," she told me. "Don't spill any," she said. "It's said that long ago they never spilled any sap. Don't spill any of that sap," she said to me. She got lots of sap then.

[11] There were barrels there called *atoobaanan*. In the evening, when the sap buckets were full, the women carried the sap and poured it into them, straining the sap through a cloth. In the morning there were three barrels full, so they hung the kettles. They boiled sap inside, not outside; when they boiled sap, they put it there.

[12] What I did was stand by the fire watching things so they didn't boil over, holding a fir bough, while the women stoked the fire. If it boiled over, I dipped the bough in the kettle. That's what I did all day.

[13] There was one pail there where they poured what they had when they finished boiling. By night, that single pail, the one that hung last in the row, just the one pail there, was syrup. There

go, mii i'iw zhiiwaagamizigan. Gabe-dibik ezhi-ishkodewang
imaa miinawaa gigizheb azhigwa ziikoobiiginamowaad i'iw.

[14]   Ogii-kiziibiiginaan-sh iko iniw akikoon. "Giziibiiginik ongo
akikoog," gii-ikido. Miinawaa gimiwang, mii i'iw apii
giziibiiginigaadewan iniw ayi'iin biskitenaaganan, apane gii-
kiziibiiginang.

[15]   Gaawiin ginwenzh ogii-kanawendanziin. Mii go ingo-
ombigamizigan ikidom, eni-izhi-biina'ang makakong, wiigwaasi-
makakong, ombigamizigewaad, eni-izhi-biina'amowaad imaa i'iw
ayi'ii, i'iw ziinzibaakwad.

[16]   Miinawaa adaawewininiwan ogii-adaamigowaan ziiga'iganan.[7]
Miish ko gii-adaawewaad bakwezhiganan, aniibiish, bimide, waa-
miijiwaad. Miinawaa ingiw ikwewag gii-wenda-ginzhizhawiziwag
madaabiiwaad, ezhi-bagida'waawaad daashkikwadininig, mii imaa
iniw asabiin onaabiiginaawaad. Iniw giigoonyan niibowa
onisaawaan. Mii ezhi-abwewaad iniw giigoonyan, gaye wii-
izhi'aawaad igo. Maagizhaa odoonzwaawaan maagizhaa
odabwenaawaan.

[17]   Miish azhigwa, miish azhigwa ishkwaagamizigeyaang, miish
azhigwa aniibiishensan ayaamagak. Ishkwaagamizigeyaang, mii
ezhi-asiginamaang akina gegoo giziibiiginamaang gaye iniw
biskitenaaganan ezhi-dakobidooyaang. Mii ezhi-madaabii-
goziwaad, jiigibiig izhi-goziwag. Imaa akina gegoo gii-
asiginamaang. Miish imaa endaawaad imaa jiigibiig,
wewebanaabiiwaad. Ogii-adaawaagenaawaan iko iniw
giigoonyan. Gii-paatayiinowag giigoonyag. Aabita-zhooniyaans
ingo-dibaabiishkoojigan iko gii-izhi-miinaawag ogaawan. Apane
go wewebanaabiiwaad imaa jiigibiig.

[18]   Mii azhigwa mawinzong, azhigwa mawinzowaad iniw miinan.
Mii[8] ezhi-giiweyaang akawe. Miinawaa go da-o-gitige akawe, o-
gitiged, a'aw mindimooyenh o-gitiged. Gii-michaani ogitigaan.
Gii-michaani iko ogitigaan a'aw mindimooyenh gaa-izhi-gitiged.

was a fire there all night and in the morning they strained it.

[14]   She washed the kettles. "Wash these kettles," she said. And if it rained, then the sap buckets were washed; she was always washing them.

[15]   She didn't keep the syrup long. They say that the results of each sugaring should be put away as you go into the boxes, birch bark boxes, so as they sugared off, they put in the sugar.

[16]   The storekeeper bought sugar cakes from them. They used to buy flour, tea, lard, whatever they wanted to eat. Those ladies worked hard going to the shore and setting a net through a crack in the ice. They got lots of fish. Then they roasted the fish or fixed them in other ways. They might boil them or roast them by the fire.

[17]   Then when we got done boiling sap, there were leaf-buds on the trees. When we got done boiling sap, we gathered everything together, washed the sap buckets, and tied them up. Then they moved camp down to the shore, moved to the lake. We gathered everything up. They lived there by the lake and fished. They used to sell the fish. There were lots of fish. They were given a nickel a pound for walleyes. They were always fishing there by the lake.

[18]   Then in berry-picking time, they picked blueberries. But first we went home. First the old lady went to do the planting. Her garden was big. The garden the old lady planted was big.

[19]   Mii azhigwa jiigayi'ii wii-aabita-niibininig. Miish aanind, miish azhigwa opiniin giizhiginid miinawaa ezhi-maajaayaang, babaa-mawinzoyaang. Mii go ingiw bebezhigooganzhiig gichi-ziibiing iko ingii-izhi-mawinzomin. Bagiwayaanegamig omaajiidoonaawaa. Mii iwidi mawinzoyaang waa-adaawaageyaang iniw miinan. Miish akeyaa bakwezhiganan ezhi-adaawewaad, miinawaa ziinzibaakwad, miinawaa adaawewaad aniibiish, makade-mashkikiwaaboo,[9] ge-wii-miijiwaad igo. Miinawaa ishkwaa-mawinzoyaang, mii ezhi-biidooyaang aanind. Mii ezhi-gibaakobidood nookomis maagizhaa gaye ninoshenh. Mii go akina gegoo ezhi-gibaakobidood.

[20]   Miish akeyaa gaa-izhi-bimaadiziwaad. Akina gegoo ogii-gibaakobidoon. Mawinzoyaan gaye niin. Akina gegoo ingii-ozhitoon.

[19]   Then it was close to the middle of the summer. Some of the potatoes were full-grown and we left to go around picking berries. We used horses and went to pick at the Mississippi. They took along a tent. We went berry-picking in order to sell the blueberries. Then they bought flour, sugar, tea, coffee, and whatever they wanted to eat. And after we got through picking berries, we brought some of them back there. My grandmother, or maybe my aunt, canned them. She canned everything.

[20]   That's how they lived. She canned everything. I picked berries too. I made everything.

Iskigamiziganing

[1]   Miinawaa mewinzha ko iwidi waasa ingii-taamin.
Ingoji go nisimidana daso-diba'igan daa-ikido a'aw gichi-
mookomaan.

[2]   Bebezhigooganzhiin iko ogii-odaabii'aawaan, miish imaa ba-
izhaayaang imaa iskigamiziganing gii-izhi-wiinde. Mii imaa gii-
ayaanig i'iw odiskigamizigewigamig a'aw mindimooyenh. Mii
i'iw gii-ozhitood. Gaawiin igo ingezikwendanziin gaa-izhitood
iskigamizigewigamig. Indigo waakaa'igan izhi-naagwad.

[3]   Miish imaa naawayi'ii ezhi-onakidood i'iw iskigamiziganaak[1]
ezhi-wiindeg. Niiwin eyishkwe-ayi'ii obadakinaanan iniw
mitigoon, obadakinaawaan. Miish ezhi-aazhawaakosidoowaad
imaa i'iw mitig. Miish miinawaa odadaakwaakoga'aanaawaan
wawiinge gaye obishagikodaanaawaan iniw mitigoon. Miish imaa
iniw agoodakikwaanan ayaamagak. Enda-onizhishinoon iniw
agoodakikwaanan.

[4]   Miish[2] ingiw akikoog agoojinowaad. Bezhig a'aw akik niigaan-
agoojin iwidi. Miish imaa ani-ziiginamowaad apane go imaa ini-
zhiiwaagamideg i'iw. Mii ezhi-zhiiwaagamiziganikewaad.

[5]   Miish azhigwa giizhigamideg, mii i'iw ziinzibaakwad,
ziinzibaakwad azhigwa zhiiwaagamideg.

At the Sugar Camp

[1]   And a long time ago we used to live far away. It was about thirty miles as the white man would say.

[2]   They used to drive horses when we came here to Iskigamiziganing 'The Sap Boiling Place', as it was called. That's where the old lady's sap-boiling lodge was. She made it. I don't remember how she made that sap-boiling lodge. It looked like a house.

[3]   In the middle she put up what's called an *iskigamiziganaak* 'sap boiling frame'. She put up four sticks, [two] on each end, they put them up. They laid a stick across [each set of end poles]. Then they chopped some short sticks and carefully peeled them [to go over the cross sticks]. The kettle hangers were [attached to them] there. The kettle hangers were really nice.

[4]   That's where the kettles hung. One kettle hung there at the front. That's where they kept pouring it as it thickened into syrup. That's how they made syrup.

[5]   Then when it was done boiling, the sugar thickened into syrup.

[6]   Gaawiin odagwaashimaasiwaawaan. Gozigwani a'aw akik.
Gozigwan i'iw zhiiwaagamizigan. Miish eyiidawayi'ii ezhi-
minjiminamowaad i'iw mitig, ozhooshkonaanaawaa,
ozhooshkwaakonaanaawaa, ozhooshkwaakonaanaawaan iniw
akikoon. Miish gaawiin jaagizosiin imaa; ingiwedig-sh aanind
endakamidemagak.

[7]   Mii i'iw ayi'ii ziinzibaakwadwaaboo, oziikoobiiginaanaawaa[3]
gaye, ayi'ii bagiwayaanish i'iw odaabajitoonaawaa
ziikoobiiginamowaad i'iw zhiiwaagamizigan. Apane gaa-
izhichigewaad.

[8]   Ginwenzh imaa gii-ayaamagad i'iw iskigamizigewigamig izhi-
wiinde. Gaawiin noongom wiikaa ingoji niwaabandanziin
geyaabi, mii iniw.

[9]   Mii go endaso-ziigwaninig, bi-maajaad, bi-maajaawaad, bi-
maajaayaang, mii eta go datakobidood wiigob ge-aabajitood
miinawaa apakwaadang. Giishpin-sh goon niibowa abid imaa,
omangaanibaadaanaawaa miinawaa. Gaawiin mitakamig
zhingishinziiwag. Mii ezhi-desa'oniked, dibishkoo go nibaagan.
Mii nibiiwakamigaag eni-apiichi-ningideg i'iw ayi'ii, i'iw ayi'ii aki,
imaa biindig. Aanish, mii go apane, mii go gaye niibaa-dibik
ezhi-iskigamizigewaad. Gaawiin agwajiing gii-tazhi-
iskigamizigesiin mewinzha anishinaabe.

[6]   They didn't just take it off the fire. The kettle
was heavy. The syrup was heavy. Holding the
[short peeled] stick on both ends, they slid it, slid
it along on a stick, slid the kettle along on a stick.
It didn't get burnt there then, but the other ones
were left to boil.

[7]   They used a rag to strain the syrup. They were
always doing that.

[8]   That sap-boiling lodge, as it was called, was
there a long time. I never see any of them
anywhere today.

[9]   Every spring when they came over, when she
came over, all she [grandmother] had to do was
tie it up using the inner bark of the basswood and
cover it. If there was a lot of snow there, they
shovelled it out again. They didn't lie down to
sleep on the bare ground. She made a platform
just like a bed. The ground was wet as long as it
kept thawing out there inside. Well, they kept
boiling sap there through the night. Long ago the
Indian didn't boil sap outside.

Ombigamizigewin

[1]   Mewinzha ko gii-iskigamizigeyaang a'aw nookomis. Mii i'iw ombigamiziged, mii imaa niibawiyaan. Mii i'iw neyakokwaanens izhi-wiinde, jekaagaminamaan[1] i'iw.

[2]   Miish azhigwa wii-kiizhideg i'iw[2] ziinzibaakwad, "Mikwam naazh!" Mii[3] ezhi-maajiibatooyaan iwidi agamiing, mikwam okoshing naanag.

[3]   Mii azhigwa wii-kiizhidenig, onisidawinaan ezhi-naagwadinig i'iw ayi'ii ziinzibaakwad wii-kiizhidenig. Ezhi-gwaaba'ang mitigwemikwaan i'iw odaabajitoon. Mii ezhi-gwaaba'ang mii i'iw ayi'ii ziinzibaakwad ombigamiziged. Mii imaa ezhi-ziiginang mikwamiing. Waa, niminwendam, niminwendam gichi-niibowa ozhitooyaan i'iw bigiwizigan, miijiyaan. Mii i'iw apane gaa-izhichiged a'aw nookomis.

[4]   Miish i'iw ezhi-ziiga'iganiked, wiigwaasan-sh iko ogii-aabajitoonan, wiigwaas ezhi-bajiishkinang.[4] Miish i'iw ayaabajitood i'iw ayaad, ziiga'iged iniw ziiga'igaansan zhiishiigwaansag gii-izhinikaazowag[5] iko. Mii iniw ziiga'iganan ziiga'igeng imaa wiigwaasing.

[5]   Miish azhigwa naseyaawangwaaning oziiginaan i'iw azhigwa mashkawi-ayaanig i'iw ayi'ii ombigamizigan, naseyaawangwed, i'iw ziinzibaakwad ozhitood. Niibowa, enda-niibowa ayaamagad imaa ziinzibaakwad.

[6]   Miish i'iw, "Giziibiigin, Naawakamigook, a'aw akik!" indig. "Gego ziigwebinangen! Ganawendan i'iw!" indig. Mii ezhi-giziibiiginag. Gizhaagamideg nibi indaabajitoon giziibiiginag

Sugaring Off

[1]   A long time ago my grandmother and I used to boil maple sap. When she sugared off, I stood there. I dipped in that little carved paddle called the *neyakokwaanens*.

[2]   When the sugar started to get done, "Get the ice!" So I took off running down to the shore where the ice piles up to get some.

[3]   She recognized just what the sugar looked like when it was about to finish cooking. She used a wooden ladle to scoop it out. She scooped it up when it sugared. Then she poured it on the ice. My, I was really happy making that maple sugar taffy and eating it. That's what my grandmother always did.

[4]   She used birch bark then to make sugar molds, forming the bark into cones. That's what she used when she cast sugar cones, which used to be called *zhiishiigwaansag*. Those were the cakes that formed when they poured it into the bark.

[5]   When the boiled sugar hardened, she poured it into the sugaring trough and stirred to granulate it, making it into sugar. There was a lot, a whole lot of maple sugar there.

[6]   And then she said this to me, "Wash the kettle, Naawakamigook! Don't spill it! Take care of it!" she told me. So I washed the treaty kettle using

a'aw okaadakik, ezhi-giziibiiginag. Miish ezhi-ayaayaan eni-izhi-
maawandoonamaan.

[7]   Mii endaso-ombigamiziged, aangodinong gaye niizhing
ombigamiziged, giishpin mino-giizhigadinig, gigizheb
mizhakwadinig. "Onizhishin i'iw ziinzibaakwad," ikido,
mizhakwak ombigamiziged.

[8]   Miish eni-izhi-ganawendamaan akikong, miish i'iw niibowa
ayaamaan i'iw giziibiiginakokwaanaaboo gii-izhi-wiindemagad.
Enda-wiishkobaagamin.

[9]   "Naawakamigook, ombigamizigen gaye giin!"

[10]   Mii iidog gagwejichigeyaan. Mii ezhi-ombigamizamaan i'iw
giziibiiginakokwaanaaboo,⁶ iskigamizamaan gaye niin. Miish o'o
ombigamizamaan, ozhitooyaan gaye niin ziiga'igaansan. Gaawiin
iko gii-makadewaasinoon. Gii-onizhishinoon.

[11]   Apane go ogii-piini'aan iniw akikoon. Mii gaa-izhichigeyaan
gaye niin i'iw.

[12]   Mii sa go i'iw.

hot water. That's what I was up to as she gathered things up.

[7]   She sugared off every time it boiled down, sometimes twice if it was a nice day, if it was clear in the morning. "That sugar is nice," she said when she sugared off in clear weather.

[8]   And then as I tended the kettle, I'd get a lot of kettle-washing liquid, called _giziibiiginakokwaanaaboo_. It was really sweet.

[9]   "Naawakamigook, you sugar off too!"

[10]   I must have tried it. I sugared off the kettle-washing liquid, and I too did the boiling. And then I sugared off and I too made sugar cones. They weren't black. They were nice.

[11]   She was always cleaning the kettle. That's what I did too.

[12]   That's it.

Naseyaawangwaan

[1]   Gii-agaashiinyiyaan iko omaa nookomis gii-pi-iskigamiziged. Mii eta go gii-pezhigoyaan, gii-ikwezensiwiyaan, gii-ikwezhenzhishiwiyaan. Miish iko ayi'ii, nibaawaad ayaangodinong maagizhaa gaye naadoobiiwaad, mii ezhi-gimoodiyaan i'iw ayi'ii naseyaawangwaan. Imaa ayi'iing waanashkaag imaa gii-wenda-nibiikaa mewinzha ezhi-gimoodiyaan naseyaawangwaan. Miish iidog, gaawiin dash iidog ingii-mindidosiin.

[2]   Gaawiin michaasinoon i'iw naseyaawangwaan. Mii ko ezhi-booziyaan imaa babaamishkaayaan imaa ayi'iing waanashkobiiyaag i'iw naseyaawangwaan. Azhigwa madwe-ombigamizigewaad madwe-wanitoowaad iko aandi i'iw, ezhi-gaazoyaan. Ayaangodinong igaye imbapakite'igaaz giishpin mikigaadeg imaa gimoodiyaan naseyaawangwaan, baamishkaayaan imaa megwejiishkiwag.

The Sugaring Trough

[1]   When I was small, my grandmother used to come over here to boil sap. I was the only one when I was a little girl, when I was a naughty little girl. Sometimes while they were sleeping or maybe while they were hauling sap, I'd steal the sugaring trough. Long ago there was a puddle there with lots of water in it, so I stole the sugaring trough. I must not have been very big.

[2]   The trough wasn't very big. I used to get in that trough and paddle it around in the puddle. Then when I heard them boiling sap down and wondering where they had misplaced it, I'd hide. Sometimes I got a licking when it was found out that I'd stolen the sugar trough for paddling around there in the mud puddle.

Ingii'igoshim

[1]   Mewinzha imaa ko gii-pi-dazhi-iskigamizige a'aw nookomis, gichi-mewinzha go. Miish i'iw gezikwendamaan.

[2]   "Gii'igoshimowag ingiw abinoojiinyag ini-ziigwang," ikido. Gigizheb[1] ingoding goshkoziyaan, "Naawakamigook,[2] mamoon akakanzhe," indig. "Zinigwiingwenidizon," gaa-izhi-zinigwiingwenidizoyaan i'iw akakanzhe.

[3]   "Gego ganage daangandangen," ikido. "Gego gaye zhaashaagwandangen mitigoons. Giga-waabamig a'aw giizis booch. Giganawaabamig a'aw giizis," indig.

[4]   Maajaayaan, gaawiin gegoo ingii-miijisiin, gaa-izhi-maajaayaan. Miish igo imaa iskigamiziganing izhi-wiindeg imaa, gaa-izhi-maajaayaan.

[5]   Niwenda-maanendam. Gaawiin niwiisinisiin. Imbakade babaa-ayaayaan imaa, mii ko ezhi-mamooyaan mitigoons. Gomaa go inigokwaa i'iw mitigoons, ayi'ii i'iw aninaatigoons i'iw. Mii ezhi-bookobidooyaan. Wiishkoban dash i'iw. Mii i'iw waa-shaashaagwandamaan, ezhi-aagawewetaayaan imaa ji-ganawaabamisig a'aw giizis, aagawewetaayaan imaa mitigong, gaa-izhi-zegiziyaan. Gaa-izhi-maajaayaan miinawaa imaa-sh neyaashiiwang abi gichi-asin. Gichi-mindido a'aw asin imaa ebid. Anishinaabeg imaa asemaan odizhiwinaawaan apane imaa, iniw asemaan. Amanj iidog i'iw izhichigewaad, biindaakoonaawaad imaa iniw asiniin, iniw asemaan.

I Fast

[1]   Long ago my grandmother used to boil sap here, a very long time ago. This I remember.

[2]   "The children fast along toward spring," she said. When I got up in the morning, she said to me, "Naawakamigook, get some charcoal. Rub it on your face," so I rubbed the charcoal on my face.

[3]   "Don't take a taste of anything," she said. "And don't chew on twigs either. The sun will see you for sure. The sun is watching you," she said to me.

[4]   I didn't have anything to eat as I went along. I left from Iskigamiziganing, as the sugar camp is called.

[5]   I was just feeling sad. I didn't eat. I got hungry hanging around there, so I took a twig. The twig, a maple twig, was kind of big, so I broke it in half. It was sweet. I wanted to chew on it and I got behind a tree so the sun couldn't see me because I was afraid. I set off for the point where the big rock sat. The rock that was there was very big. The Indians always take tobacco there. I don't know why they do but they make an offering of tobacco to that rock.

[6]   Mii dash i'iw nanaamadabiyaan imaa agiji-asin, ganawaabamag
a'aw mikwam. Gegaa go azhigwa niigoshkaa a'aw mikwam.
Nanaamadabiyaan, enda-gizhaate. Ingii-waabamaa imaa,
niwenda-minwaabamaa meziwezid asemaa, ezhi-mamag mii a'aw
meziwezid, bakwemag. Wa, niwenda-minopwaa, mii a'aw
asemaa—wa gichi-zaziikoyaan. Ingoding igo baanimaa go wenji-
giiwashkweyaan, giiwashkweyaan. Niwenda-giikiibingwash,
niwii-shishigagowe gaye, gaa-izhi-gawishimoyaan imaa agiji-asin.

[7]   Mii iidog imaa gaa-izhi-nibaayaan. Ingii-kiiwashkweshkaag
a'aw asemaa. Azhigwa wenaagoshig, eni-onaagoshig, azhigwa
giiweyaan, giiweyaan azhigwa.
[8]   Enda-agaasaani i'iw ayi'ii, ayi'ii wiigwaasing iidog gaa-
ozhitoogwen onaagaans, enda-agaasaani onaagaans, mina'id i'iw
ayi'ii nibi. Eshkwaa-minikweyaan,[3] agwajiing gaa-izhiwidood, gii-
agoodood gii-peshibii'ang akakanzhe aabiding.

[9]   "Niizhogon," ikido, "ji-gii'igoshimowag," gawishimoyaan
miinawaa. Azhigwa miinawaa gegizhebaawagak gweshkoziyaan,
mii gaawiin indashamigosiin.
[10]   Niminwendam, niminwendam-sh igo gaye, booch onzaam
niibowa inanokiim azhigwa ozhiitaang iskigamizigeng. Manisem.
Niin dash indigoo ji-gii'igoshimoyaan.

[11]   Mii gaa-izhi-segiziyaan i'iw mikwendamaan i'iw gii-
shaashaagwandamaan mitigoons, miinawaa asemaa gii-
agwanemag imaa. Niizhogon sa go ingii-kii'igoshim. Azhigwa
eni-dibikak, mii gaa-izhi-ashamid a'aw mindimooyenh,
manoomin miinawaa ayi'ii.
[12]   Akiwenzii ko ingii-ayaawaanaan, ezhi-maadaajimod
dadibaajimotawid, anooji-gegoo aadizookawid. Gaawiin-sh
inganwendanziin ko gaa-ayinaajimod.
[13]   Mii eta go minik miinawaa gekendamaan gaa-izhichigeyaan.

[6]   I was sitting there on top of the rock watching the ice. The ice was just about broken up. It got real hot while I was sitting there. I saw some plug tobacco there and it looked good to me, so I took that plug and bit off a piece. My, that tobacco tasted good to me—oh, I was spitting hard. A little while later I started to get dizzy from it. I was just sleepy and I wanted to puke, so I lay down on the top of the rock.

[7]   I must have gone to sleep there. The tobacco made me dizzy. In the evening, towards evening, I went home.

[8]   She must have made a little cup of birch bark, just a tiny cup, and she gave me a drink of water. When I finished drinking, she took it outside, hung it up, and made a single mark on it with charcoal.

[9]   "It's two days," she said, "that you'll fast," and I lay down again. In the morning when I got up again, she didn't feed me.

[10]   I was kind of glad [that I was fasting] as there certainly was a lot of work to be done in getting ready for boiling sap. There was woodcutting to be done. But I was being told to fast.

[11]   I got scared remembering about how I chewed on the twig and put tobacco in my mouth. I fasted for two days. Then when it got dark, the old lady again fed me wild rice.

[12]   We used to have an old man there and he began telling me stories, telling me all sorts of legends. I don't remember what he told me about.

[13]   That's all I remember of what I did.

Ishkode-jiimaan

[1]   Miinawaa gichi-mewinzha agaawaa go ingezikwendaan. Mii eta go imaa gikendamaan namadabiyaan jiigibiig. Maagizhaa gaye gaa-wewebanaabiiwaagwen, maagizhaa gaye gaa-ishkwaa-iskigamizigewaagwen. Gii-paakibii'an sa wiin igo.

[2]   Namadabiyaan ganawaabandamaan gichi-jiimaan bimibidemagak naawagaam. Dibi-sh iidog gaa-ipidegwen i'iw gichi-jiimaan. Miish ingiw zhingwaakwag[1] ezhi-wawikwapizowaad. Mii imaa niibawiwaad imaa, ganawaabamagwaa ingiw.

[3]   Miish ingoding gaa-izhi-gagwejimag a'aw mindimooyenh, "Gichi-jiimaan ina ko gii-ayaamagad?" ingii-inaa.

[4]   "Enyan'," ikido, "mewinzha giiwenh gii-paatayiinowag zhingwaakwag omaa Misi-zaaga'iganiing. Mii go gaa-izhi-gashki-dibiki-ayaag gaa-apiichi-baatayiinowaad ingiw zhingwaakwag. Ingodozid, ingodozid maagizhaa gaye niizhozid apiichishinoog ingiw zhingwaakwaandagoog,[2] binaakwiiwaad. Aangodinong, gaawiin awiiya gidaa-noondawaasiin bimweweshing, apiichishinowaad ingiw zhingwaakwaandagoog[3], binaakwiiwaad. Miinawaa go aniibiishibagoon gichi-mitigoog igaye. Miish ishkode-jiimaan iko omaa gaa-ayaamagad," gii-ikido.

[5]   Iwidi-sh iidog ayi'ii—amanj ezhinikaadegwen i'iw ziibi imaa Zaagiing wenji-maajitigweyaag—mii giiwenh imaa gaa-ini-ipideg i'iw gichi-jiimaan. Gichi-mewinzha gii-michaa iidog i'iw ziibi.

26

The Steamboat

[1]   Again I barely remember about long ago. All I remember is sitting on the shore. Maybe they were fishing or had just finished boiling sap. The lake was open anyway.

[2]   I was sitting there watching a big boat go across the middle of the lake. I don't know where that boat was going. There were pine trees in bundles. I was watching men standing on them.

[3]   So once I asked the old lady, "Did there used to be a big boat?" I said to her.

[4]   "Yes," she said, "long ago there were lots of pine trees here at Mille Lacs Lake. There were so many pines that it was dark. The fallen pine needles lay a foot or two deep. The fallen pine needles lay so deep that sometimes you couldn't hear anyone coming. There were leaves and big trees. There used to be a steamboat here," she said.

[5]   Over there—I don't know what they call that river there at Vineland where it starts—that's where the big boat went. Long ago that river must have been big.

[6]   Miish iwidi Gibaakwa'iganing odizhi-wiindaanaawaa
anishinaabeg, miish iwidi gii-ayaad a'aw daashkiboojigan. Miish
iko iwidi gaa-izhiwinindwaa ingiw zhingwaakwag gichi-
mewinzha. Dibi-sh gaa-izhaamagadogwen i'iw ishkode-
jiimaanish. Gaawiin ingikendanziin dibi gaa-izhiwijigaadegwen.[4]

[6]   There was a sawmill there at Onamia, which the Indians call Gibaakwa'iganing 'At the Dam'. That's where they used to take those pines long ago. I wonder where that old steamship went to. I don't know where it might have been taken.

Iskigamiziganaatigoon

[1]   Miinawaa mewinzha a'aw iko mindimooyenyiban, akina gegoo ingii-waawiindamaag. Aanind eta go inganwendaanan.

[2]   Miish i'iw gaa-ikidod, "« Mii i'iw ayi'ii iskigamiziganaak, » gii-ikidowag iko, « gaawiin giiwenh awiiya odaa-manisaadanziin i'iw, » gaa-izhi-gina'amaagooyaang iko gete-iskigamiziganaatigoon ji-manisaadamaang."

[3]   "Mii giiwenh awiiya manisaadang mii iniw iskigamiziganaatigoon ezhi-bookogaadeshing. Mii gaa-izhi-gina'amaading mewinzha ji-manisaadanziing iniw gete-iskigamiziganaatigoon.

The Sap Boiling Poles

[1]   And a long time ago my late grandmother used to tell me all sorts of things. I only remember some of them.

[2]   She said, " 'One should not chop the sap boiling frame for firewood,' they used to say, so we were forbidden to chop up the sap boiling poles for firewood.

[3]   "If anyone chopped up the sap boiling poles for firewood, he'd break his leg. There was a prohibition long ago against the chopping up of the old sap boiling poles for firewood."

Gii-paagijigewaad Animikiig

[1]   Miinawaa, mii i'iw omaa akeyaa—amanj iidog ge-
izhinikaadamowaambaanen[1]—omaa neyaashiiwan iwidi
iskigamiziged a'aw mindimooyenh. Gaawiin a'aw inzhishenh gii-
pi-izhaasiin mii i'iw apii. Agaawaa go, agaawaa go
ingezikwendaan iwidi iskigamizigeyaang. Mii eta go niizh
oshkiniigikweg, niizh ingiw oshkiniigikweg, miinawaa gaye niin
miinawaa-sh a'aw mindimooyenh, iskigamizigewaad. Miish ko
mewinzha iniw wiigiwaaman ko gii-kagaanwaawan,
gagaanoondewan. Imaa biindig ko gii-tazhi-iskigamizigewag.
Gaawiin wiikaa agwajiing gii iskigamizigesiiwag. Mii ingiw
wiigwaasabakwayan miinawaa-sh ingiw apakweshkwayag imaa,
imaa michayi'ii.
[2]   Miish azhigwa go ani-ziigwang. Aaniish naa geyaabi ogii-
kiziibiiginaanaawaan iko mii iniw biskitenaaganan—akina gegoo
ayaabajitoowaad owii-kiziibiiginaanaawaan—miinawaa gaa-izhi-
ozhitoowaad waaginogaanens. Miish imaa akina gegoo
biina'amowaad, ishkwaagamizigewaad. Mii miinawaa ziigwang,
mii miinawaa imaa ba-izhaawaad miinawaa nanaa'itoowaad
owiigiwaamiwaa.
[3]   Miish imaa gii-ayaayaang, miish azhigwa wii-asiginamowaad.
Mii azhigwa ji-ishkwaa-iskigamizigeng. Gaawiin gaye ani-
maanaadadinig, ogii-mamoosiinaawaan i'iw
ziinzibaakwadwaaboo, ishkwaagaanig, mii ezhi-ishkwaataawaad.
Miish azhigwa, oo waa, animikiig—gii-wenda-zegwewemagad—

32

When the Lightning Struck

[1] It was up here—I don't know what I should call it—the next point over, where the old lady was boiling sap. My uncle didn't come that time. I barely remember when we were boiling sap over there. There were just the two young women, me, and the old lady boiling sap. It used to be that long ago those wigwams were long, they were long lodges. They used to boil sap there inside. They never boiled sap outside. There were birch bark coverings and, down at the bottom, cattail mats.

[2] It was along towards spring. They were still washing the sap buckets—they would wash everything they used—and then they made a little domed lodge. They put everything in there when they got through boiling sap. And when it was spring again, they came back and fixed up their wigwam.

[3] We were staying there and were then going to gather things up. It was after sap-boiling time. When it starts to go bad, they wouldn't take any sap; they quit at the last run. And then, oh goodness, thunder, it was really rumbling and the thunder was coming. Goodness, the women were

bi-noondaagoziwaad ingiw animikiig. Waa, enda-zegiziwag, enda-zegiziwag, mii ingiw ikwewag, niibowa mitigoon.

[4]   "Oo, yay indaanis," ikido, "daga naa, daga naa izhaadaa imaa waakaa'iganing." Besho imaa waakaa'igan, gichi-mookomaan ko gii-ayaa. "Izhaadaa imaa waakaa'iganing," ikido. Ogii-nagadenimaawaan gichi-mookomaanan imaa gaa-taanijin, gaa-izhi-maajiiba'idiyaang iwidi ezhaayaang. Ayi'ii ko wewebizon imaa gii-agoodemagad gichi-mitigong, wewebizon imaa. Iniw ko oozhishenyan iko wa'aw gichi-mookomaan ba-mawadisigowaagwen. Wewebizon imaa gii-agoode. Mii imaa eni-apatooyaan. Aaniish naa animikiikaag, iwidi biidwewidamoog animikiig. Mii imaa apatooyaan.

[5]   "Naawakamigook gego, wewiib," indaano-igoog. Mii go imaa eni-apatooyan ko akawe ezhi-wawenabibagizoyaan imaa, gichi-wewebizoyaan. Baanimaa go naa gichi-baashkakwa'amowaad ingiw animikiig. Apane go gikendamaambaan. Indigo godotaagaansan madwesinoon. Baanimaa go miinawaa gikendamaan waasechiganing ninamadab indinendam, jiigayi'ii indinendam. Mii eta go, amanj-sh iidog gaa-izhiwebiziwaanen. Mii eta go imaa minik gezikwendamaan, gichi-besho gii-bapakite'igewaad ingiw manidoog, mewinzha, mewinzha mii imaa gii-iskigamizigeyaang. Gaawiin geyaabi ingikendanziin amanj iidog apii gaa-koziwaangen. Amanj isa go gaa-iniginiwaanen.

really scared, really scared because there were lots of trees around.

[4] "Oh, no, my daughter," she said, "come on, come on, let's go to that house." There was a house nearby where a white man was staying. "Let's go to that house," she said. They were friends with the white people living there, so they just started running there. There was a swing hanging there on a big tree. The white man's grandchildren must come and visit them. A swing hung there. That's where I started running to. Well, it was thundering, the sound of the thunder was coming. That's where I was running to.

[5] "Naawakamigook, don't, hurry," they said to me in vain. I was starting to run there and I leapt on and swung hard. All of a sudden there was a clap of thunder. That's the last I remember. It was just like little bells ringing. All of a sudden I came to and thought I was sitting by a window. That's all, I don't know what happened to me. That's all I remember about when the lightning struck long ago where we were boiling sap. I still don't remember when we moved camp. I don't know how big I was.

NIIBING

SUMMER

Gichigamiiwashkoon

[1]   Miinawaa mewinzha gichigamiiwashkoon
mamood zaaga'iganiing, miish iniw. "Ode'imini-giizis," gii-ikido
ko, "jibwaa-aabita-niibing."

[2]   Mii asemaan ezhi-bagidinaad, azhigwa wii-mamood iniw
ayi'iin gichigamiiwashkoon.[1] "Gaawiin giiwenh awiiya odaa-izhi-
mamoosiinan," gii-ikido ko.

[3]   Apane ingii-naanaagadawaabamaa gaa-izhichiged. Miish i'iw
jiimaaning-sh, boozi wiigwaasi-jiimaaning gaye. Mii ezhi-
bakwajibidood, mii iniw gichigamiiwashkoon, ikidowag,
izhinikaadenig.

[4]   Mii azhigwa niibowa ezhi-bakwajibidood, mii ezhi-ayaad ezhi-
agwaasidood, mii ezhi-maawandoopidood. Mii ingoji go
nisimidana, ingoji go odizhi-maawandoopidoonan. Mii ezhi-
giishkizhang iwidi ojiibikaawaninig.

[5]   Mii dash imaa namadabiyaan iko maamiijiyaan mii iniw. Ingii-
kina'amaag-sh[2] wiin. "Gego miijiken niibowa!" ingii-ig. Enda-
minopogwadoon ojiibikaawang iniw gichigamiiwashkoon.

Bulrushes

[1]   Long ago she got bulrushes from the lake. "In June," she used to say, "before the middle of the summer."

[2]   She put the tobacco out when she wanted to get bulrushes. "No one is supposed to take them otherwise," she used to say.

[3]   I always watched what she did with great interest. She got in the canoe, a birch bark canoe. Then she pulled up the *gichigamiiwashkoon*, as they are called.

[4]   She pulled up a lot of them, took what she got to shore, and tied them up. She tied them in bundles of about thirty. Then she cut them off at the roots.

[5]   I used to sit there eating them. But she forbid me to do that. "Don't eat much!" she said to me. Bulrush roots taste real good.

Jiimaan

[1]   Mewinzha agaawaa ingezikwendaan—amanj iidog
gaa-iniginiwaanen—madaabiiyaan. Jiimaan imaa gii-ate. Miish
gaa-izhi-booziyaan. Maagizhaa gaye iwidi ishkwe-ayi'ii gaa-
inaandawewaanen. Gaawiin imaa ingikendanziin minik.

[2]   Imaa inaabiyaan igo, waasa azhigwa ayaamagad i'iw jiimaan,
noondawagwaa ikwewag, niswi maagizhaa gaye niiwin,
nookomis miinawaa go ninoshenh, miinawaa go ninoshenyag
niizh, biijiba'idiwaad, bi-mawiwaad, aanind
biidaadagaaziiba'idiwaad,[1] gaa-izhi-zegiziyaan.

[3]   Ingikendaan wiin igo zegiziyaan. Maagizhaa gaye gaa-
kwaashkwaniwaanen. Baanimaa dash igo miinawaa gikendamaan
iwidi ganawaabamagwaa ingiw giigoonyag, eniwek igo naa anooj[2]
ezhi-naagoziwaad. Agwadaashiinsag ingiw. Aangodinong gaye
enda-besho inganawaabamigoog. Mii eta go imaa minik gaa-
gikendamaan. Maagizhaa gaye gaa-agwaabiiginigoowaanen.

40

Canoe

[1]   I can barely remember long ago—I
don't know how big I was—going down to the
shore. There was a canoe there so I got in it. I
must have climbed down to the far end. I don't
remember much.

[2]   When I took a look, the boat was far out and I
heard some ladies, maybe three or four of them,
my grandmother and my aunt, two of my aunts,
running towards me, crying as they came, some of
them running right into the water, and so I got
scared.

[3]   I remember that I was scared. I must have
jumped. Then I remember looking at fish of all
different colors. They were sunfish. Sometimes
they came real close and looked at me. That's all I
have remembered. I must have been picked up
out of the water.

Gii-mawinzoyaang

[1]   Mewinzha, mii go iwidi Gabekanaansing gii-
taayaang, ani-ziigwang ishkwaa-iskigamiziged. Mii i'iw ezhi-
wewiibitaad, bagidiniged. Anooj igo gegoo bagidinang i'iw
gitigaan ogii-ayaan a'aw mindimooyenh. Mii ba-izhi-maajaad,
ishkwaa-bagidiniged bi-wewebanaabiiyaang imaa Misi-
zaaga'iganiing. Gii-adaamaawag iko giigoonyan. Mii eta go gaa-
izhi-izhichiged a'aw mindimooyenyiban gii-anokiitaazod.

[2]   Wewebanaabiiyaang gabe-giizhig, niwenda-ayekoz iko.
Giigoonyag niibowa indebibinaanaanig. Mii ezhi-biini'aad. Ogii-
kijinagizhiinaan,[1] ishkwaa-biini'aad, mii ezhi-maadoomaad gii-o-
adaawaaged. Giigoonh-kiwenzhiinh gii-inaa ko a'aw gaa-adaawed
iniw, aabita-zhooniyaans ingo-dibaabiishkoojigan iniw ogaawan.

[3]   Ingoji go ingo-anama'e-giizhigad maagizhaa gaye midaasogon
debiseyendang, ani-dagoshinaang iwidi endaayaang.
Indoodaabii'iwemin[2] igaye iwidi Gabekanaansing. Mii azhigwa
zaagiging gitigaan, akina go gegoo azhigwa giizhibagaag iniw
aniibiishan.
[4]   Mii ezhi-wewiibitaayaang ningwaja'iged, ningwaja'waad igaye
opiniin, gichi-gigizheb amadinid jibwaa-mooka'aninig, ji-o-
bashkwashkibidoowag i'iw gitigaan. Mii ko ezhi-mawiyaan.
"Indinigaa'ig," indinendam.

When We Went Berry-Picking

[1]   A long time ago, we lived at Portage Lake in the spring after she [my grandmother] finished boiling sap. She hurried to plant the garden. The old lady planted all kinds of things in that garden she had. When she got through planting, she left for here at Mille Lacs Lake where we went fishing. The fish used to be bought from them. All that old lady did was work for herself.

[2]   I used to get real tired as we fished all day. We caught lots of fish. Then she cleaned them. She took the guts out and when she finished cleaning them, she took them on her back and went and sold them. The one that bought the walleyes, at five cents a pound, was called Giigoonh-kiwenzhiinh 'Old Man Fish'.

[3]   After about a week or ten days, when she thought she had enough, we came back home. We drove a team to Portage Lake. The garden was just coming up then and all the leaves were fully grown.

[4]   She hurried to hoe, to hoe the potatoes, and early in the morning before the sun was up, she woke me to go and weed the garden. I used to cry. "She's mean to me," I thought.

[5]   "Azhigwa mooka'ang jibwaa-gizhaateg wewiib o-ningwaja',"
indig iko, "ingiw opiniig!" Akina gegoo ingii-kitigaadaamin.[3]

[6]   Miish ingiw ikwewag iko gii-ayaawag niizh oshkiniigikweg
miinawaa-sh gaye niin. Miinawaa dash a'aw niiyawen'enh bakaan
gii-taawag. Ikwezensan gaye wiinawaa ogii-ayaawaawaan. "O-
mawinzodaa ambe iwidi Gichi-ziibiing," ikidowag.

[7]   Nashke dash gaawiin indebashkinesiimin imaa odaabaaning.
Gaawiin indebashkinesiimin imaa ditibidaabaaning,
debibinangidwaa niizh ingiw bebezhigooganzhiig, ezhi-
debibinaawaad onapinaawaad. Akina gegoo omaajiidoonaawaan
iniw akikoon, bakwezhiganan, akina sa gegoo waa-aabajitoowaad
wii-wiisiniwaad.

[8]   Mii ezhi-bimishkaad, mii a'aw niiyawen'enh, inzhishenh, mii
ezhi-bimishkaawaad. Miish imaa amanj iidog akeyaa gaa-ini-
ayina'owaagwen, gaa-ini-ayina'ogwen. Jiimaan ogii-aabajitoon.
Zezabegamaag akeyaa gii-ini-izhaawag miinawaa iwidi
Zezabegamaag, mii miinawaa iwidi ingoji gaa-izhi-
gakiiwewidood i'iw jiimaan, miish iwidi Gichi-ziibiing. Miish
iwidi gii-nagishkawangidwaa, iwidi Gichi-ziibiing, ingoji go
iwidi.

[9]   Miish azhigwa ani-onaagoshig bagamidaabii'iweyaang, mii
azhigwa gegaa dibikak. Mii i'iw gabe-giizhig ezhi-
bimidaabii'iweyaang. Mii azhigwa ani-onaagoshig azhigwa ezhi-
ayaayaang, ezhi-onakidooyaang.

[10]   Gaazhagens igaye indayaawaa. Gaawiin niwii-naganaasiin.
Agaashiinyi a'aw gaazhagens, mii ezhi-dakonag. Miish i'iw
onakidoowaad i'iw ayi'ii, jiibaakwewaad. Bagiwayaanegamigoon
ogii-ayaanaawaan. Giizhakidoowaad iniw bagiwayaanegamigoon
ezhi-dakonag a'aw ingaazhagensim. Ingosaa ingoji ji-izhaad.
Anooj gegoo ninoondaan. Gookooko'oog nwaandaagoziwaad
bizindawagwaa, ingosaa gookooko'oo ji-debibinaad.

[11]   Namadabiyaan gaye niin jiigishkode awazoyaan daki-
ayaamagad, awazoyaan dakonag ingaazhagensim. Miish gaa-izhi-
zegizid. Ogii-kotaan i'iw ishkode ganabaj gichi-boodawaadenig

[5]   "Now that the sun is up, you'd better hurry
and go hoe those potatoes before it gets hot," she
told me. We had planted all sorts of things.

[6]   There were two women there as well as me.
My namesake's family lived at a different place.
They too had a little girl. They said, "Let's go
berry-picking at the Mississippi."

[7]   You see, there wasn't enough room in the
wagon for us. There wasn't enough room for us
in the wagon so we caught two of the horses and
they harnessed them when they caught them. We
took everything along, kettles, flour, everything
they wanted to have to eat.

[8]   So my namesake, my uncle, went by canoe,
they went by canoe. I don't know which way they
paddled, which way he paddled. He used a canoe.
They went through Bay Lake and over there
somewhere they portaged the canoe to the
Mississippi. We met them over there at the
Mississippi somewhere.

[9]   It was towards evening and almost night when
we drove up there. It took all day to drive there.
It was toward evening by the time we got there
and set up camp.

[10]   I had a kitten. I wouldn't leave it behind. The
kitten was small so I held it. They set up camp
and cooked. They had tents. As they finished
putting them up, I was holding my kitten. I was
afraid it would go some place. I heard all sorts of
things. Listening to the hooting of the owls, I
was afraid that one would catch it.

[11]   It was cool so I was sitting by the fire getting
warm and holding my kitten. It was scared. It was
afraid of the fire, maybe from seeing the flames. It

ganawaabandang. Gaa-izhi-zegizid, miish gaa-izhi-bishigonag, gaa-izhi-gwaashkwanid imaa ishkodeng, nawadinaawaad gichi-mawiyaan, nawadinaawaad, aatebinaawaad. Gaa-izhi-banzod ingaazhagensim, gaawiin-sh wiin gii-nibosiin.

[12]   Miish i'iw gegizhebaawagak azhigwa ayaawaad, obimoomaawaan igaye akikoon, mawinzowaad. Mii ko ezhi-mawiyaan biminizha'igeyaan indaano-wii-tazhitaa.

[13]   Mii azhigwa ani-onaagoshig, azhigwa niibowa ayaamowaad iniw miinan, mii ezhi-onapijigewaad. Bezhig igo onapijige, miish niinawind ezhi-naganigooyaang. Miish a'aw mindimooyenh miinawaa bezhig a'aw ikwe ezhi-maajaawaad Oshki-oodenaang iwidi izhidaabii'iwewaad o-adaawaagewaad iniw miinan.

[14]   Mii akeyaa gaa-onji-bimaadiziwaad adaawaagewaad iniw miinan, adaawewaad bimide miinawaa bakwezhiganan miinawaa ziinzibaakwad waa-aabajitoowaad igo. Mii eta akeyaa gaa-izhi-bimaadiziwaad mewinzha ingiw anishinaabeg, gii-anokiitaazowaad. Ishkwaa-mawinzoyaang, bi-giiweyaang, mii azhigwa giizhiging gegaa i'iw gitigaan. Akina gego atitemagak, ezhi-mawinzoyaan anooj igo gegoo.

[15]   Mii akeyaa gaa-izhi-bimaadiziyaang mewinzha. Mii sa go i'iw.

got scared and slipped away from me, and when it jumped in the fire, they grabbed it, as I was bawling, and put out the fire on it. My kitten was kind of singed but didn't die.

[12] Early in the morning they got ready and packed pails for berry-picking. I chased after them, crying, wanting to play.

[13] Toward evening, they had a lot of berries, so they harnessed up. One of them harnessed up and then they left us. The old lady and a woman started off for Brainerd, driving there to sell the blueberries.

[14] That's the way they made their living, selling berries and buying lard, flour, sugar, whatever they needed. That's the only way the Indians made their living long ago, always working on their own. After we got through picking berries, we went home and the garden was almost ready then. Everything was ripe, and we picked all sorts of things.

[15] That's the way we used to live long ago. That's it.

Mikinaakoonsag

[1]   Mewinzha Gabekanaansing ingii-taamin. Miish a'aw ninoshenh, bezhig wa'aw ninoshenh, "Adaawewigamigong izhaadaa," ikido. Miish wii-wiiji'iweyaan. Niwii-wiijiiwaa adaawewigamigong izhaad.[1] Ziinzibaakwadoons iko nimiinig a'aw Waandane gii-inaa a'aw adaawewinini.

[2]   Niwenda-ondendam wii-wiiji'iweyaan gaa-pi-izhi-wiijiiwag. Waasa ingii-izhaamin ingoji go naanan maagizhaa gaye ingodwaaswi diba'igan.

[3]   Miish eta go miinawaa imaa gezikwendamaan imaa ini-bimoseyaang miikana, odaabaanikana. Mii eta go eniginid a'aw odaabaan. Inzhaashaaginizide[2] gaye, basikawaanagwaa ingiw asiniinsag imaa[3] ani-bimoseyaan.

[4]   Baanimaa go imaa gaa-bimooded mikinaakoons enda-agaashiinyi. Mii imaa izhi-inaabiyaan indigo naa gaa-wanoodewaad mikinaakoonsag. Mii go bijiinag gii-paashkaawe'owaad.

[5]   "Wewiib,"[4] ikido aabanaabamid, "jibwaa-onaagoshig ji-dagoshinaang iwidi endaayaang."

[6]   "Gaawiin,"[5] indinaa, "niwii-naganaasiig ingiw mikinaakoonsag.[6] Dibi ge-izhaawaagwen."

[7]   Enda-nishkaadizi. "Wiiwegin imaa gigoodaazhishing! Maamigin! Zaaga'iganiing ga-ani-izhaamin," ikido.

[8]   Mii imaa endazhitaayaan maamiginagwaa baabii'id imaa, maamiginagwaa ingoji go nisimidana, niibowa sa go

The Little Snapping Turtles

[1]   Long ago we lived at Portage Lake. One of my aunts said, "Let's go to the store." I wanted to go along. I wanted to go with her to the store. The storekeeper, Waandane he was called, used to give me candy.

[2]   I was determined to go along, so I went with her. We went a long way, maybe five or six miles.

[3]   And then I remember again that we were walking along in the road, the wagon road. It was only as big as a wagon. I was barefoot and kicked the stones as we walked along.

[4]   All of a sudden there was a real small turtle crawling along. When I looked there, there were a lot of turtles crawling around. They had just hatched.

[5]   "Hurry up," she said turning to look at me, "so we get home before evening."

[6]   "No," I told her, "I won't leave these little turtles. I wonder where they are going."

[7]   She was just mad. "Wrap them in your skirt! Pick them up! We'll go by a lake on our way," she said.

[8]   And so I got busy and picked them up while she waited for me, picked up about thirty, a

mikinaakoonsag,[7] imaa ingoodaazhenzhishing ezhi-
wiiweginagwaa, bimoseyaang.

[9]   Gomaapii dash igo azhigwa geget zaaga'igan imaa ayaamagad.
"Mii imaa o-bagidin," ikido, "mii ingiw mikinaakoonsag."[8] Mii
ini-bimoseyaang gaa-izhi-izhaayaang imaa jiigibiig, miish imaa
bebezhig ezhi-bagidinagwaa imaa nibiikaang.

[10]   "Ingosaag ji-gibwanaabaawewaad."

[11]   "Gaawiin," ikido, "mii imaa endazhiikewaad ingiw
mikinaakwag,"[9] ikido. Miish ezhi-bagidinagwaa imaa bebezhig,
ganawaabamagwaa maamaajiikwazhiwewaad. Enda-
wawiyadendaagoziwag.

[12]   Mii eta go imaa minik gezikwendamaan.

whole lot of those turtles, and wrapped them in my little skirt as we walked along.

[9] Sure enough after a while there was a lake. "Go and put those turtles in," she said. As we went by the shore, I released them one-by-one in the water.

[10] "I'm afraid they'll drown."

[11] "No," she said, "that's where snapping turtles live," she said. And so I put them down one-by-one and watched them swim away. They were so cute.

[12] And that's all I remember of that.

Bemezhising

[1]   Iwidi ko gaa-taayaang Gabekanaansing, miish a'aw inzhishenh nandawasimwed iko. Bebezhigooganzhiig ingii-ayaawaanaanig.

[2]   Miish ingoding gaa-izhi-gichi-animikiikaag niibaa-dibik, gegizhebaawagadinig—dibi iidog waa-izhaagwen—gaa-izhi-nandawasimwed, nandawaabamaad bebezhigooganzhiin. Godotaagan iko ogii-ayaanaawaa ingiw bebezhigooganzhiig. Agaaming giiwenh iwidi gii-debwewesinini i'iw godotaagan, gaa-izhi-maajaad iidog naanaad iniw bebezhigooganzhiin, ani-babimosed jiigibiig. Nisogamaawan iniw zaaga'iganiin imaa.

[3]   Miish i'iw, amanj giiwenh inendam bezhig zaaga'igan ani-bimosed jiigibiig, indigo giiwenh gaa-ani-naweshkosininig iniw mashkosiinsan miinawaa go mitigoonsan, gichi-biingeyendang giiwenh aaniin gaa-izhiwebak.

[4]   Miish giiwenh i'iw gaa-izhi-maada'adood. Miish miinawaa imaa gaa-izhi-gakiiwenigwen, awegwenan dinowa, ingoji go enigokwadeyaag i'iw miikana. Mii i'iw enigokwadeyezhisininig. Gaa-izhi-waabandang, gaa-izhi-gikendang wegonen dinowa i'iw imaa bemezhisininig. Wegwaagi giiwenh gichi-mishiikenyan, gaa-izhi-naanaad iniw bebezhigooganzhiin iwidi awas-ayi'ii.

[5]   Mii sa giiwenh ingiw bebezhigooganzhiig gaa-izhi-gotamowaad wii-aazhogewaad imaa wii-aazhooshkaawaad imaa bimikawenid iniw gaa-aazhogenijin. Wiikaa giiwenh ogii-kashki'aan gii-aazhogewinaad iniw bebezhigooganzhiin.

[6]   Miish eta go i'iw gaa-inaajimod.

What Leaves a Trail

[1] When we lived there at Portage Lake, my uncle used to look for the horses. We had horses.

[2] Once there was a great thunderstorm in the night and in the morning—I wondered where he was going—he went looking for the horses. The horses used to have a bell. The bell was heard from across the lake, so he must have gone there to get the horses, walking along the shore. There are three lakes joined together there.

[3] As he walked along the shore of one lake, he wondered about how the grass and the twigs got all broken up; he was really puzzled about what had been going on.

[4] So he followed the trail. Whatever sort of thing it was, it must have crossed there at the portage and was as wide as the trail. That's how wide its track was. When he saw that, he knew what sort of thing it was that left the trail there. You see, it was a huge mud turtle, so he went to fetch the horses further along.

[5] The horses were scared to cross where the trail had been left by the thing that crossed. It took him a long time to lead the horses to cross.

[6] That's all he told about that.

Wese'an

[1]   Mewinzha gaye ingikendaan igo gichi-
giishka'aakwewigamig iko gii-tagon iwidi Misi-zaaga'iganiing
agaaming, amanj igo iwidi apii. Mii iwidi akina gii-anokiiwaad
ingiw anishinaabeg. Eni-gashkanokiijig,[1] mii iwidi o-anokiiwaad
ingiw anishinaabeg. Geyaabi-sh igo ingii-taamin iwidi ayi'iing
Gabekanaansing, niinawind iwidi ingii-taamin, gaa-pi-izhi-
maajaad a'aw inzhishenh. Gii-niimi'idiim imaa neyaashiing.
Maagizhaa gaye gaa-aginzogwen, amanj iidog igo.

[2]   Mii azhigwa eni-onaagoshig, azhigwa enda-zegizi
nookomisiban. Dibi iwidi gaa-onjibaawaagwen ingiw
manidoog, maagizhaa gaye akeyaa wenji-mooka'ang. Gaawiin
giiwenh iwidi akeyaa daa-onjibaasiiwag ingiw manidoog. Waa,
enda-zegizi a'aw nookomisiban. "Naawakamigook, daga iwidi
izhaadaa," indig, "iwidi ayi'ing, imaa i'iw gitigaan ateg." Gichi-
moonikaan imaa gitigaan endanooyaang. "Izhaadaa imaa!" ikido.
"Eniwek igo naa ba-zeginaagwak," ikido. Mii imaa azhigwa gaa-
izhi-biindigeyaang, imaa azhigwa imaa, miinawaa ko ingoji
onzikaamagad i'iw ayi'ii noodin, babagamaanimak, gaa-o-izhi-
biindigeyaang imaa gichi-waanikaaning imaa gii-
nanaamadabiyaang.

[3]   Ingoding igo azhigwa wiikaa go azhigwa aabaakawad.
Diba'igiiziswaan indayaawaanaan. Ingoding azhigwa zaagikweni.

Tornado

[1] I remember that long ago there used to be a great big logging camp on the other side of Mille Lacs Lake, I don't know how far. That's where all the Indians were working. The Indians who were able to went to work there. We were still living over there at Portage Lake, so my uncle came over here from there. They were having a dance up at the point. Maybe he belonged in there as a member, I don't know.

[2] Then toward evening my grandmother got real scared. I don't know where the thunder came from, maybe from the east. The thunder never comes from that way. Goodness, my grandmother was really scared. "Naawakamigook, come on, let's go over there," she said to me, "over there where the garden is." There was a big root cellar there where we kept the vegetables. "Let's go there," she said. "It's looking even more frightning," she said. As we went in there, the wind was coming from every direction, beating down hard, so we went in the dugout and sat down.

[3] After a while, it suddenly calmed down. We had a clock. Then she stuck her head out. "The

"Mii gii-pimaanimak," ikido, gaa-izhi-zaaga'amaang imaa, giiweyaang imaa endaayaang gii-o-nibaayaang, besho go imaa, nibaayaang.

[4]   Miish wayaabang gaa-pi-izhi-dagoshing mii a'aw inzhishenh. Miish bi-dibaajimod, "Eniwek igo naa gaa-gichi-nichiiwak," ikido, "iwidi neyaashiing. Mii go naa gegaa gaa-izhi-bakobiiyaashid a'aw indoodaabaanenzhish," ikido, gaa-izhi-diitibaashininid iniw odoodaabaanan. "Bezhig-sh giiwenh iwidi gii-onjibaa," ogii-wiinaan igo ezhinikaazonid iniw ininiwan. "« Gii-pagamiba'iwewag, » ikido. « Mii go giiwenh akina gaa-izhi-webaashiwaad² ingiw nabagisagoog, » ikido, inaajimo giiwenh a'aw inini, « akina gaa-izhi-webaashiwaad ingiw nabagisagoog. Miinawaa go amanj igo daswi iniw waakaa'iganan gaa-piigwaasinogwen. » Miish giiwenh a'aw inini dibaabandang aaniin apii, aaniin ezhiwebadinig gaa-izhi-zaagikwenid imaa obagiwayaanegamigoonsing. Mii imaa gii-waabamaad iniw gichi-binesiwan, biijibizonid. Mii ko giiwenh iwidi ishpiming izhi-ayaanid iniw ayi'iin, iniw oningwiiganan mii akina gegoo ezhi-ombibideg, miinawaa ezhi-naazhibideg. Miish iidog gaa-izhi-bazhizikaagowaad mii gaa-izhi-ombaangeninid imaa ayaawaad." Mii gaa-inaajimod iko mewinzha. Mii iidog a'aw Wese'an gaa-inind.

wind has gone by," she said, so we went outside
and just a little ways home to sleep.

[4]   The next day my uncle came. He was telling us,
"There was a really big storm," he said, "over
there on the point. My old buggy almost blew
into the lake," he said, his buggy having been
knocked down by the wind. "One guy came from
over there," and he told the name of the guy.
" 'They came in running,' he said. 'All of the
boards blew away,' he said, that man told, 'all of
the boards blew away.' I don't know how many
buildings were blown down. That guy looked to
see how far the cloud was and to see what was
happening, and he stuck his head out of his little
tent. That's when he saw a big bird there, flying
toward them. It was up in the sky and every time
it flapped its wings, everything went up and came
down again. It passsed over them as it raised its
wings." That's what he told about long ago. It
must have been the one called Wese'an 'Tornado'.

Gii-o-bapashkobijigeyaang
I'iw Gitigaan

[1]   Mewinzha gaye, mewinzha go, gaawiin igo aapiji gichi-mindimooyenyiwisiin iidog a'aw mindimooyenh, gaanitaawigi'id. Gaa-izhi-ayaad bezhig-sh iko iwidi, Zezabegamaag gii-ayaa. Adaawewininiikwe ko ingii-inaanaan. Ingoji go naanodiba'igan, maagizhaa gaye niso-diba'igan apii, imaa gaa-taayaang iwidi dash iko gii-adaawewininiikwewi a'aw; gaa-izhi-nandomaad bezhig go iniw ikwewan awiiya ji-o-bashkwashkibidaagod ogitigaan. Gii-mindimooyenyiwi a'aw adaawewininiikwe. Giiaakozi, enda-aakozi.

[2]   Mii dash a'aw nookomis, "Niin igo inga-o-bashkwashkibijige indaanis," odinaan iniw ikwewan. "Naawakamigookwe ingawiijiiwaa," ikido.

[3]   Mii sa azhigwa gegizhebaawagadinig aapiji gaa-izhinawapwaaniked, maagizhaa gaye bakwezhiganan gaamaajiinaagwen miinawaa akikoonsan—maagizhaa gaye waaaniibiishikegwen imaa, gaa-onji-maajiinaad iniw akikoonsan, akikoon, akikoonsan igo—gaa-izhi-maajaayaang. Miish azhigwa gwayak gaa-izhi-izhaayaang. Gaawiin miikanaang ingiiayizhaasiimin. Mii azhigwa iwidi gaa-ani-izhi-izhaayaang.

[4]   Ingoding imaa ini-bimoseyaang, bezhig igo zaaga'igaans. Agaasaa go zaaga'igaans. Zhiishiib imaa gii-paa-ayaa, ininishib; mamaad iniw asiniin, gaa-izhi-bakite'waad. Mii sa gaa-izhiniiwana'waad. Oo, minwendam, minwendam niiwana'waad iniw zhiishiiban, ezhi-de-niiwana'waad, gaa-izhi-debibinaad. Gaawiin

When We Went and
Weeded a Garden

[1]   Long ago the old lady, she wasn't so very old, raised me. There used to be a person there at Bay Lake. We called her Adaawewininiikwe, 'lady storekeeper'. It must be five, maybe three miles away from our place to where she had a store, and she wanted one of the women to go weed her garden for her. The storekeeper was an old lady. She was sick, real sick.

[2]   "I'll go and weed her garden, my daughter," my grandmother told the woman. "I'll go with Naawakamigookwe," she said.

[3]   Real early in the morning, she made a lunch, maybe she took bread along and a little pail—I guess she took along the little pail because she wanted to make tea in it—and then we left. We went straight through. We didn't follow the road. We just went right there.

[4]   As we walked along, we came across a little lake. That lake was small. There was a duck there, a mallard, and she picked up a stone and hit it. She killed it. She was very happy that she killed the duck, and she went and got it. It wasn't very

igo naawij imaa gii-ayaasiin, besho go imaa. Miish imaa gaa-izhi-
ayaad, gaa-izhi-bashkobinaad, mii iniw zhiishiiban, gaa-izhi-
boodawed imaa, banzwaad.

[5]   "Oo, Naawakamigook, mii ji-wiisiniyang," ikido a'aw
mindimooyenh, Gichi-aakogwan, gaa-kiizhi-banzwaad. "Oo, yay,
gaawiin sha naa gegoo mookomaan gibimiwidoosiimin," ikido.
"Babaa-nandawaabam imaa asin gaanizid," indig. Miish niin gaa-
izhi-gwiinawaabamag. Gaawiin ninisidawinawaasiin awenen dino
asin a'aw ge-nandawaabamag. Ingoding bazigwii, maajaad imaa
babaa-ayinaabid imaa jiigibiig igo gaye go nawaj baa-ayinaabid
imaa. Ingoding igo ogii-madwe'waan[1] iniw asiniin. Wa, azhigwa
biidaasamosed. Azhigwa wegwaagi, mii a'aw asin enda-giinizi.
Miish iniw gaa-aabaji'aajin gii-kiishkizhwaad iniw zhiishiiban,
gaa-izhi-jiibaakwaanaad imaa iniw akikoonsan bemiwinaajin.

[6]   Wa, gichi-wiisiniyaang. Enda-minwaagamin igaye naboob
miinawaa bakwezhigan gii-nawapoyaang; ezhi-maajaayaang.

[7]   Gii-agaasaani azhigwa ogitigaan gaa-o-bashkwashkibidood.
Aanish naa niwiidookawaa gaye niin bangii go imaa; azhigwa
onaagoshig gaye gaa-izhi-giizhiitaad, imaa adaawewigamigong
biindiged, dibaajimod, dibaajimoyaang gii-kiizhiikamaang
gitigaan. Wa, diba'amaagod iniw adaawewininiikwen, adaawed
meneziyaang, adaawed igo. Dibishkoo, bakwezhigaansan
miinawaa ziinzibaakwadoons indashamig a'aw adaawewininiikwe;
miinawaa aapiji maajaayaang. Mii azhigwa onaagoshig
dagoshinaang aapiji imaa endaayaang.

[8]   Mii sa go i'iw.

far out in the lake, but just close. Then right there she plucked the duck, built a fire, and singed it.

[5]   "Oh, Naawakamigook, we're going to eat," the old lady, Gichi-aakogwan, said after she got through singeing it. "Oh no, we haven't even got a knife along," she said. "Look around there for a sharp stone," she told me. I couldn't spot any. I didn't know what sort of stone I was looking for. Pretty soon, she stood up, went to the shore, and started looking around right along there. Then she started noisily pounding on a stone. Then she came over. All of a sudden that stone was real sharp. That's what she used to cut up the duck which she cooked in the little pail she was carrying.

[6]   Oh boy, we had a big dinner. The soup was delicious with the bread we'd packed for lunch. Then we left.

[7]   The garden she went to weed was small. Well, I helped her a little there, and then when it was getting to be evening she finished, went into the store, and said that we had finished the garden. The lady storekeeper paid her and she bought what we needed. The storekeeper fed me things like cookies and candy, and we started off again. It was getting late in the evening when we came home.

[8]   That's it.

Egwanigaazod Odaabaan

[1]   Miinawaa mewinzha, amanj iidog gaa-taso-biboonagiziwaanen, maagizhaa gaye ishwaaswi, maagizhaa gaye zhaangaso-biboonagiziwaanen, imaa bi-wewebanaabiiyaang miish igo a'aw ninoshenyiban imaa, Ozhaawashkobiikwe gii-inaaa, miinawaa ingiw ikwewag gii-wewebanaabiiyaang. Ogii-adaawaagenaawaan iko mii iniw giigoonyan imaa, adaawaagewaad, adaawewaad waa-miijiwaad. Gaawiin go gaye gii-kiiwashkwebiisiiwag. Mii eta go adaawewaad bakwezhiganan jibwaa-gitigeng, imaa gii-pi-izhaayaang. Waasa-sh igo imaa gii-ayaamagad. Minisiiwinini gii-inaa ko akiwenzii gaa-adaawewininiiwid. Gii-waabishkawedoon. Agaawaa go ingikenimaa.

[2]   Amanj dash iidog i'iw gii-pi-anoonigooyaan. Nashke-sh sa naa ingo-diba'igan igo imaa apii indayaamin, iwidi onigamiinsing gii-izhaayaan,[1] gii-inanoozhiwaad. Ganabaj mazina'igan ingii-miinigoog. Mii iwidi gaa-izhaayaan iwidi, gaa-izhaayaan. Gete-miikana ingii-ani-babima'adoon, waasa go naa ingo-diba'igan. Wegodogwen iidog gaa-naadiwaanen imaa.

[3]   Bi-washki-giiweyaan, bi-washki-giiweyaan, aaniish naa anooj gegoo inganawaabandaan igaye bi-ganawaabamagwaa ingiw bineshiinyag, bimoseyaan. Miinawaa go gegoo ingii-initam aabanaabiyaan. Gii-biijidaabii'iwewag iwidi, aya'aa odaabaan, mii go ezhi-agwanigaazod, bizhikiwan wedaabii'aajin. Maagizhaa gaye gaa-pagijwebinamowaanen iniw gaa-anoonigooyaanin wegodogwen gaa-anoonigoowaanen, bakebatooyaan. Mii go naa mashkosiing igaye imaa ezhi-bimaadagaaziiyaan, ezhi-

Covered Wagon

[1]   A long time ago—I don't even know how old I was, maybe eight or nine—my aunt who was called Ozhaawashkobiikwe, the other ladies, and I came to fish. They used to sell fish there and buy what they wanted to eat. Nobody got drunk. They just bought flour before planting and came over here. It was a long way. Minisiiwinini, 'Island Man', was the name of the old man who was the trader. He had white whiskers. I barely remember him.

[2]   I don't know why but I was told to—you see, we were about a mile away—they told me to go over there to the little bay. Maybe they gave me a piece of paper. That's where I went. I followed the old road, a long way, a mile. I don't remember what I was going there for.

[3]   On my way home, I was looking at all sorts of things, watching the birds as I walked along. I heard something and looked back. They were coming in a covered wagon, driving an ox. I must have dropped what I was told to go after, whatever it was, and run off the road. I waded right through the meadow. I'd heard that

bimaadagaaziiyaan. Ingii-noondam iko *gypsies*, amanj iidog
ezhinikaanaawaagobanen, gijiipiziyag iko gii-inaawag, omaa
gimoodiwaad abinoojiinyan. Waa, mii go imaa megwe-
mashkosiw miinawaa go waabashkikiing, gichi-bimibatooyaan.
Besho azhigwa ini-ayaayaan gichi-baabiibaagiyaan gichi-
mawiyaan. Miish azhigwa biijiba'idiwaad ingiw ikwewag.

[4]   "Aaniin?"

[5]   "*Gypsy* imbiminizha'ogoog," gichi-giiwanimoyaan,
"imbiminizha'ogoog. Jiibisenyag niwaabamaag.
Biijidaabii'iwewag. Bizhikiwan odoodaabii'aawaan, amanj iidog
minik. Bezhig-sh eta iwidi biijidaabii'iwe, amanj iidog igo minik.

[6]   "Oo, yay, yay, yay," ikido. "Geget ina go gibiminizha'ogoog?"

[7]   "Enyan' imbiminizha'ogoog," indikid.

[8]   "Miish azhigwa madaabiiwaagwen," ikido. "Daga o-
giimaabamaadaanig," ikido mii a'aw Ozhaawashkobiikweban.
Miinawaa zhaaganaashiimowag akina go. "O-giimaabamaadaanig.
Geget ji-ayaawaagwen gijiipiziyag," ikido,[2] azhigwa
maadaawanidiyaang.

[9]   Miish imaa, imaa jiigibiig—amanj iidog
ezhinikaadamowaambaanen imaa jiigibiig imaa, azhigwa, mii
imaa miikana enamog—gii-ayaa imaa. Gii-abi imaa a'aw
odaabaan. Gii-bakwenemagad. Miinawaa-sh igo aaniish enda-
zoongide'e. Aaniish naa nisiwag ikwewag gaye niin. Enda-
zoongide'ewag naazikawaawaad. Bizhikiwag gaye imaa
dananjigewag ganawaabamangidwaa.

[10]   Waa, enda-minwendam minwendam a'aw akiwenzii, miinawaa
mindimooyenh. Dazhi-jiibaakwewag. Enda-minwendam.

[11]   "Aa, gigosigowaa a'aw," odinaan.

[12]   "Ingii-waabamaa iwidi ikwezens. Ingii-waabamaa iwidi awiiya,
indinendam," ikido, "bakebatood. Indaano-baabiibaagimaa,"
ikido.

gypsies—I don't know what they are called—
gijiipizi they used to be called—used to steal
children here. Well, I'm running hard through the
grass and the swamp. So as I got near, I hollered
loud and cried. Then the ladies came running.

[4]   "What's the matter?"

[5]   "Gypsies are chasing me," I lied in a big way,
"they're chasing me. I saw gypsies. They're
driving here. They're driving oxen, I don't know
how many there are. There's just one coming, I
don't know how many others."

[6]   "Oh my goodness," she said. "Are they really
chasing you?"

[7]   "Yes they're chasing me," I said.

[8]   "They must be going down to the lake now,"
she said. "Come on, let's go and take a peek at
them," Ozhaawashkobiikwe said. They were all
speaking English. "Let's go and sneak a peek at
them. I guess it is possible that they're gypsies,"
she said, and we started off in a group.

[9]   There along the shore—I don't know what they
would have called it there along the shore where
the road ran—it was there. The wagon was there.
There was smoke. Well, she was just brave. There
were three women as well as me. They were just
brave and went up to them. The oxen were
grazing there and we watched them.

[10]   Well, the old man was really happy and also the
old lady. They were cooking there. He was really
happy.

[11]   "So, she's afraid of you," she said to them.

[12]   "I saw a girl over there. I thought I saw
someone over there," he said, "running off the
road. I tried to call to her," he said.

[13]   "Gigosigowaa. Jiibisenyag inendam," ikido.

[14]   Waa, aaniish naa niwenda-mayagenimaag. Aaniish naa gaawiin
inganawaabamaasiin. Niwaabamaag-sh wiin iko mazinaakizod
a'aw odaabaan agwanigaazod miinawaa bizhikiwan
odaabii'aawaad.

[15]   Imaa, oo, gaagiigidowaad, amanj iidog gaa-ikidowaagwen.
Dibi gaa-izhi-goziwaagwen, mii ingiw ezhi-goziwaagwen. Aa,
gaagiigidowaad imaa. Iwidi Gakaabikaang iidog iwidi akeyaa
onjibaawag, ikido. Nisogon bi-dazhitaawag bimidaabii'iwewaad.

[16]   Eyaawaad minwendamowaad igaye waabamaawaad, aaniish
naa apii, gaawiin gichi-mookomaan gii-ayaasiin mewinzha,
minwendamowaad gaganoonaawaad.

[17]   "Haaw, ikwezensidog, aa, gaawiin na akawe gidaa-wiisinisiim.
Gaawiin akawe gidaa-wiisinisiim," ikido. Wegwaagi iniw aya'aan
maskodesiminan miinawaa gookooshan imaa ezhi-dagozonid.
Oo, yay, waa enda-minwanjigeyaang imaa gii-kichi-zegi'iwaad
ingiw gichi-mookomaanag. Ginwenzh igo ogii-mawadisaawaan
waawiindamaagowaad iniw gichi-mookomaanan wenjibaanid[3]
miinawaa ezhaanid iwidi. Iwidi akeyaa Mazhii'iganing ganabaj,
ingoji gii-o-gabeshi a'aw gichi-mookomaan.

[18]   Mii sa gaa-izhiwebiziyaan. Anooj ingii-izhiwebiz gii-
ikwezensiwiyaan. Gaawiin indaa-giizhaajimosiin.

[13]   "She's afraid of you. She thinks you're gypsies," she said.

[14]   My, I thought they were strange. Well, I'd never actually seen one. I used to see them in pictures with covered wagons and driving oxen.

[15]   They talked there—I don't know what they said. I wondered where they were moving to. Oh, they kept talking there. They came from over there by Minneapolis. It took them three days driving.

[16]   [The ladies] were glad to be there and to see them, for at that time long ago there weren't white people around, and they were happy to talk to them.

[17]   "Well, girls, don't you want to eat first? Don't you want to eat first," he said. Why look, there were beans and pork cooking in there. Oh, my goodness, we sure ate well there though I had been really scared by those white people. They visited with them for a long time and the white people told them about where they came from and where they were going. Perhaps the white man went over towards Garrison to camp.

[18]   That's what happened to me. All sorts of things happened to me when I was a little girl. I couldn't tell all of it.

Miskwaadesiwag

[1]   Miinawaa aabiding megwaa go ayaawangid a'aw gwiiwizens, jibwaa-wiidigeyaan igo gaye niin, bagiwayaanegamig gaa-izhi-naajinizha'ang a'aw mindimooyenh. Miish iwidi, iwidi waawaashkeshiwi-zaaga'iganiing, mii iwidi ji-bagamibideg. Aanawi go imaa mazina'iganiiwinini ko gii-pimi-ayaa, onzaam-sh gii-michaa babagiwayaanegamig. Miish gaa-izhi-bagamibideg mazina'igan ji-naadiyaang i'iw bagiwayaanegamig, iwidi waawaashkeshiwi-zaaga'iganiing.

[2]   Ingoding sa go gigizheb, "Naawakamigook, onapizh ingiw bebezhigooganzhiig," ikido. "Naadig i'iw babagiwayaanegamig. Wiijiiw gishiime," indig.

[3]   Mii azhigwa imbwaanawi'aanaanig ingiw bebezhigooganzhiig wii-tebibinangidwaa. Niiwin ingii-ayaawaanaanig. Bezhig-sh igo ozaawizi a'aw bebezhigooganzhii gaa-izhi-debibinangid. Miish imaa, imaa imbezhigoopijige, odaabaanens, bezhigoopijigeyaan. Waa, enda-gichi-gagaawinaweyendaagozi a'aw bebezhigooganzhiiwish, gitimi. Aano-bakite'wangid, mii ezhi-azhetaad. Oo, yay sa gichi-ginwenzh. Ingoding igo azhigwa gaa-izhi-maajiibatood. Waasa azhigwa ingii-izhi-waaninishkaamin. Ingoji midaaso-diba'igan inga-izhaamin, iwidi waawaashkeshiwi-zaaga'igan apii imaa gaa-taayaang.

[4]   Mii[1] go apane ani-mikawangidwaa ingiw miskwaadesiwag bimoodewaad. Miish igo gwiiwizhenzhish Makoons, "Haw, niwii-amwaag ingiw," indig.

[5]   "Gaawiin gosha naa,"—aaniish[2] naa inzhaaganaashiim.

68

Mud Turtles

[1]   And once when we had that boy with us before I got married, the old lady sent for a tent. The tent was to come to Deer River. Although a mailman came by, the tent was too big for him. A notice came for us to go get the tent in Deer River.

[2]   So early one morning, "Naawakamigook, harness the horses," she said. "Go for the tent. Go with your little brother," she told me.

[3]   I couldn't catch the horses. We had four of them. One of the horses was brown and that was the one I caught. I hitched up one horse to the wagon, I hitched one up. Oh, that horse was just stubborn and lazy. We hit the horse, but he just backed up. Oh my, it took a long time. Then he started off running. We went the long way around. We'll go about ten miles along Deer Lake from where we lived.

[4]   We kept finding little turtles crawling along. That boy, Makoons, said to me, "So, I'm going to eat them."

[5]   "No!" I'm speaking English, you know.

69

[6]   "Gaawiin gidaa-dagoshimaasiwaanaanig," ikido. "Giga-
ginjiba'igonaanig," gaa-izhi-mikwendamaan waa-inag.

[7]   "Aazhigijishim," indinaa. "Aazhigijishim ingiw bimi-
azhegiiweyang idash ga-bimi-maamiginaanaanig. Gaawiin ingoji
daa-izhaasiiwag," indinaa.

[8]   Waa, ikogabaad, aazhigijishimaad iniw miskwaadesiwan,
maajiiba'igoyaang, azhigwa iwidi ishkwaa-naawakweg o-
dagoshinaang, maagizhaa gaye jibwaa-naawakweg. Azhigwa
miinawaa imbi-washki-giiwemin. Mii miinawaa bi-waabamaad
ingoji go naanan, apane gaa-pi-izhi-gwiinawaabamaad iko iniw
gaa-aazhigijishimaajin gaa-izhi-nishkaadiziitawid.
[9]   "Gidaano-gii-inin awiiya ji-mamaad," indig, "mii iniw
miskwaadesiwan." Mii i'iw gii-aazhigijishimaad, gii-
aazhigijishimaad, maagizhaa gaye gaa-kwekibagizowaagwen.
Ingoji sa go naanan, maagizhaa gaye ingodwaaswi gaa-pi-
mikawaagwen. Wa, enda-minwendam ezhi-minjimishkawaad
imaa bimidaabiiba'igoyaang.
[10]   Azhigwa imaa gii-biidaanakwad, indigo enadog wii-nichiiwad,
ezhi-naagwak, manidoog bi-noondaagoziwaad agaaming.
"Miinawaa imaa akikong, imaa akikong o-bagidin. Gaawiin daa-
gidoodesiiwag," indinaa. Waa, niwenda-zhiingendamawaa mii
iniw miskwaadesiwan iidog ji-gabaashimaad, iidog wii-amwaad.
Mii imaa, maagizhaa gaye imaa, awegwen sa iidog dinowa akik,
maagizhaa gaye okaadakik. "Mii imaa o-ashi," indinaa. "Gaawiin
daa-gidoodesiiwag," indinaa.
[11]   Mii gii-o-aaba'wangid ingiw bebezhigooganzhiig i'iw
bagidinangid. Waa, gaa-izhi-gichi-nichiiwak, gaa-izhi-gichi-
nooding gichi-animikiikaag, gichi-gimiwang. Agaawaa ingii-
pagamiba'iwemin imaa endaayaang biindigeba'idiyaang. Azhigwa
onaagoshin aapiji.
[12]   "Mii azhigwa ji-o-boodaweyaan. Niwii-amwaag
miskwaadesiwag," ikido, mii a'aw gwiiwizens, Makoons.
[13]   "Maajaan," indinaa.

[6] "We can't take them that far," he said. "They'll run away from us." I thought over what I was going to tell him.

[7] "Turn them on their backs," I told him. "Turn them on their backs, and then on our way back home we'll collect them. They won't go anywhere," I told him.

[8] Oh, he jumped off, turned the turtles on their backs, and we drove along, getting there after noon, maybe before noon. Then we turned around for home. He saw about five, but couldn't spot the other ones he'd turned over, so he got mad at me.

[9] "I told you someone would pick up those little turtles," he said to me. He had turned them on their backs, but maybe they'd turned themselves right side up. He must have found about five or six. Oh, he was just glad, and he held them down with his feet as we drove along.

[10] There was a cloud coming then, and it looked like it was going to storm; the manitous could be heard across the lake. "Go put them in a pail. They won't crawl out," I told him. Oh, I didn't like it that he might cook and eat those turtles. I don't remember what kind of pail it was, maybe a treaty kettle. "Go put them there," I told him. "They won't crawl out," I told him.

[11] We went to unhitch the horse and let him loose. Oh, there was a big storm with lots of wind, thunder, and rain. We barely made it running into the house. It was already evening.

[12] "I'll go build a fire. I want to eat those little turtles," the boy, Makoons, said.

[13] "Go on," I told him.

[14]   Azhigwa gii-piidaasamose. Niin igo imbi-giikaamig. "Aaniish i'iw gii-pagidinadwaa akina," indig.

[15]   "Gaawiin ingii-pabaamenimaasiig," indinaag. "Ingosaag mii iniw miskwaadesiwag. Gaawiin ingii-pabaamenimaasiig.

[16]   "Mii akina gaawiin awiiya ingiw miskwaadesiwag imaa ayaasiiwag," ikido, "akina gaa-izhi-gidoodenid ingiw miskwaadesiwan.

[17]   Onzaam niibowa gii-kimiwan. Miish gaa-izhi-gidoodenid iniw miskwaadesiwan. Gaawiin ogii-amwaasiin.

[14]   Then he walked in. He scolded me. "Well, the turtles were let go," he told me.

[15]   "I didn't bother them," I told them. "I'm afraid of those little turtles. I didn't bother them."

[16]   "There aren't any turtles there," he said. "All of the turtles crawled out."

[17]   It rained so much all of the turtles crawled out. So he didn't get to eat the turtles.

Minisiiwikwe

[1]   Mii imaa endaawaad ingiw *Shagobays* inaawag, onigamiinsing izhi-wiinde. Miish iwidi ishkwe-ayi'ii gii-wenda-onizhishin. Miish iidog imaa gii-ayaawaad akiwenzii miinawaa mindimooyenh miinawaa odaaniwaan. Enda-onizhishi giiwenh a'aw ikwe.

[2]   Mii giiwenh ingoding gaa-izhi-wani'aawaad. Maagizhaa gaye gaa-o-bagizonigwen, amanj sa iidog igo, gaa-izhi-wani'aawaad iniw odaaniwaan. Maagizhaa gaye odayi'iiman imaa gaa-atenigwen o-bagizod a'aw ikwe. Mii sa apane, apane, ezhi-bimosewaad jiigibiig, mawiwaad—aandi iniw odaaniwaan gaa-inikaanid, aandi gaa-izhaanid iniw odaaniwaan, aaniin gaye gaa-izhiwebizinid—apane go amanj gegaa gabe-niibin.

[3]   Ingoding-sh iidog igo azhigwa eni-dagwaagininig gaa-izhi-nagishkawaawaad gii-biidaasamosewan giiwenh. Enda-mino'owan miinawaa dibishkoo sa go gii-nanaa'iigwen miinawaa gii-nazikwe'ogwen. Oo, yay, ini-nawadinaawaad.

[4]   "Ka bekaa, gego daanginishikegon! Eniwek igo enigaa'iyeg apane mawimiyeg," odinaan giiwenh iniw oosan miinawaa ogiin, "enigaa'iyeg mawimiyeg apane. Mii iwidi ayaayaan noongom," odigoon giiwenh, "iwidi minisaabik, mii iwidi ayaayaan. Apane go iwidi ge-izhi-ayaayaambaan," ikido giiwenh a'aw ikwe. "Mii dash, mii dash i'iw gaawiin ginwenzh ga-bi-wiij'-ayaawisinooninim."

Lady of the Island

[1]   It's there where the Shagobays live at Onigamiinsing as it is called. It's real nice over there at the end of it. An old man and old lady were living there with their daughter. That lady was very beautiful.

[2]   One time they lost her. Maybe she went for a swim, I don't know how but they lost their daughter. Her clothes must have been left there where she had gone swimming. They walked along the shore crying all the time—where had their daughter disappeared to, where had their daughter gone, and what had happened to her— they did this nearly all summer.

[3]   Then as it was beginning to be autumn, they met her walking toward them. She was well dressed, just like she was dressed up and had done her hair. Oh, my, they were just going to grab her.

[4]   "No, wait, don't touch me! You have done me a grave injustice by always crying for me," she told her father and her mother. "You have done me a grave injustice by always crying for me," she said to them. "Over there on the rock island, that's where I am now. I will always be there," that lady said. "I will not stay with you long."

[5]   Mii giiwenh geget, amanj iidog maagizhaa gaye ingo-giizis,
maagizhaa gaye ingo-anama'e-giizhigad, mii sa gaa-izhi-aakozid,
gaa-izhi-nibod a'aw ikwe. Miish giiwenh gaa-inaad iniw oosan
miinawaa omaamaayan, "Mii iwidi danenimishig." Miish i'iw gii-
nibod. Miish i'iw, miish iidog iwidi noongom ayaagwen a'aw
ikwe. Mii[1] iwidi ayaagwen noongom a'aw ikwe.
[6]   Mii[2] sa go i'iw.

[5]   Sure enough, I don't know, maybe in a month, or maybe in a week, the lady took sick and died. She told her father and her mother, "Think of me as being over there." Then she died. That lady must be there now. It's over there where that lady must be now.

[6]   That's all.

DAGWAAGING

FALL

Imbagida'waamin

[1]   Miinawaa ko mewinzha gezikwendamaan o-
bagida'waad, mii ezhi-wiijiiwag. Mii iwidi Gabekanaansing, awas
idash igo iwidi ani-aanikegamaag i'iw zaaga'igan. Mii iwidi
ena'oyaang. Mitigo-jiimaan-sh indaabajitoomin. Azheboye dash.

[2]   Miish iwidi o-bagida'waad azhigwa onaagoshininig. Aanish,
mii go naganaad iniw odasabiin, mii go ji-gimoodimind. Mii
iwidi binda'amowaad ingiw odoonibiinsag. Ikido, "Gichi-
mamaandidowag ingiw odoonibiinsag." Miish iko iwidi ezhi-
aazhawaabiiginaad iniw odasabiin.

[3]   Gaawiin igo gisinaasinoon igo aapiji go azhigwa ini-
dagwaagig. Gaawiin igo gichi-gisinaasinoon, mii ezhi-
gawishimoyaang imaa jiigibiig, ezhi-gawishimoyaang imaa
jiigibiig ganawenimaad iniw odasabiin, jiichiigawiganebinag imaa
zhingishinaang, apane go ezhi-anoozhid ji-jiichiigawiganebinag.

[4]   Miish i'iw, miish i'iw maadaajimod. Enda-mizhakwak
ayaangodinong, miish i'iw maadaajimotawid eyinagoojininid iniw
anangoon. Gaawiin-sh ingezikwendanziin[1] waawiinaad iniw
anangoon akeyaa eyinagoojininid. "Odaadawa'amoon," odinaan
"nesoogoojinijin, miinawaa iniw Gichi-anangoon. Mewinzha gaa
wiikaa gii-wanishinziiwag ingiw niibaa-dibik."

We Set a Net

[1]   And I remember that long ago when she [my grandmother] would go to set the net, I'd go with her. It was there at Portage Lake, on the other side, where another lake joins it. That's where we went. We used a wooden boat. She rowed.

[2]   That's where she went in the evening to set the net. Well, if she just left her net there, it was stolen from her. She caught tullibees there. She said, "The tullibees are bigger there." That's where she strung her net across.

[3]   It wasn't cold although it was getting to be fall. It wasn't very cold so we lay down there on the shore where she could watch the net and I scratched her back as we lay there; she always had me scratch her back.

[4]   Then she started to tell stories. Sometimes when it was really clear, she told me about how the stars hang in constellations. I don't remember what she told me about the way the stars hang. "Orion's Belt," she told me, "the three that hang together, and the North Star, the great star. Long ago they never got lost at night."

[5]   Enagoojininid iniw anangoon, mii go gaa-izhi-
waawiindamawid. Mii iidog iko ezhi-nibaayaan megwaa
dibaajimod, miinawaa gichi-gigizheb azhigwa amadinid,
wiikobinaad iniw odasabiin, miinawaa giiwe'oyaang.

[5]   And so she told me about how the stars hang
in constellations. Maybe I fell asleep while she
talked, and early in the morning she woke me up,
pulled in her net, and we rowed home.

Naazhwashkak Baashkizigan Gii-madwezigeyaan

[1]   Mewinzha gaye—agaawaa go ingezikwendaan—
bezhig a'aw Jiipaawenh gii-inaa a'aw ikwezens. Gii-aakozi iidog.
Miish imaa agwajiing imaa zhingishing agawaateyaanig jiigi-
zaaga'igan iko gaa-taayaang imaa Gabekanaansing, imaa. Gii-
piidaasamose inzhishenyiban, bi-namadabid. "Aapiji aakozi,"
odinaawaan, mii iniw ikwezensan.

[2]   Namadabiyaan imaa ganawaabamagwaa, mii i'iw niwenda-
minwaabamaag ingiw. Enda-anwaatin. Niwenda-minwaabamaag
ingiw owaazisiig, bimaawadaasowaad gichi-niibowa, iniw
owaazisiinsan. Zhiishiibag imaa gii-paa-agomowag,
ganawaabamagwaa imaa.

[3]   "Apegish amwagwaa ingiw," ikido a'aw ikwezens. "Apegish
amwagwaa ingiw," ikido, mii iniw zhiishiiban.

[4]   Miish a'aw inzhishenh, "Da, niiyawen', da, niiyawen' maajaan,
naadin i'iw imbaashkizigan," ikido, "niizhwashkad. Gego
baamendangen. Mii eta go izhi Dookisin. Oga-bina'aan," indig.

[5]   Waasa dash igo ingii-apatoo. Gaawiin aapiji waasa gitigaan
imaa naawayi'ii gii-ayaamagad, miinawaa imaa
minjikanaakobijigan, imaa gii-maajiibatooyaan iwidi. Miish iwidi
eni-bagamibatooyaan, Dookisin aya'aa mazinigwaaso, miish
manidoominensan. "Niiyawen'enh giiwenh obaashkizigan owii-
ayaan," indinaa. "Zhiishiibag iwidi agomowag. Owii-
paashkizwaan," indinaa.

When I Shot Off
the Double-Barrelled Gun

[1]   Long ago—I can barely remember—there was a girl called Jiipaawenh. She was sick. She was lying outside in the shade by Portage Lake where we used to live. My uncle walked over and sat down. They said of that girl, "She's real sick."

[2]   I was sitting there watching them, really enjoying watching them. It was just calm. I was really enjoying watching the bullheads, a whole school of little bullheads. There were ducks in a flock on the water and I was watching them.

[3]   "I wish I could eat them," the girl said. "I wish I could eat them," she said, meaning the ducks.

[4]   My uncle said, "Hey, my namesake, hey, my namesake, go and get my gun, the double-barrelled one. Don't mess with it. Just tell Dookisin. She'll take it down," he said.

[5]   I ran there, a long way. Not very far away was where the garden and a fence were, and that's where I took off running. When I got over there, Dookisin was doing beadwork embroidery. "My namesake wants his gun," I told her. "There is a flock of ducks over there on the water. He wants to shoot them," I told her.

[6]   "Hmm," ikido, bazigwiid, bina'ang i'iw baashkizigan, niizhwashkad. Enda-gozigwan igaye. "Gego ganage baamendangen," ikido. "Ganabaj onashkinade," indig.

[7]   "Oonh," indinaa, bi-maajaayaan. "Enda-gichi-michaa i'iw baashkizigan," indinendam. Imaa naawi-gitigaan imbimose. "Amanj giiwenh enendaagwadogwen," indinendam, "ji-madwezigeyaan i'iw baashkizigan." Mii go niizh iniw ayi'iin, obwaamensan gii-izhi-wiindewan iko iniw ayi'iin, wegodogwen iidog dinowan, niizh igo. Mii gaa-izhi-maagobidooyaan, gaa-izhi-maagobidooyaan iniw ayi'iin ji-madweweg, wawaabamagwaa. Niizh igo, mii gaa-aazhigidaabikinamaan, bagijwebinamaan. Waa, apane go noondamaambaan, gichi-madweweg.

[8]   Amanj iidog apii gaa-izhi-ditibasikaagoowaanen. Mii eta go zaasitamaan. Mii imaa zhingishinaan imaa, baanimaa go awiiya wenji-nawadiniwaad, awiiya gichi-mawiwaad, gwekwekiwebiniwaad. Mii go gaye niin ezhi-gichi-mawiyaan.

[9]   Mii[1] eta go imaa minik gezikwendamaan. Ingagwejimigoog ingoji ji-inikoozowag, wiindamawadwaa mii eta go madwezigeyaan, geyaabi nitawagan gaa-izhi-madweweg.

[6]   "Hmm," she said, and she stood up and took down the double-barrelled gun. It's kind of heavy too. "Don't bother it at all," she said. "I think it's loaded," she told me.

[7]   "Oh," I said to her and started coming back. "It's a great big gun," I thought. I was walking along in the middle of the garden. "How would it be," I wondered, "if I were to shoot off the gun." There were two hammers, "little hindquarters" they're called, whatever they are. I squeezed them so it would go bang while I looked at [the ducks]. I drew both of them back and let go. Goodness, I just heard a big bang.

[8]   I don't know how far I was knocked. All I heard was a sizzling sound. I was lying there when all of a sudden people grabbed me, crying, and turned me over. I started crying just hard too.

[9]   That's all I remember. They asked me if I got hit anywhere and I told them that I just took a shot and my ears were still ringing.

Mikinaakwag

[1]   Iwidi gaye gaa-taayaang Gabekanaansing,
gomaapii go iwidi zaaga'igaans ayaamagad. Minisaabikowan.
Miish igo ani-dagwaagig ini-gashkading, mii ezhi-wiijiiwag
inzhishenh. Miish naa niineta ingii-agaashiinh,
giboodiyegwaazhonenzhish, gaa-izhi-wiijiiwag
bimidaabiiba'igoyaang. Miish iwidi ezhaad zaaga'igaansing. Enda-
onizhishin i'iw zaaga'igan. Minisiiwan, miish ingiw mikinaakwag
iidog imaa izhaawaad bibooninig. Obabaa-bapazhiba'waad iniw
mikinaakwan niibowa go. Gaye niin idash, mii ingiw aya'aag,
ingiw miskwaadesiwag, mii ezhi-inag ji-debibidawid ji-
bazhiba'amawid gaye niin. Miish imaa apaginaad imaa ayi'ing
agidiskwam, mii go wewiib. Maagizhaa gaye gaa-kisinaagwen.
Mii go gaawiin mamaajiisiiwag, mii ingiw mikinaakwag; oo,
ingoji go niishtana maagizhaa gaye nisimidana gichi-
mikinaakwan. Mii go giikajiyaang, bi-maajaayaang, bi-
giiweyaang.
[2]   Miish azhigwa nookomis,[1] wiigiwaam ogii-ozhitoon imaa gaa-
taayaang, agwajiing. Waasa go iwidi ogii-ozhitoon.
Wiigwaasabakwayan ogii-ayaanan iwidi gii-ozhitood. Miish iwidi
dazhiikawaawaad, mii iniw mikinaakwan, ganawaabamagwaa. Mii
ezhi-gaaskizwaawaad,[2] mii iniw mikinaakwan, ezhi-agoonaawaad,
ezhi-miinidiwaad aayaabita.
[3]   Besho-sh gaye wiinawaa gii-taawag, mii a'aw inzhishenyiban.
Ayi'ii imaa gii-taawag, miish gaa-izhi-ozhitoowaad waakaa'igaans
mitigoogamigoons. Aanish naa gii-michaani i'iw endaawaad, gii-
ishpimisagokaadeni, mii go gaye niinawind dibishkoo. Miish gaa-

Snapping Turtles

[1]   We were living over there at Portage Lake where there is a little lake not far away. There is a rock island there. In the fall when it started to freeze, I went along with my uncle. I was the only one there when I was small, with little bib overalls on, so I went along with him riding in the sleigh. He was going to that little lake. The lake is real nice. There's an island there where the snapping turtles go in the winter. He went around spearing a lot of those snapping turtles. I told him to catch and spear the little mud turtles for me. He threw them on top of the ice just quickly. It must have been cold. Those big snapping turtles didn't even move; there were maybe twenty or thirty of them. We were cold and we left to come home.

[2]   My grandmother made a wigwam outside there where we lived. She made it a ways away. She had some birch bark rolls for making it. That's where they butchered the turtles as I watched. They smoked the turtles, hanging them up, and divided them half to each.

[3]   My late uncle and his family lived close by. They lived in a little wooden house they had made. Well, their regular place was big and had a second floor like our place. They made the little

izhi-ozhitoowaad mitigo-waakaa'igaans imaa, mii eta go bezhig
gii-abiwinikaadeg ji-giikajisigwaa. Niizh igo abinoojiinyan ogii-
ayaawaawaan.

[4]   Miish ingoding baanimaa go dagoshing, gii-gichi-ishpate.
Gegaa go ingii-pakademin; gaye gichi-ishpate. Misan iko gaye
niibowa ingii-atoomin, azhigwa bi-dagoshing. "Mii sa naa akina
ingiw mikinaakwag, gaawiin awiiya," ikido, ikido mii a'aw
inzhishenh. "Awegwenag naa. Wenda-gichi-mamaangizidewag
naa ingiw. Mii iidog naa gaa-izhi-niigoshkamowaad i'iw
waasechigan," ikido, "imaa onji-biindigewaad," ikido, "imaa-sh
makakosagong abinid iniw mikinaakwan gii-amwaawaad," mii
gaa-ikidod inzhishenyiban. Gii-gichi-ishpate go apii. Gaawiin-sh
ingikendanziin amanj iidog, amanj iidog i'iw apii i'iw
gikinoonowin[3] gaa-izhisinogwen.

log cabin right there, just a single room, so they wouldn't get cold. They had two children.

[4]   Once he came over after a deep snow. We were almost in hunger as the snow was really deep. We used a lot of firewood, so he came over. "All those turtles are gone," my uncle said. "I don't know what they are. They have really big feet. They must have broken the window," he said, "and got in through there and eaten the turtles in the barrel," that's what my uncle said. The snow was really high that time. I don't know exactly what year that was.

Indinigaaz, Indinigaaz
Manidoominensag

[1] Mewinzha gii-agaashiinyiyaan, agaawaa go ingezikwendaan, mii ko imaa neyaashing ba-izhaawaad midewiwind.

[2] Miish ingiw ikwewag gibichiitaawaad, ayaangodinong jiibaakwewag. Miish i'iw ezhi-namadabiwaad giiwitaashkode[1] imaa boodawaadenig. Miish iniw manidoominensan endazhiikawaajin mazinigwaasowag.

[3] Miish gaye niin imaa namadabiyaan. Mii ko ezhi-makamagwaa iniw manidoominensan. "Naawakamigook," ikido bezhig a'aw ninoshenh, "aaniin nanda babaa-zaagidon imaa iniw wiigiwaaman!"

[4] Ingikinoo'amaag-sh ge-ikidoyaan. "Giga-miinigoo manidoominensag. Mii mewinzha gaa-izhichigeng." Inzhaagwenim isa. Ingagiibaadiz. Indagaashiinh. Nimisawenimaag gaye ingiw manidoominensag, gaa-izhi-agwazhe'id[2] moshwen. "Imaa wiigiwaaming izhaan. Miish babaa-ikidon, « Indinigaaz, indinigaaz manidoominensag. »"

[5] Gaa-izhi-maajaayaan niwenda-zoongide'e. Miish imaa niibawiyaan ishkwaandeming, gii-wiigiwaamigewag. Mewinzha gii-maawanji'idiwaad midewiwaad, gii-wiigiwaamigewag ingiw anishinaabeg. Gaawiin waakaa'iganing gii-ayaasiiwag maawanji'idiwaad imaa wiigiwaaming. Anooj gii-onjibaawag.

[6] Naaniibawiyaan, "Indinigaaz, indinigaaz manidoominensag."[3] Mii imaa naaniibawiyaan. Gegaa ko inginjiba'iwe. Baanimaa go ikwe zayaagewed. Ogii-bi-dakonaan manidoominensan gomaa go

I'm Poor, I'm Poor in Beads

[1]   I barely remember about long ago when I was little and they used to come here to the point for the Midewiwin.

[2]   Sometimes when the women took a break, they cooked. They sat around the fire. They did beadwork embroidery.

[3]   I sat there too. I used to take the beads away from them. "Naawakamigook," said one of my aunts, "why don't you go around and beg there at the wigwams."

[4]   She taught me what to say. "You'll be given beads. This is what they used to do long ago." I was hesitant. I was foolish. I was small. But I wanted the beads badly, so she covered me with a shawl. "Go there to the wigwams. Go around and say, 'I'm poor, I'm poor in beads'."

[5]   So I bravely took off. I stood there by the doorway as they lived in wigwams. Long ago when the Indians got together for the Midewiwin they lived in wigwams. They weren't in houses when they gathered there but in wigwams. They came from different places.

[6]   I stood there [singing], "I'm poor, I'm poor in beads." I stood there. I almost ran away. After a while a lady appeared. She had some beads on her

minik, bi-asaad imaa nimoshweming. Gaa-izhi-maajaayaan
miinawaa iwedi bezhig wiigiwaam: "Indinigaaz, indinigaaz
manidoominensag."[4]

[7]   Mii imaa naaniibawiyaan gomaapii go miinawaa bezhig
mindimooyenh zaagewe. Gomaa go minik manidoominensan
imaa bi-apagidawid, niwenda-onzaamaapi'ig.

[8]   Gaa-izhi-maajaayaan miinawaa, mii go apane bebaa-ikidoyaan
i'iw. Ingoji go naanan ezhaayaan iniw wiigiwaaman. Miish igo
enda-niibowa indayaawaag ingiw manidoominensag. Anooj igaye
inaanzowag. "Haw, mii minik ge-ayaawagwaa," indinendam, gaa-
izhi-giiwebatooyaan.

[9]   Ani-biindigeyaan, oo yay, niwenda-onzaamaapi'igoog. Mii
dash ezhi-gagwejimagwaa, "Aaniin dash i'iw ezhichigeyaan,"
waabamaawaad iniw nimanidoominensiman.

[10]   "Mewinzha giiwenh," miish a'aw mindimooyenh, nookomis,
mamaadaajimod, "mewinzha mii gaa-izhichigewaad anishinaabeg
gegoo gii-maneziwaad, maagizhaa gaye anishinaabe-
ziinzibaakwad,[5] wegodogwen[6] igo ge-maneziwaad. Miish i'iw
ekidod zaagido. Mii bebaa-izhi-izhaawaad, babaa-
nandodamaagewaad gegoo maneziwaad."

[11]   Mii gaa-inaajimod a'aw mindimooyenh, awiiya ge-bakaded,
ezhi-maajaad iniw wiigiwaaman babaa-nandodamaaged, akina,
niibowa gegoo wiisiniwin ezhi-miinind.

[12]   Mii i'iw.

hand and came and put them in my shawl. So I went on to another wigwam, "I'm poor, I'm poor in beads."

[7] I stood there a while and another old lady appeared. She threw quite a few beads to me, laughing just hard at me.

[8] And so I went on around and kept saying the same thing. I went to about five wigwams. Then I had lots of beads. They were all different colours. "Well, that's how many I want," I thought, so I ran home.

[9] As I came in, my goodness, they were laughing hard at me. As they looked at my beads, I asked them, "Why am I doing this?"

[10] "Long ago," began my grandmother, "the Indians did that when they were short of anything, maybe maple sugar or whatever they were short of. Then one said _zaagido._ They went around begging when they were short of something."

[11] The old lady told that when anyone was hungry, he went around to the lodges and begged, and so was given lots of food.

[12] That's it.

Awiiya Imbiminizha'og

VERSION I

[1]   Iwidi ko Gabekanaansing gii-taayaang, gaa-pi-izhi-maajii-goziyaang gii-wewebanaabiiwaad, imaa Misi-zaaga'iganiing.

[2]   Niizh ikwewag imaa gii-ayaawag, oshkiniigikweg ashi-ningodwaaswi. Bezhig-sh a'aw gii-ozosodamwaapine. Miish gaa-izhi-igooyaan ingoji naawakweg, nookomis gaa-izhi-anoozhid, "Giin gizhiikaabatooyan, maajiibatoon naadin i'iw mashkikiwaaboo iwidi neyaashing," gaa-izhi-maajaayaan, gaa-izhi-miizhid[1] asemaan, gaa-izhi-miizhid asemaan.

[3]   Miish iwidi ingii-wiiji'aa ko iwidi bezhig gwiiwizens, indinawemaa, gaa-izhi-maajii-dazhitaayaang, Gebe-giizhig gii-izhinikaazo, gaa-izhi-maajii-dazhitaayaang imaa jiigibiig babaamibatooyaang.[2] Gaawiin-sh ingii-maaminonendanziin azhigwa onaagoshig. Gaa-izhi-giizhiikaang mashkiki a'aw mindimooyenh;[3] "Wewiib, maajaan," indig. "Wewiib, giiwen. Giga-ani-gotaaj," indig. "Azhigwa onaagoshin," ikido, gaa-pi-izhi-maajiibatooyaan.

[4]   Miish imaa baa-izhi-dazhitaayaan akawe imaa. Miish aya'aa Biiswejiwang, Biiswejiwang iko ingii-kosaa. Gii-piijibatoo, mitigoons bi-dakonang wii-pi-bapashanzhe'od. "Maajaan[4] wewiib," indig. "Azhigwa dibikad," ikido, bi-izhi-maajiibatooyaan megwayaak.

[5]   Medaabiibatooyaan imaa, medaabiibatooyaan iko gaa-pi-inamog ozide-miikanens, miikanens, medaabiibatooyaan. Ziibiins imaa ayaamagad. Mitig imaa aazhawaakosin. Miish imaa bi-

Something Chases Me

Version 1

[1] We were living over at Portage Lake, but we moved camp here to Mille Lacs Lake and went fishing.

[2] There were two women there, young women, of sixteen years. One had tuberculosis. Around noon, I was told, told by my grandmother to get something, "You run fast, run and get the medicine there on the point," so she gave me tobacco and I ran off.

[3] I used to pal around with one boy, a relative of mine named Gebe-giizhig, and we started to play, running around on the shore. I wasn't thinking about it being evening. When the old lady finished the medicine, she said to me, "Hurry, go. Hurry, go home. You'll get scared," she said to me. "It's already evening," she said, so I ran off.

[4] But first I played around there. I was afraid of [an old man], Biiswejiwang. He ran up to me holding a stick as if to hit me. "Get going, hurry," he told me. "It's already night," he said, so I ran off through the woods.

[5] I ran along the shore where the footpath coming this way went. There was a stream there. A log crossed it. As I ran along, I looked back to

bimibatooyaan gaa-izhi-aabanaabiyaan awiiya ji-biminizha'od
geyaabi, Biiswejiwang wenji-aabanaabiyaan.

[6]   Gichi-animosh iwidi gii-piijibatoo. Makadewizi a'aw animosh,
biigwawe, gagaanwaakwawe a'aw animosh. Gii-piijibatoo iwidi.

[7]   "Awegwen giiwenh wedayigwen," indinendam, gaa-pi-izhi-
maajiibatooyaan. Mii ko aabanaabiyaan, mii ko gaye wiin a'aw
animosh ezhi-noogibatood, ganawaabamag, miinawaa
maajiibatooyaan. Mii miinawaa ezhi-biminizha'od. Mii a'aw
animosh baabiijibatood imaa ishkweyaang. Jiibegamigoon-sh iko
imaa niibowa gii-atewan. Gaa-sisegiziyaan, enda-mindido a'aw
animosh.

[8]   Miish azhigwa besho biijibatood gichi-baabiibaagimag
ninoshenh, gichi-baabiibaagimag. Miish igo gegaa
dibikaabaminaagwak azhigwa miinawaa imaa aazhogeyaan imaa
ziibiinsing. Ingii-piijibatoo.

[9]   "Aaniin endiyan?" indig.

[10]   "Imbiminizha'og animosh," indinaa, gaa-izhi-nawadinang i'iw
nininj, gaa-ani-izhi-maajaayaang, gaa-pi-izhi-maajaayaang imaa ko
besho waaginogaan. Mii imaa endaayaang wewebanaabiiwaad
mindimooyenyiban, gii-pi-maajiibatooyaang, bi-izhi-
maajiibatooyaang. "Wewiib," ikido, "wewiib. Awegwen iidog
wedayigwen," indig. "Aaniin enanokiiyan iwidi baa-ayaayan,"
indig.

[11]   Miish gaa-izhi-wiindamawag, "Ginwenzh ogii-tazhiikaan i'iw
mashkiki gii-ozhitood, gii-naadid iwidi megwayaak." Gaawiin
niwiindamawaasiin babaa-dazhitaawag akawe.

[12]   Baandigeyaang imaa wiigiwaaming, akiwenzii ko ingii-
ayaawaanaan, miish a'aw akiwenzii wiindamawaad, "Animoshan
obiminizha'ogoon." ikido, inaabiwaad agwajiing. Gii-namadabi
iwidi ganawaabamiyangid. Gichi-mindido.

see if anyone was still following me, I looked back
because of Biiswejiwang.

[6]   A huge dog was running toward me. The dog
was black and bushy, with long hair. It was
running toward me.

[7]   "Whose dog is that," I wondered, and I started
running this way. Whenever I looked back, the
dog too stopped running and looked at me, and I
started running. It chased me again. It was
coming just behind me. There used to be a lot of
graves there. I was scared; that dog was really big.

[8]   Then it ran up close and I yelled to my aunt. It
was almost dark now and I was crossing the
stream. I ran here.

[9]   "What's the matter with you?" she said to me.

[10]   "I was being chased by a dog," I told her, and
so she took me by my hand, and we left, coming
closer to the wigwam. That's where we lived
when my grandmother and the others went
fishing, that's where we ran to. "Hurry," she said.
"Hurry, I don't know whose dog it is," she told
me. "What are you doing hanging around there?"
she said to me.

[11]   So I told her, "She took a long time to make
the medicine because she went to get it in the
woods." I didn't tell her about playing around
first.

[12]   When we got in the wigwam, she told the old
man we had there about it, "She's being followed
by a dog," she said, and they looked outside. It
was sitting there looking at us. It was huge.

[13]   Miish a'aw akiwenzii ezhi-wawenabid imaa, odoopwaaganan
zaka'waad, zagaswaad. "Gego zaaga'angen," ikido. "Maagizhaa go
gaye gaawiin animosh aawisiin a'aw," ikido. "Gaawiin awiiya
odayan omaa izhi-naagozisiiwan," ikido.

[14]   Miish eta imaa minik gekendamaan.

[13]   So the old man sat down, lit his pipe and smoked. "Don't go outside," he said, "Maybe it's not a dog at all," he said. "Nobody's dog here looks like that," he said.

[14]   That's all I remember.

Awiiya Imbiminizha'og

[1]   Mewinzha gii-ikwezensiwiyaan—ingii-ashi-
bezhigo-biboonagiz—imaa go ingii-taamin gii-
wewebanaabiiyaang, imaa waaninigamiiyaag. Gii-ayaawag iko gii-
wewebanaabiiwag anishinaabeg. Giigoonh-adaawewinini gii-ayaa
imaa Onigamiinsing. Miish imaa gii-adaawaagewaad iniw
giigoonyan, ingiw anishinaabeg.[1]

[2]   Miish igo bezhig a'aw ikwe gii-aakozi. Miish gaa-izhi-
anoonigooyaan mashkikiwaaboo ji-naadiyaan iwidi Neyaashiing,
ingoji go niizho-diba'igan apii maagizhaa gaye ingo-diba'igan
ashi-aabita. Jibwaa-bimamog imaa miikana, mii eta ozide-miikana
miinawaa odaabaanikana gaa-inamog. Miish gaa-izhi-
maajiibatooyaan, gii-miinigooyaan asemaa.

[3]   Miish iwidi Neyaashiing, bezhig iwidi ogii-ozhitoon ko—
awegwen iidog dinowa akiwenzii—mashkikiwaaboo. "Haaw,
baabii'ishin," indig, baa-dazhitaayaan imaa, ginwenzh igo.
"Haaw, ingiizhitoon, noozis. Ambe, maajaan," indig.

[4]   Mii azhigwa onaagoshig. Anishinaabeg gichi-niibowa imaa gii-
taawag, imaa anishinaabeg okogewaad. Niibowa imaa gii-taawag
imaa anishinaabeg. Gaa-pi-izhi-maajaayaan. Imaa-sh igo gii-pi-
ishkwegewag—Biiswejiwang gii-inaa ko a'aw inini. Akiwenzii
"ingitigaan" ingii-ig. "Ingitigaan" ingii-ig. Niwii-wiidigemig sa
go giiwenh nitaawigiwag. Miish a'aw, bezhig a'aw
indoodawemaawikaawinag ingiw ininiwag, Biiswejiwang inaa,

Something Chases Me

VERSION 2

[1]   A long time ago when I was a little girl—I was eleven—we lived and fished there at the bay between the points. The Indians used to fish. There was a fish buyer at Vineland. That's where the Indians sold their fish.

[2]   One girl was sick. So they told me to go get medicine at the point, about two or maybe one and a half miles away. Before the road went through, there was only a footpath and a wagon trail going there. So I started running having been given tobacco.

[3]   Up at the point there was, I don't know, some kind of old man who used to make medicine. "Okay, wait for me," he told me, and I played around there for quite a while. "Okay, I got it done, grandchild. You can go now," he told me.

[4]   It was evening then. A lot of Indians lived there bunched together. A lot of Indians lived there. So I started going back. On the end of the village lived a man called Biiswejiwang and his family. An old man, he called me "my garden." "My garden" he called me. He wanted to marry me when I grew up. That one, one of the men I'm kind of related to as a cousin, Biiswejiwang, broke off a stick. "Hurry up and go! Don't you

bookobidood i'iw mitigoons. "Wewiib maajaan. Gigikendaan na azhigwa dibikaabaminaagwak. Gidani-gotaaj," indig.

[5] Aa, niibowa mitigoog gii-ayaawag imaa gete-odaabaanikana, odaabaan eta go ezhaawaad, bebezhigooganzhiig. Gaa-pi-izhi-maajaayaan. Ingoding igo aabanaabiyaan gaa-biijibatood enda-gichi-ginoozi a'aw inini. Imbiminizha'og, gichi-enigok maajiibatooyaan. Ziibiins imaa bimitigweyaa, mitig imaa aazhawaakoshing, mitigoog igo niizh. Gaawiin-sh igo aapiji dimiisinoon i'iw ziibiins, aazhawigaaziibatooyaan miinawaa ezhi-aabanaabamag. Enda-gichi-mindido. Mii go ezhi-aazhawigwaashkwanid imaa ziibiinsing, gichi-enigok bimibatooyaan. Jiibegamigoons ko imaa gii-paatayiinadoon. Gichi-niibowa imaa gii-atewan, jiibegamigoon, anishinaabe-jiibegamigoon. Gichi-aayaazhikweyaan. Mii go imaa aabanaabiyaan, geyaabi ko biminizha'od. Gichi-aayaazhikweyaan, bimibatooyaan gichi-enigok. Mii^2 gaa-izhi-noondawiwaad ingiw ikwewag, biijiba'idiwaad.

[6] "Aaniin," indig.

[7] "Awiiya imbiminzha'og," indinaag.

[8] "Animosh gosha naa a'aw," ikidowag. "Dibi naa wenjibaagwen," ikidowag. Enda-gichi-mindido a'aw animosh. Ozaawizi. Waabishkizi omaa okweganaang. Mii imaa ani-biminizha'oyangid. Wayiiba azhigwa imaa biindigeyaang. Aaniish naa zegiziyaan ezhi-mawiyaan imaa biminizha'od. "Gidaano-inin ji-wewiibishkaayan," indig. Mii go imaa ba-izhi-biindiged a'aw gichi-animosh, gaa-izhi-biindiged a'aw animosh.

[9] Miinawaa imaa akiwenzii ko ingii-ayaawaanaan. Aazhawakiwenzhiinh gii-inaa. Akiwenzii ingii-ayaawaanaan. Ingoding igo omamaan iniw odoopwaaganan—ginwaakoziwan—onashkina'aad. Mii imaa nanaamadabid a'aw animosh. Zagaswaad, eshkwaa-zagaswaad, ingoding igo eni-izhi-zaaga'ang a'aw animosh. Ingii-owiiyawen'enyinan dash a'aw akiwenzii. "Niiyawen'enh," indig, "gaawiin animoshiwisiin a'aw omaa ba-

know it's already getting dark. You'll get scared,"
he told me.

[5]   There were a lot of trees there on an old wagon
trail, with room enough for horses to go through
with wagons. So I started coming. Then I turned
around to look and there was a real tall man
running towards me. He was following me, so I
started running just hard. There was a creek there
with a log, two logs, lying across it. That creek
wasn't very deep, and I waded right across and
looked back at him again. He was really big. He
jumped right across at the creek, and I ran real
hard. There were a lot of graves there. There were
a whole bunch of graves there, Indian graves. I
started screaming. I looked back there and he was
still following. I screamed real loud and ran just
hard. The ladies heard me and came running.

[6]   "What's the matter," she said to me.

[7]   "Somebody is following me," I told them.

[8]   "Goodness, it's a dog," they said. "I wonder
where he came from," they said. That dog was
just big and brown. It was white here around the
collar. It started following us. In a little while we
went inside. Well, I was scared and crying at
being followed there. "I told you to hurry," she
said to me. That big dog came right in, that dog
came right in.

[9]   And we used to have an old man there. He was
called Aazhawakiwenzhiinh. We had that old
man. After a while he took his pipe—it was
long—and filled it. That dog was sitting there. He
smoked and when he got through smoking, the
dog went out. I was namesake to that old man.
"My namesake," he said to me, "that wasn't a dog

biindiged," ikido. "Mii imaa iniw ozidan, bakaan izhi-
naagwadiniwan," indig. Oo, yay, gichi-zegiziyaan.

[10]   Miish igo i'iw, miish igo i'iw, mii i'iw apii ajidamoog niizh
ingii-pami'aag, aya'aag misajidamoog. Niizh ingii-ayaawaag. Gii-
agaashiinyiwaad ingii-tebibinaag, gii-pami'agwaa.

[11]   Ingoding-sh igo mindimooyenh baa-dazhitaayaan iwidi
jiigibiig, giigoozensag ingiw imbabaa-debibinaag. Niwenda-
minwenimaag ingiw giigoozensag, nooji'agwaa, imaa baa-
dazhitaayaan iwidi bishigiishkibikaakweyaag. Imaa mitigokaa sa
go. Baanimaa go gaa-biidaasamosed a'aw mindimooyenh.
"Ambe, noozis," indig. "Wewiib," indig. Gaawiin gegoo
inzegimigosiin. "Mitigominan imaa indayaanan ingiw
gidajidamoomag," indig. Mii imaa gaa-ani-izhi-wiijiiwag. Bimose.
Miish imaa degoshinaan wiigiwaaming, miish i'iw ekidod, "Gego
miinawaa ingoji daa-izhaasiin, Naawakamigookwe," ikido.
"Awiiya iwidi enda-ginoozi gayaagiimaabamigojin," indig. "Mii
ko ezhi-aagaweweyaakotaad. Enda-gichi-ginoozi a'aw inini,"
ikido, odinaan iniw mindimooyenyan. Gaa-izhi-zegimigooyaan.

[12]   Miish i'iw bezhig a'aw ikwe waaj'-anokiimag,[3] waandamawag
i'iw gaa-izhiwebiziyaan gii-ikwezensiwiyaan.

[13]   "Mii go naa goshkomiyan, mii go naa ezhi-goshkomiyan,"
ikido. "Niwenda-wapaa'igoog gaawashkwebiijig," ikido,
"dapaabamagwaa ko gichi-gigizheb gaa-izhi-goshkoziyaan," ikido.
"Bengang," ikido, "dapaabiyaan," ikido. "Aaniish naa
indanokiimin gaye dapaabiyaan," ikido, "imaa endaawaad. Mii go
naa ezhi-nisidawinawaasiwag eniwek igo naa genoozid a'aw
bemosed. Mii ezhi-gwiinawi-mikwenimag awenen a'aw," ikido.
"Enda-gichi-ginoozi," ikido. "Aaniish naa niibin a'aw bemosed
mii iwidi akeyaa ezhaad neyaashiiwaninig," ikido.

that came in here," he said. "His feet were
different," he told me. Oh, my, was I scared.

[10]   At that time, I was taking care of two squirrels,
grey squirrels. I had two of them. I had got them
when they were small and took care of them.

[11]   One time there was an old lady where I was
playing along the shore catching minnows. I really
liked to catch them and play with them there
where it was dark in the woods along the shore.
There were a lot of trees there. After a while an
old lady came over. "Come, grandchild," she said
to me. "Hurry," she said to me. She didn't say
anything to scare me. "I've got acorns for your
squirrels," she told me. I followed her there. She
walked. We got to the wigwam and she said,
"Don't let Naawakamigookwe go anywhere
again," she said. "There's somebody real tall
secretly looking at her over there," she said to me.
"He'd go back behind the trees. That man is real
tall," she said, she told the old lady. So I got
scared.

[12]   I told a lady I work with what happened to me
when I was a little girl.

[13]   "You surprised me, you surprised me with
that," she said. "The drunks just kept me awake,"
she said, "and I looked out of the window early
in the morning when I woke up," she said. "It
was quiet," she said, "when I looked out," she
said. "Well, it was because we were working, and
I looked out," she said, "there at their place.
There was a tall person I couldn't recognize
walking along. I couldn't think of who that was,"
she said. "He was just real tall," she said. "Of
course it was summer and the walker was heading
toward the point," she said.

[14]   "Oo, yay," indinaa. "Awegwen naa a'aw," indinaa.

[15]   "Awegwen iidog," ikido. "Gaawiin ingikenimaasiin," ikido.

[16]   Miish a'aw, miish i'iw gii-maadaajimotawid. "Gaawiin awiiya
iwidi daa-daasiin imaa wanako-neyaashi. Gii-taawag iko iwidi
anishinaabeg, ingodogamig. Bezhig iwidi inini gii-taa, gaa-izhi-
nibod. Mii miinawaa gaa-izhi-adaawangewaad oshk'-aya'aag, mii
i'iw waakaa'igan, miinawaa iniw oniijaanisan imaa gaa-izhi-
nibonid. Miinawaa imaa aabiding akiwenzii gii-adaawanged
miinawaa mindimooyenh. Mii miinawaa a'aw akiwenzii gaa-izhi-
nibod. Gii-ishpatenig, gaawiin, gaawiin ogii-kashki'aasiin ji-
izhiwinaad aakoziiwigamigong iniw odakiwenziiyiman, imaa. Gii-
mamaajide'eshkaawan, miish gaa-izhi-nibonid igaye. Ingoding-sh
gaa-izhi-zakideg i'iw waakaa'igan."

[17]   Miish i'iw ekidod, "Mii go naa gaye mikwendamaan," ikido,
"imaa eshkwesing i'iw waakaa'igan," ikido, "mii imaa ezhi-
goziwaad, ajina go imaa aano-ayaa awiiya," ikido, "mii ezhi-
goziwaad," ikido. "Ayamanisowag giiwenh imaa," ikido. Mii
ekidod a'aw ikwe.⁴ "Gaawiin imaa awiiya daa-ayaasiin. Miish igo
noongom ezhi-bizhishigwaag i'iw waakaa'igan, oshki-
waakaa'igan-sh igaye i'iw, gotamowaad imaa wii-ayaawaad.
Amanj iidog ezhiwebak. Awiiya iidog ayaa."

[18]   Miish imaa ingoding, ingoding, ingii-mawadisaa imaa
niinimoshenh a'aw. Ayaangodinong inga-ani-mawidisaa
niinimoshenh.⁵ Amanj iidog igo aabiding igo ingii-kagwejimaag
ingiw, dibishkoo go gegoo gekendang, ingii-o-gagwejimaa aaniin
sa go, amanj iidog gaa-izhiwebiziwaangen. "Giga-wiindamoon
naagaj," indig. "Azhigwa-sh wiin igo giwiindamoon," ikido,
"asemaa, azhigwa ani-ziigwang, asemaa imaa bagidin," ikido.
"Jiigaatig imaa o-ningwakamigin asemaa," ikido. "Enda-ginoozi
a'aw, maagizhaa gaye maji-aya'aawish," ekidogwen. "Enda-
ginoozi," ikido. "Mii bebaa-izhi-naanaazikang iniw
waakaa'iganan. Mii imaa akeyaa endaayeg ezhaad," ikido.

[14]   "Oh, my," I told her. "I don't know who that was," I told her.

[15]   "I wonder who it was," she said. "I didn't know him," she said.

[16]   Then she started telling me a story. "Nobody will live there on the end of that point. There used to be some Indians living there, one household. One man lived there, and then he died. And then a young couple rented that house and one of their children died there. And once again an old man and old woman rented it. Then again the old man died. As the snow was deep, she wasn't able to get her old man to the hospital. He had a heart attack and then he too died. Then after a while the house burned down."

[17]   Then she said, "I just remember," she said, "it's the last house there," she said. "They move away, anyone who stays there a while," she said. "They just move away," she said. "They sense something there," she said. Then the lady said, "Nobody can stay around there. Now that house is empty, a new house too, as they're afraid to stay there. I don't know why it happens. Somebody's there."

[18]   One time, I was visiting my cousin. From time to time I'll go visit my cousin. I ask him what I don't know—it's like he knows things. I went to ask him why it's happening to us. "I'll tell you after a while," he said to me. "Right now I'll tell you," he said, "to offer tobacco towards spring," he said. "Put tobacco under the ground by the tree," he said. "He's real tall, maybe he's an evil being," I think he said. "He's real tall," he said. "He goes from house to house. He was walking toward your place," he said. "Go put tobacco no

"Asemaa maanoo ashi," indig. Miish geget gaa-izhichigeyaan.
"Miinawaa giizhikaandag agoozh imaa endaayan." Aaniish naa
mii azhigwa gaa-izhi-asag a'aw giizhikaandag imaa
ishkwaandeming. Mii gaa-inaajimotawid, "Awiiya iidog geyaabi
imaa ayaa."

matter what," he told me. And we certainly did that. "And hang a cedar bough there where you live." Well, then I put a cedar bough there at the door. What he told me was, "There's still somebody there."

"Ingitigaan"

[1]   Miinawaa gichi-mewinzha iko gii-pi-izhaa imaa neyaashing a'aw mindimooyenh. Mewinzha go imaa gii-pimidaabii'iwe. Amanj iidog gaa-izhichigewaagwen, maagizhaa gaye gaa-midewiwaagwen. Gaawiin ingikendanziin. Ingii-kagiibaadiz. Indagaashiinh.

[2]   Bimidaabii'iwed imaa, miish igo maadaanimiziyaan. Bezhig ko a'aw akiwenzii ingii-wenda-gichi-gosaa. Gichi-jaagigaabaw gii-inaa a'aw akiwenzii. Eniwek igo gaa-kosag a'aw akiwenzii.

[3]   "Ingitigaan," indig. Miish gaa-onji-gosag, niwii-wiidigemig giiwenh nitaawigiwag. Imaa waakaabiyaang iwidi, maagizhaa gaye wiigiwaaming, maagizhaa gaye gaagiigidowaagwen, maagizhaa gaye gaa-mawadishiwewaangen. Mii ko ezhi-negwaabamag a'aw akiwenzii, geyaabi ko ingii-kanawaabamig. Mii i'iw apane.

[4]   Mii ko aangodinong iko giiweyaang igaye miinawaa bi-izhaayaang bi-wiiji'iweyaan. Mii i'iw ziibiins idash imaa gii-ayaamagad. Bapashkwaaminisensing izhi-wiinde i'iw ziibiins. Mii imaa ba-izhi-basangwaabiyaan imaa. Miish booch ji-gagwejimid a'aw akiwenzii ba-dagoshinaang. Oo, yay, eniwek sa gaa-kosag a'aw akiwenzii. Gii-michaani iniw omisad.

[5]   Miish i'iw ekidod, "Gigii-pi-inaab ina imaa inziibiinsiming?" indig, ezhi-wewebikwetawag, basangwaabiyaan.

"My Garden"

[1]   Long ago the old lady used to come this way to the point. Long ago she drove there with a team. I didn't know what they were doing, maybe they were having the Midewiwin. I didn't know. I was foolish. I was small.

[2]   On the way there, I started to get scared. There was one old man I was really afraid of. The old man's name was Gichi-jaagigaabaw. I was pretty scared of that old man.

[3]   He said to me, "*Ingitigaan* 'my garden'." I was scared of him because it was said that he wanted to marry me when I grew up. We were sitting around in the wigwam, maybe they were talking or visiting. When I looked out of the corner of my eye at the old man, he was still looking at me. He was always doing that.

[4]   Sometimes we used to go home, and when we went back again I came along. There was a creek there. That creek is called Bapashkwaa-minisensing. That's where I shut my eyes on the way here. The old man certainly would question me when we arrived. Oh, goodness, I was really scared of him. His belly was huge.

[5]   This is what he'd say, "Did you peek at my creek on your way here?" he'd say to me, so I'd shake my head, my eyes closed.

[6]   Mii sa go ezhichiged noongom, ingoji waabamangid. Mii sa
eta go ganawaabamid, ganawaabamid. Eniwek igo gaa-kosag
a'aw akiwenzii. Mii gaa-onji-gosag, "Ingitigaan" gii-izhid.

[6] This is what he did wherever we saw him. He just looked at me and looked at me. I was pretty scared of that old man. I was really scared of him because he said "Ingitigaan 'my garden' " to me.

Gichi-jaagigaabaw

[1]   Mii go i'iw apii go mewinzha gii-niibin. Ganabaj
wii-niimi'idiiwag, ganabaj. Aanish apane bimidaabii'iwewaad bi-
izhaawaad Misi-zaaga'iganiing, ezhi-wiiji'iweyaan. Waasa ko iwidi
Gabekanaansing, ingoji go niishtana maagizhaa gaye nisimidana
daso-diba'iganedogwen. Gichi-waasa sa ko ingii-inendam.
Gaawiin dash niwii-naganigoosiin, azhigwa dash igo ba-izhi-
wiiji'iweyaan.

[2]   Miish imaa bimidaabii'iweyaan, mii ko imaa ziibiins
Bapashkwaaminishensing izhi-wiindeg, mii ko ba-izhi-
basangwaabiyaan. Gaawiin niwii-pi-inaabisiin, mii Gichi-
jaagigaabaw oziibiinsim gii-ikido. Ingii-kosaa a'aw akiwenzii,
aapiji.

[3]   Mii dagoshinaang omaa neyaashiing, jiibaakwewaad. Gii-
odewe'igani ko a'aw Gichi-miskogiizhig, gii-inaa inzhishenh. Gii-
odewe'iganiwag, maagizhaa gaye Zhingwaakwakiwenzhiinh,
awegwen iidog.

[4]   Mii imaa jiibaakwewaad ingiw ikwewag, wii-sagaswe'iwewaad,
izhiwidoowaad imaa niimi'idiiwigamigong. Babaa-dazhitaayaan
jiigibiig imaa neyaashiing, giigoozensag imbabaa-debibinaag.
Anooj sa go imaa asiniinsan imaa. Baanimaa go imaa inaabiyaan
agidaaki gaa-namadabid, mii a'aw Gichi-jaagigaabaw gii-inaa. Oo,
yay, gichi-zegiziyaan.

[5]   "Aaniin imaa ezhichigeyan?" ikido a'aw akiwenzii,
maajiibatooyaan gichi-enigok, gopiibatooyaan, owa gichi-

Gichi-jaagigaabaw

[1]   It was a summer long ago. Perhaps they were going to have a dance. They always drove a team when they went to Mille Lacs Lake so I came along. It's a long way from Portage Lake, it must be about twenty or thirty miles. I used to think it was very far. They didn't want to leave me behind so I had to come along.

[2]   We drove by a creek called Bapashkwaaminishensing where I used to shut my eyes. I didn't want to take a look as Gichi-jaagigaabaw had said that it was his creek. I was afraid of that old man, very afraid.

[3]   When we arrived at the point, they cooked. Gichi-misko-giizhig, as my uncle George Pine was called, had a drum. They had a drum; maybe it was Zhingwaakwakiwenzhiinh, John Pine, I don't know who.

[4]   The women cooked there for the feast and took it to the dance lodge. I was playing around on the shore at the point catching minnows. There were all sorts of stones there. Suddenly I looked up and there was Gichi-jaagigaabaw as he was called sitting on top of the hill. Oh, goodness, I was very scared.

[5]   "What are you doing there?" that old man said, so I ran off just hard, running inland. My, I was

zegiziyaan. Nanaamadabiyaan iwidi bakwezhiganikewag ingiw
ikwewag.

[6]   Ozaasakokwaanaawaan iniw bakwezhiganan, enda-gichi-
niibowa, imaa ganawaabiyaan aaniin iidog ge-izhichigeyaan. Mii
a'aw akiwenzii imaa ingosaa ji-amod. Aanish, mii gaye i'iw ezhid,
"Giwii-amon," indig iko aangodinong. Miinawaa niwii-
wiidigemig. Oo yay, eniwek sa gaa-kosag.

[7]   Miish ayaayaan, gaa-izhi-gimoodiyaan bezhig a'aw gichi-
zaasakokwaan ji-asag imaa anaamayi'ii imaa
ingoodaazhenzhishing. Niisaakiiweyaan imaa, miish iwidi geyaabi
gii-namadabi. Maagizhaa gaye gaa-kizhaatenigwen. Gii-namadabi
geyaabi a'aw gichi-akiwenzii, gichi-mindido, gaa-izhaayaan imaa.

[8]   Mii go gaye i'iw ezhid gaawiin iwidi indaa-izhaasiin i'iw ayi'ii,
omiikaans giiwenh i'iw nibinaadookana, omiikanens giiwenh.
Miish giiwenh, oganawendaan imaa. Mii i'iw, miish iwidi akeyaa
opime-ayi'ii gaa-onji-izhaayaan, gaa-onji-apatooyaan.

[9]   Mii miinawaa iwidi akeyaa gaa-ani-izhaayaan opime-ayi'ii,
iwidi namadabid ganawaabamag iwidi agidaaki,
akwaandaweyaan. Mii gaye gaawiin indizhaasiin imaa
omiikaansing. Opime-ayi'ii igo imaa indani-bimose. Ashamag
iniw imbakwezhiganan, oonh enda-minwendam, minwendam,
"Oo, ho," ganawaabamag imaa amwaad imbakwezhiganan.

[10]   "Ha, mii gaawiin gidaa-amosinoon. Mii gii-tebisiniiyaan.
Gegaa go indebisinii," gaa-izhi-niisaakiiweyaan miinawaa.

[11]   Miish ingiw ikwewag imaa jiibaakwewaad imaa, ginagaapiwaad
igaye. "Gaawiin dash naa awiiya animosh ayaasiin?"

[12]   "Animoshag dash wiin igo baatayiinowag."

[13]   "Gaawiin na omaa besho bi-onji-izhaasiin animosh? Oonh,
ingii-metasinaa bakwezhigan."

[14]   Oo, niwenda-zegiz. Gaawiin gaye debisiniisiin a'aw Gichi-
jaagigaabaw, nanaamadabiyaan, miinawaa imaa ingoji
ayinaabiwaad gaa-izhi-giichigobinag miinawaa bezhig a'aw

really scared. I sat down for a while where the women were making bread.

[6]   They were frying a whole lot of bread and I was watching, wondering what to do. The old man that I was afraid would eat me up was there. Well, sometimes he said to me, "I want to eat you up." He even wanted to marry me. Oh goodness, I was really scared of him.

[7]   While I was there, I stole one of the big pieces of fry bread to tuck under my little old skirt. I went down the hill where he was still sitting. It must have been really hot. That old man was still sitting there—he was very fat—and I went there.

[8]   Another thing that he had told me is that I was not to go on his trail, the water-carrying trail, his trail. It was that he was supposedly looking after it. That's why I went a different way, why I ran off to one side.

[9]   And so again I went a different way, off to one side, watching him sitting there on the hill, and I climbed up the hill. I didn't go on his trail. I walked off to one side. When I fed him that bread, he was just glad, "Oh, ho." I watched him eating the bread.

[10]   "Hah, I won't eat you up. I'm full. I'm almost full," so I went down the hill.

[11]   The women were still cooking, and also giggling. "There aren't any dogs here, are there?"

[12]   "But there's lots of dogs here."

[13]   "Did a dog ever come near here? Oh, I'm missing some bread."

[14]   Oh, I was just scared. Gichi-jaagigaabaw wasn't full. I sat around and when they looked off in another direction, I pulled out another piece of

zaasakokwaan, miinawaa ji-waabamigoosiwaan, gaa-izhi-niisaakiiwebatooyaan miinawaa.

[15]   Mii gaawiin omiikaans indizhaasiwaan a'aw akiwenzii. Ingotaan, namadabid imaa gaa-o-izhi-ashamag miinawaa iniw zaasakokwaanan.

[16]   Oo, wa, enda-minwendam, minwendam ashamag iniw bakwezhiganan, namadabid imaa, mii a'aw gichi-akiwenzii. "Haa, mii debisiniiyaan. Mii gaawiin gidaa-amosinoon. Miish eta go imaa minik gekendamaan. Amanj gaa-ayizhiwebiziwaanen.

fry bread so they wouldn't see me, and ran down the hill again.

[15] I didn't go on the old man's trail. I was afraid of it with him sitting there, so I went over and fed him the piece of fry bread.

[16] Oh, my, he was just glad that I was feeding him that bread, that big old man sitting there. "Hah, I'm full. I won't eat you up." That's all I remember. I don't know what happened to me after that.

Manoominikeng

[1]   Maajii-manoominikewaad ingiw anishinaabeg, mii
i'iw, ingiw oshkaabewisag ezhi-maajaawaad
nandawaabandamowaad manoomin. Miish ezhi-
maajinaazha'ondwaa baa-waabandamowaad, miish ingoji
minwaabandamowaad. Mii i'iw, mii imaa aanind ezhaawaad,
Onigamiiwanishinaabeg, Gibaakwa'iganing iko gii-izhaawag.
Miinawaa ingiw Neyaashiwanishinaabeg imaa Eshkwegamaag gii-
izhaawag, gaye niinawind iwidi Gabekanaansing, mii gaye
niinawind iwidi Manoominaganzhikaansing ezhaayaang.[1]

[2]   Mii ezhi-ozhigewaad[2], wiigiwaamikewaad, ozhiitaawaad,
ozhiitaawaad azhigwa wii-pawa'amowaad. Giizhiitaawaad
azhigwa gii-ozhigewaad, mii ezhi-maajaawaad,[3] azhigwa
bawa'amowaad. Bezhig igo boozi gichi-aya'aa. Gaawiin gii-
paatayiinosiiwag zaaga'iganiing, ingoji go niishtana jiimaanan,
maajaawaad.

[3]   Miish giizhigininig, mitaawangaanig, mii imaa endazhi-
bawa'amowaad. Mii biidoowaad azhigwa, ezhi-gidasiged a'aw
mindimooyenh gidasiged, ezhi-biinitoowaad i'iw manoomin.
Giizhaa gaye odoozhi'aawaan iniw bootaaganan. Mii imaa
ayaangodinong endazhi-mimigoshkamowaad, maagizhaa gaye
bootaagewag.

[4]   Miish giizhitood i'iw manoomin, gaawiin odaa-miijisiin, gaa-
izhi-gina'amaagooyaan ji-miijisiwaan. Mii akawe, miish ezhi-
zagaswe'iwed, asemaan ezhi-bagidinaad, dazhimaad iniw
manidoon miinawaa bineshiinyan, giizisoon, akina go gegoo,

122

Ricing

[1]   When the Indians were to start ricing, the officials went looking for rice. They were sent to search for a place that looked good. Some Indians, the Cove Indians, used to go to Onamia. The Point Indians went to Eshkwegamaag, and we at Portage Lake went to Little Rice Lake.

[2]   They built wigwams there and prepared to knock rice. When they were done building, they went out and knocked rice. One of the elders embarked first. There weren't many people on the lake then; about twenty canoes went out.

[3]   And when the rice was ripe, they knocked it in the sandy places. Then they brought it to where the old lady did the parching and they cleaned the rice. They had previously made a mill for dehusking rice. Sometimes they jigged the rice there or else they pounded it.

[4]   When she finished the rice, no one was supposed to eat any, so I was forbidden to eat any. First she gave a feast in which she offered tobacco and talked about the manitous and thunderbirds, and the sun, and all such things,

asemaan asaad. Ishkwaa-gaagiigidod, mii ezhi-miijiyaang i'iw manoomin.[4]

[5]   Waabaninig, mii azhigwa ezhi-bawa'amowaad, ezhi-bawa'amowaad azhigwa. Miish i'iw biidoowaad i'iw manoomin, gichi-neningodoonag. Miish gaawiin ingikendanziin amanj gaa-izhitoowaagwen i'iw. Gichi-neniibowa i'iw manoomin agwaasijigaadeg miinawaa bezhig a'aw gidasige. Aangodinong niizhogon onikanisidoonaawaa i'iw manoomin. Mii ezhi-makadewiminagak i'iw manoomin. Mii go nisogon ge-nikanisidoowaad, mii go wewiib eta go ezhi-gidasamowaad, gaawiin daa-gichi-makadewiminagasinoon. Mii i'iw anishinaabe-manoomin.

[6]   Giishpin idash agwaa'oodoowaad, wewiib igo baasamowaad, gidasamowaad, mii ezhi-ozhaawashkwaag i'iw manoomin. Enda-onizhishin. Mii eta go gizhaagamideng, ezhi-agonjichigaadeg i'iw manoomin. Enda-gichi-onizhishin.

[7]   Mii imaa apane gaa-taayaang gaye niinawind Gabekanaansing, apane eta go ezhi-gidasiged a'aw mindimooyenh, miinawaa dash ingiw bewa'angig, apane ezhi-biinitooyaang i'iw manoomin. Aangodinong ishkwaa-aabitaa-dibikak, mii nibaawaad ingiw gichi-aya'aag.

[8]   Mii dash ezhi-ayaad ayaangodinong gaye iniw mazaanan, amanj ezhi'aagwen, amanj ezhi'aagwen iniw mazaanan. Mazaanens ginigawising i'iw ayi'ii manoomin biisaamagak, aangodinong gaye mii i'iw ne'inang.

[9]   Miinawaa aanind ingiw anishinaabeg, mii ezhi-wanii'igewaad wanii'igewaad. A'aw mindimooyenh gaye dakobidood, ayaangodinong giishpin baatayiinak ingoji manoomin ezhi-dakobidood. Mii eta go ezhichiged i'iw, miinawaa ishkwaa-dakobidood, miinawaa ezhi-gidasiged. Miish, miish imaa giishpin wazhashk imaa ozhitood i'iw ayi'ii endaad, wazhashkwiish, mii imaa ezhi-wanii'iged, mii a'aw mindimooyenh. Mii ezhi-dasoonaad iniw wazhashkwan, miish ezhi-gijiigibinaad, wawiinge ezhi-giziibiiginaad ji-miskwiiwisig. Miish imaa biina'ang i'iw ayi'ii jibwaa-baasonid, mii imaa ezhi-biina'ang ozhaawashko-

and put tobacco out. When she finished speaking, we ate the rice.

[5] In the morning they started knocking rice again. They brought the rice in by great canoe loads. I don't know what they must have done with it all. A great amount of rice was unloaded and one of them did the parching. Sometimes they left the rice there for two days. Then the rice turned black. If they left the rice for three days, they just parched it quickly so it wouldn't be coal black. That was Indian rice.

[6] If they dried and parched it immediately on taking it from the lake, then the rice was green. It was very nice then. It was just put in hot water and soaked. It was real nice.

[7] When we were living at Portage Lake the old lady was always parching rice, and maybe a few of the ones who knocked rice, and we were always cleaning rice. Sometimes it was after midnight when the adults went to sleep.

[8] Sometimes she had broken rice. I don't know what she did with it. Chaff was mixed with the fine rice, and sometimes she stored it away.

[9] Some of the Indians set traps. The old lady tied rice; if there was a lot of rice in a place, she tied it up. That's all she did; after she was finished tying then she parched again. If a muskrat made its home there, a lodge, the old lady set a trap. When she got a muskrat in the trap, she skinned it and washed it out carefully so it wasn't bloody. Before the skin dried up, she put green rice in it. When it was filled with a lot of rice, she sewed it shut and after she put it in, she hung it up in the

manoomin. Gichi-niibowa ko debashkineg imaa i'iw manoomin, ezhi-giboogwaanaad, ishkwaa-biina'ang ezhi-agoonaad imaa wiigiwaaming. Miish eta go i'iw manoomin, miish eta go ezhi-dipaabaawadoong gichi-niibowa imaa debashkinemagad manoomin.

[10]   Ayaangodinong gaye mii ezhi-nikanisidoowaad, onikanisidoonaawaa, omaa miinawaa aangodinong niizhogon, mii apii miinawaa bewa'amowaad. Mii go awiiya niigwa'ang i'iw manoomin, mii ezhi-inind ji-agwaa'od. Giishpin idash igo wii-shazhiibitang, mii ezhi-niigwa'igaadenig ojiimaan. Miish eta go weweni eta go apane bawa'amowaad eta go. Gaawiin gaye giiwashkwebiisiin. Amanj sa go gegoo gichi-neniibowa giizhitoowaad i'iw manoomin. Ishkwaa-manoominikewaad, miinawaa ezhi-mamoowaad iniw odapakwaaniwaan miinawaa iniw ayi'iin obootaaganiwaan, akina gegoo na'inamowaad, ezhi-giiwewaad.

wigwam. When that rice was put in hot water, it just swelled right up.

[10]   Sometimes they left the rice undisturbed for two days and then knocked again. If anyone broke up the rice he was told to leave the lake. If he would not obey, his canoe was broken up. They always riced only the right way. They didn't get drunk. I don't know how much rice they finished, a whole lot. When they were done ricing, they again took the wigwam coverings, mats, and their mills, put everything away, and went home.

Bootaaganikewin

[1]   Ingii-wiidookawaa ko inzhishenyiban gii-ozhi'aad
iniw bootaaganan. Ingii-minjiminamawaa. Mii ezhi-
giishkiboodood i'iw mitig, ezhi-gwayakoboodood. Mii ezhi-
bajiishkiga'ang miinawaa mii ezhi-onikonaad iniw mitigoon, ezhi-
bapajiishkikonaad, ingoji ji-minoshininid igo ji-waawiyezinid iniw
bootaaganan. Mii giizhikonaad; mii ezhi-atood, mii ezhi-
waaniked; miish ezhi-atood mashkosiwan.
Gagaanwaakwadiniwan iniw mashkosiwan imaa etoojin. Miish
i'iw ezhi-atood ayi'ii oziisigobimizhiins, ezhi-waawiyaaginang.
Miish ezhi-minjimishkoodood iniw mashkosiwan. Mii miinawaa,
miish iniw nabagisagoon bijiinag ezhi-baabiichishimaad imaa.
Miish iko imaa gii-minjiminamawag ganawaabamag.

[2]   Miish gaa-kiizhishimaad iniw aya'aan, iniw mitigoon
wenikonaajin, giizhikan, miish imaa ezhi-ginjida'ang i'iw
wayaawiyeyaanig mitig. Mii ezhi-ginjida'ang imaa. Indigo-sh igo
akik ezhi-naagozid a'aw. Mii miinawaa giiwitaashimaad iniw
nabagisagoon. Mii miinawaa ezhi-atood ayi'ii, ayi'iin, iniw
oziisigobimizhiinsan. Mii ezhi-minjiminigemagak. Miish ezhi-
waawiyezid imaa. Miish igo gaawiin gaye bingwi imaa daa-
ipidesinoon. Mii ezhi-wenda-ganawenimangid igo weweni gaye
ji-nisaabaawesig ezhi-badagwana'wangid, maagizhaa gaye
wiigwaasabakway imaa gimiwang, niibaa-dibik sa go gaye
aabaji'aasiwangid.

[3]   Mii imaa endazhi-mimigoshkamowaad, miinawaa go
aangodinong bootaagem ikidom, bootaagaadamowaad i'iw
manoomin. Miish ani-dibikak, ishkwaa-aabaji'angid, mii ezhi-

Making a *Bootaagan*

[1]   I used to help my uncle when he
made a bootaagan. I held it for him. He cut a log,
then sawed it straight. Then he pointed one end
and carved some wooden pieces, pointing them so
they'd fit well and make the bootaagan round.
When he was through carving them, he dug a pit
and put grass in it. It was long grass that he put
in it. Then he put in a willow strip bent into a
circle. He pressed the grass down. Then he fitted
the boards together in it again. I held them as I
watched him.

[2]   After he got done fitting in those things, the
pieces of carved cedar, he tapped in the round
piece of log. He tapped it in there. It looked just
like a pail. He formed the boards into a circle.
The he put in the willow strips. It held then. It
was round. No sand could get in there. We took
care of it properly so it didn't get wet, covering it,
perhaps with a birch bark roll, when it rained or
at night when we weren't using it.

[3]   That was where they trampled the rice, or,
sometimes, so it is said, they pounded the rice.
When it got to be night and we were through

129

badagwana'wangid ji-nisaabaawesig, mii a'aw bootaagan, miinawaa bingwi maajii-ipidesinog. Mii miinawaa ishkwaa-aabadizid, ishkwaa-manoominikewaad, mii akina ezhi-giichigonaad na'inamowaad iniw ayaabajitoowaajin. Miish igo endaso-manoominikeng, mii go ezhi-aabaji'aad iniw bootaaganan. Ogii-ozhi'aan apane.

[4]   Mii sa go i'iw.

using it, we covered that mill up so it wouldn't get wet and so no sand would start getting into it. When it was through being used and they were done picking rice, they took it apart and stored away the parts. Whenever there was ricing, he used the bootaagan. He was always putting it together.

[4]   That's all.

Gichi-ingodobaneninj

[1]   Miinawaa gaa-izhiwebiziyaan manoominikeng.
Mii go bijiinag igo oshki-manoominikewaad igo, giizhigewaad,
bezhig iwidi babaa-bawa'am. Mii ezhi-biidood i'iw manoomin.
Miish wewiib ezhi-zhingaatenamowaad ji-baatenig. Ishkwaa-
naawakwe go. Mii ezhi-ayaawaad, gii-paatenig miinawaa, wewiib
ezhi-gidasamowaad. Mii i'iw ozhaawashko-manoomin wii-
ayaamowaad, wii-miijiwaad.

[2]   Aangodinong igaye zagaswe'iwewag oshki-ayaamowaad i'iw
manoomin. Miish wewiibitaawaad imaa. Miish imaa
niiyawen'enyiban ishkwaa-mimigoshkang, azhigwa ezhi-
nooshkaatoonid iniw niiyawen'enyiban wiiwan, ezhi-
nooshkaatoonid i'iw manoomin.

[3]   Miish i'iw baasaag iwidi ipidemagad nooshkaachigaadeg i'iw
manoomin. Miish apane ezhi-ganakinamaan miijiyaan. Mii go
apane go ezhi-miijiyaan. Miish ekidod a'aw ikwe, Dookisin gii-
inaa ko a'aw ikwe, "Naawakamigook, gego miijiken! Gego
doodangen i'iw! Giga-baasinig."

[4]   Mii ko ezhi-gimoodiyaan gichi-ingodobaneninj iko miijiyaan
i'iw manoomin. Mii azhigwa debikak, gichi-maazhi-ayaayaan,
eshkwaa-zagaswe'iwewaad, mii i'iw gaa-izhi-gichi-maazhi-
ayaayaan. Waa, enda-gichi-zegizi a'aw nookomis aaniin
ezhiwebiziwag. Gaawiin gaye awiiya nenaandawi'iwed imaa
ayaasiin. Gichi-maazhi-ayaayaan, gichi-zhazhiishigagoweyaan, mii
eta go manoomin, eta go baajiseg.

[5]   "Oonh, yay yay, baasinigo gosha wa'aw," ikido. Mii gaa-izhi-
ishkwaa-zegizid.

132

A Big Handful

[1]   Another thing happened to me during ricing. Just when they started ricing and finished the building, one of them went around knocking rice. He brought in that rice. Right away they spread it out to dry. It was after noon. What they had there dried and they parched it right away. They wanted to have green rice to eat.

[2]   Sometimes they had a feast when they first got the rice. Then they were in a hurry. After my namesake, my uncle, finished tramping the rice, his wife winnowed it, winnowed the rice.

[3]   The fine broken rice flew out when the rice was winnowed. I was always grabbing and eating it. I was always eating it. Then the lady, Dookisin she was called, said, "Naawakamigook, don't eat it. Don't do that! You'll get bloated."

[4]   I'd always steal a great big handful of rice and eat it. One night I really got sick, I really felt bad after they finished the ceremony. My, was grandmother ever scared about my condition. There wasn't any Indian doctor around there. I was very sick and kept vomiting hard, but it was only rice, only the broken stuff.

[5]   "Oh, goodness gracious, she's just bloated," she said, and so she wasn't scared any more.

Biindaakwaan

[1]   Gichi-mewinzha agaawaa go ingikendaan, miish inzhishenyiban. Gii-niizhoonagiziwag,[1] ingii-niizhoonagizimin jiimaanan, wiigwaasi-jiimaanan.

[2]   Miish ezhi-mookawaakiiyaan wii-pimishkaayaan. Miish iwidi ezhi-goziwaad ayi'ing, ayi'ing, waasa iwedi zaaga'igan. Niwanendaan ezhinikaadeg. Miish[2] iwidi akeyaa waa-izhi-goziwaad, bimidaabii'iwewag idash ingiw aanind iniw odapakwaaniwaan miinawaa odakikowaan, anooj igo gegoo ezhi-goziyaang manoominikeyaang.

[3]   Miish imaa ayi'ing gaa-onji-maajii-bimishkaawaad imaa, imaa go Gabekanaansing. Miish iwidi Zezabegamaag akeyaa gaa-ani-ina'owaad.

[4]   Ingii-mookawaakii dash. Niwii-pimishkaa gaye niin. Agaawaa go ingikendaan. Miish miinawaa iwidi dibi akeyaa gaa-ani-izhaawaagwen i'iw jiimaan. Gii-ani-gakiiwenigewag. Miish miinawaa iwidi Gichi-ziibiing, miinawaa iwidi gaa-izhi-dagoshinowaad miinawaa gaa-izhi-booziwaad. Miish iwedi Adisinaake-manoominikaaning izhi-wiinde zaaga'igan. Miish iwidi gaa-izhaawaad. Mii miinawaa iwidi ziibiing, mii ziibiins miinawaa iwidi gii-ayaamagad. Mii miinawaa iwidi gaa-ani-izhi-bimishkaawaad.

[5]   Mii gii-pagamishkaawaad iwidi, ozhigewaad ingiw anishinaabeg. Gaawiin dash gii-paatayiinosiiwag, mii eta go gii-nisogamigiziyaang ganabaj, mii iwidi mii iwidi gii-nisogamigiziyaang, mii iwidi zaaga'igan. Mii gii-kiizhigewaad, miinawaa gii-ozhi'aawaad iniw bootaaganan, giizhigewaad

Snuff

[1]   A long time ago—I barely remember—it was my uncle. They were in two canoes, we had two of them, birch bark canoes.

[2]   I started crying because I wanted to go paddling. They were moving camp to a far-off lake. I forget what it's called. Some of them drove over to where they would camp with their bark roofing, kettles, and various things; that's how we moved when we riced.

[3]   They started paddling from Portage Lake. They were travelling by boat in the direction of Bay Lake.

[4]   I cried. I wanted to go by boat too. I barely remember it. I don't know exactly which way they went with the boat. They portaged. When they got to the Mississippi, they got in the canoes again. The lake there is called Adisinaake-manoominikaaning. That's where they went. There is another river there, a little river. They paddled up that.

[5]   The Indians built wigwams when they arrived. There weren't many there; maybe there were only three wigwams of us there at the lake. When they finished building and had made the mill, they knocked rice the next day. There were only three

azhigwa wayaabaninig bawa'amowaad. Mii eta go gii-
nisogamigiziyaang imaa. Gaawiin niibowa anishinaabeg gii-
ayaasiin.

[6]   Niiyawen'enyiban-sh[3] dash iko ogii-ozhi'aan iniw
biindaakwaanan. Ogii-michi-ozhi'aan. Ayi'iing idash niwenda-
minwaabandaan wiigwaasi-makakoons.

[7]   "Gego miijiken manoomin," indigoog. "Giga-baasinig,"
indigoog ingiw ikwewag. Ikwewag imaa niizh gii-ayaawag,
ninoshenyag iidog. "Gego miijiken manoomin. Giga-baasinig,"
indigoog, gaa-izhi-gotamaan, ge-izhi-ombijiishkaayaan "ge-izhi-
ombijiishkaayan, baasinigoyan," indigoog, gaa-izhi-gotamaan.

[8]   Niwenda-minwaabandaan imaa ayi'ii, ayi'ii. Bezhig-sh a'aw
ikwe gidasige. Niwenda-minwaabandaan imaa ayi'ii atemagak,
ayi'ii wiigwaasi-makakoons. Mii go naa iidog i'iw biindaakwaani-
makakoons gaa-izhi-ayaayaan,[4] giimaabamag iko ninoshenh,
gidasiged, gaa-izhi-biindaakweyaan, gaa-izhi-agwanemwag, mii
a'aw biindaakwaan, babaa-dazhitaayaan imaa agwajiing babaa-
zaziikoyaan.

[9]   Baanimaa igo naa wenji-gizhibaabizoyaan indinendam,
gizhibaabizoyaan indinendam, zhishigagoweyaan, gaa-izhi-
bwaanawitooyaan wii-pimoseyaan.

[10]   Miish a'aw ninoshenh iidog gaa-izhi-waabamid imaa gaa-
pabaamoodeyaan, gichi-aakoziyaan, gichi-maazhi-ayaayaan, gichi-
baabiibaagimaad. Waa niwenda-zegiz, gichi-baabiibaagimaad,
babaamishkaanid anishinaaben.

[11]   "Aaniin ezhiwebizid?" Maagizhaa gaye gegaa ingii-ojibinig.
Aanish naa mashkawizii a'aw biindaakwaan iidog, biindaakweng,
gichi-baabiibaagimaad. "Aaniin ezhiwebiziyan?"

[12]   "Ambe," agwaa'owaad. Miish eta go imaa gikendamaan
miinawaa dakonid, mii a'aw, mii go ezhi-mawiwaad ingiw
ikwewag. Inzhishigagowe gaye.

wigwams of us. There weren't many Indians there.

[6]   My namesake, my uncle, used to make snuff. He made it from scratch. I really liked the look of that little birch bark snuffbox.

[7]   "Don't eat rice!" I was told. "You'll get bloated," the ladies told me. There were two ladies there, maybe my aunts. "Don't eat rice. You'll get bloated," they told me, so I was scared that my stomach would swell up, "and your stomach will swell up, if you get bloated," they told me, so I was scared of it.

[8]   I really liked the look of that thing. One lady was parching rice. I admired the looks of that thing there, the little birch bark box. I must have got the snuffbox, then I peeked at my aunt parching rice, took a pinch, put the snuff in my mouth, and went playing around outside, spitting all around.

[9]   All of a sudden I felt like I was spinning around, I felt like I was spinning, and I vomited, so I couldn't even walk.

[10]   Then my aunt saw me crawling around, really sick and in bad shape, and she called them. I was just scared and she yelled to the Indians out paddling around.

[11]   "What's wrong with her?" I must have been having convulsions. How strong that snuff must be taken in a pinch. She yelled to them. "What's wrong with you?"

[12]   "Come on!" They were getting off the lake. All I remember is that she had me in her arms and the ladies were crying. I was vomiting too.

[13]   "Wewiib, gaawiin gegoo mashkikiiwinini, wewiib. Miish iidog imaa neyaashiing bi-izhidaabiiba'igod ji-bi-naanaad iniw nenaandawi'iwenijin. Wewiib, wewiib onapijigeg,[5] naanik akiwenzii."

[14]   "Aaniin ezhiwebizid?" Miish imaa maagizhaa gaye gaa-nibaawaanen, gaawiin dash ingikendanziin.

[15]   Miinawaa gweshkoziyaan, namadabiyaan. Mii go ezhi-mino-ayaayaan. Akiwenzii imaa gii-namadabi, baapiwaad baapiwaad, ingiw ikwewag, baapiwaad sa go.

[16]   "Naawakamigook," indigoog, "gego miinawaa wiikaa biindaakweken," indigoog.

[13]   "Hurry up! There's no doctor. Hurry up! They'll have to drive to the point to get the Indian doctor. Hurry, harness up and get the old man!"

[14]   "What's the matter with her?" I must have been asleep, I don't know.

[15]   And when I woke up, I was sitting up. I felt okay. An old man was sitting there and the ladies were laughing and laughing.

[16]   "Naawakamigook," they told me. "Don't ever take snuff again," they told me.

Memegwesiwag

[1]   Miinawaa dash gaa-inaajimotawid a'aw nimaamaa.
Gii-wiidige miinawaa imbaabaayiban gaa-nibod. Imbaabaayiban
gii-nibod, gaa-izhi-wiidiged. Miish gaa-inaajimotawid.

[2]   Moozhag iko ingii-izhaamin iwidi, apane go gaa-tazhiikeyaang
ayi'iing Gwiiwizensiwi-ziibiing. Miish iwidi manoominikeyaang,
namadabiyaang ini-onaagoshig, dibaajimod gii-waabamaawaad
memegwesiwan.

[3]   "Bawa'amoog gaye wiinawaa, miish imaa Gwiiwizensiwi-
ziibiing. Washkitigweyaa imaa ziibi," ikido. "Mii imaa ani-
bawa'amaang[1]," ikido.

[4]   "Ganabaj[2] naa awiiya iwidi," ikidowan giiwenh iniw
odakiwenziiyiman, ezhi-noogishkaawaad imaa, bagidinaad iniw
bawa'iganaakoon. Geget giiwenh gii-biidweweshinoon
bawa'iganaakoon, imaa ayagwamowaad, baanimaa go giiwenh
imaa zayaagewebideg jiimaan. Niizh idash iniw ba-bawa'aminijin
imaa, namadabiwaad ganawaabamaawaad.

[5]   Miish i'iw izhi-basangwaabiwaad miinawaa wii-waabamaawaad
awenenan iniw gaa-izhi-gwiinawaabamaawaad. "Miish i'iw gaa-
ikidod « memegwesiwag, »" gii-ikido.[3] "Miish i'iw gaa-ikidod,
gagiibwaweyiingwewag ingiw memegwesiwag."

[6]   Awegwenag iidog dinowag ingiw.

The *Memegwesiwag*

[1]   Then again what my [step-]mother told me. She married again after my father died. My father died and she remarried. This is what she told me.

[2]   We always went to Boy River, we were always doing something there at Boy River. We were ricing there, and were sitting down towards evening; she was saying that they had seen Memegwesiwag.

[3]   "They too knock rice there on Boy River. The river turns there," she said. "We were knocking rice along there," she said.

[4]   "Maybe there is someone over there," her old man was saying, so they stopped there and she put down the knocking sticks. Sure enough, the sound of knockers was coming toward them where they were sitting in the water, and then a boat suddenly appeared. They sat there watching those two knocking rice.

[5]   They wanted to see who they were, but when they blinked their eyes, they disappeared from view. "He said, 'Memegwesiwag'," she said, "that's what he said; those Memegwesiwag have hair on their faces."

[6]   I wonder what kind of creatures they are.

Gii-nagishkawag A'aw Mooniyaawikwe

[1]   Mewinzha gaye ezhi-odoodemiwaad ingiw anishinaabeg. Baatayiinowan iniw odoodemiwaan: aanind igaye owaazisiin, miinawaa ma'iinganan wiin ingiw bwaanag odoodemiwaan, waabizheshiwan[1] miinawaa aanind mikinaakwan, bakaan-sh wiin ingiw anishinaabeg.

[2]   Gaawiin dash daa-izhi-wiidigendisiiwag i'iw ezhi-odoodemiwaad. Mewinzha iidog, mii akeyaa inawendiwag. Mii ingiw anishinaabeg, mii giiwenh ezhi-inawendiwaad akeyaa ezhi-odoodemindiwaad. Nashke a'aw waabizheshi, iniw waabizheshiwan gaawiin odaa-wiidigemaasiin. Amanj i'iw akeyaa inawendiwag giiwenh besho ingiw.

[3]   Miinawaa-sh ingiw migiziwag, mii giiwenh ingiw mooniyaawininiwag, mewinzha. Miish i'iw ingii-kagwejimaa nookomis, "Aaniin i'iw?"

[4]   Miish i'iw gaa-ikidod, miish i'iw gaa-ikidod, "Ingiw mooniyaawininiwag wiin ingiw migiziwan wedoodemijig bagandiziwag.[2] Gaawiin ogikendanziinaawaa gegoo go aapiji anishinaabe-izhichigewin. Gegaa go gichi-mookomaani-ayaawag. Gichi-mookomaan iidog migiziwan odoodeman."

[5]   Mewinzha dash iwidi ayi'ing ingii-izhaamin, iwidi akeyaa ayi'ing, waasa go iwidi, amanj iidog ezhinikaadegwen anishinaabewinikaadeg. Ingii-o-manoominikemin iwidi. Miish i'iw ingii-pi-waabamigonaanig iko ingiw anishinaabeg ini-onaagoshig, bi-mawadishiyangidwaa. Bimishkaawag. Gaawiin gaye awiiya odaabaanan, gaawiin gegoo miikana.

When I Met the *Mooniyaa*-Lady

[1]   A long time ago the Indians had totems. They have a lot of totems: for some, bullhead; for the Sioux, wolf; marten; and for some, different kinds of Indians, snapping turtle.

[2]   They couldn't marry each other if they had the same totem. Long ago that's how they were related to each other. Those Indians were related to each other in a way when they had the same totem. A marten, you see, couldn't marry another marten. I don't know in what way, but it is said they were related to each other real close.

[3]   And the bald eagles were the Canadians long ago. I asked my grandmother, "Why is that?"

[4]   She said, "Those Mooniyaa-people who have the bald eagle as their totem are ignorant. They don't know anything much about the Indian way. They are almost white people. The white man's totem is the bald eagle."

[5]   Long ago we went over there, a long way, I don't know what it is called in Indian. We went over there to rice. The Indians came to see us for a visit in the evening. They got around in boats. There were no cars and no road.

143

[6]   Miish a'aw bezhig ikwe babaa-naaniibawid. Enda-onizhishi
a'aw mindimooyenh. Mii gaa-pi-izhi-nawadinid, "Awenen
gidoodem," indig.

[7]   Miish i'iw enag, "Migizi." Niwenda-zegi'ig ezhi-nawadinid
wawijiimid.

[8]   "Gidinawemin," ikido. "Gaye niin aya'aa migizi indoodem,"
ikido. Miish igo ginagaapid imaa. Mii go gaabige igo ezhi-
nagadenindiyaang. Mii go imaa babaa-ginagaapid. "Gigikendaan
ina egooyang," indig.

[9]   "Gaawiin," indinaa.

[10] "Naa, mooniyaawikwe gidigoomin," ikido.

[6]   There was one lady standing around. That old lady was nice-looking. She came and grabbed me, asking me, "What is your totem?"

[7]   So I told her, "Bald eagle." I was afraid of her because of how she grabbed and kissed me.

[8]   "We're related," she said. "My totem too is bald eagle," she said. And she started giggling. We made friends with each other right away. She went around giggling. "Do you know what they call us," she said to me.

[9]   "No," I told her.

[10]   "Well, we are called Mooniyaa-lady," she said.

BIBOONG

WINTER

Makwasaagimensag

[1]   Miinawaa aabiding mewinzha mikwendamaan
ganawaabamag a'aw inzhishenh ozhitawid iniw
makwasaagimensan, izhinikaazowag ingiw aagimag,
wawaawiyeziwag. Imaa namadabiyaan ganawaabamag, waa
niminwendam, niminwendam. Enda-gichi-zoogipon agwajiing.
Miish i'iw ekidod inzhishenh, "Booch gaye niiyawen' ji-
biizikawadwaa giizhi'agwaa ji-gojichigeyan," mii gaa-izhid. Miish
imaa minik miinawaa gekendamaan imaa.

[2]   Gaa-izhi-zaaga'amaan, gichi-zoogipon, gaa-izhi-
zaaga'amowaanen, gii-maajaawaanen. Baanimaa-sh igo miinawaa
gekendamaan, dibikad; namadabiyaan niwenda-giikaj. Enda-
baatayiinowag ingiw gichi-mookomaanag gaa-ayaawaagwen.
"Aandi dash gaa-izhaayan?" indigoo.

[3]   "Oonh, waasa iwidi eko-gisinaag ingii-paa-izhaa," indinaag.
Ezhi-mawid a'aw mindimooyenh, maagizhaa gaye ingoji gaa-
wanishinowaanen, amanj iidog.

148

The Little Bear-Paw Snowshoes

[1]   Again I remember once long ago watching my uncle making me some *makwasaagimensag*, as those little bear-paw snowshoes were called; they were round. I was really happy sitting there watching him. It was really snowing hard outside. Then my uncle said, "Namesake, you'll have to put them on for a test when I'm done with them," that's what he told me. That's all I remember of that.

[2]   When I went outside, it was snowing just hard, and I must have gone out and taken off. Then I remember later that it was night; I was sitting down, just cold. There were a lot of people there, they must have been white people. "Where did you go?" I was asked.

[3]   "Oh, I went around way up north," I told them. As the old lady was crying, I guess I must have been lost.

Gego Onadinaakegon
A'aw Goon

[1]   Miinawaa noomaya wiin igo ingikendaan i'iw
onadinangid a'aw goon. Mii ezhi-nishkaadizid a'aw
mindimooyenh, "Gego, o-niigwa'ok[1] wewiib a'aw."

[2]   "Aaniin danaa, aaniish," indinaa.
[3]   "Mewinzha giiwenh abinoojiinyag onadinaawaad, mii iniw
goonan. Mii giiwenh ezhi-gichi-gisinaag. Mii awiiya ezhi-
wiindigoowid. Miish iko gaa-igooyaang, « Gego onadinaakegon
a'aw goon. »"
[4]   Geyaabi go noongom, mii enindwaa abinoojiinyag gego ji-
mazinadinaasigwaa iniw goonan. Mii giiwenh ezhi-bazigwiid
a'aw, wiindigoowid amogowaad.

150

Don't Make Snowmen

[1]   Then again not long ago I remembered about the time we were making snowmen. The old lady got mad, "Don't, go break it up quick!"

[2]   "But why, why?" I said to her.

[3]   "Long ago some children were making snowmen. Then it got very cold. Someone became a windigo. They used to tell us, 'Don't make snowmen!' "

[4]   Today children are still told not to make an image from snow. It could stand up, so the story goes, become a windigo, and eat them.

Aazhawakiwenzhiinh

[1]   Bezhig igo akiwenzii ingii-wiij'-ayaawaanaan. Ogii-odawemaawinan a'aw mindimooyenh. Aazhawakiwenzhiinh gii-izhinikaazo.

[2]   Miish iko waasa, ingii-taamin Gabekanaansing gii-izhi-wiinde. Miish a'aw akiwenzii gigizheb onishkaad, babiichiid, aniibiish gashkibidood, ziinzibaakwad miinawaa bangii bakwezhiganan, ezhi-bimoondang.

[3]   Mii dash ayi'ii misko-waabowayaan iko—gii-izhi-wiindewan mewinzha gichi-waabowayaanan—mii i'iw egwazhed. Miinawaa gaawiin wiikaa gii-kiichiwakwaanesiin. Gii-waabizhagindibe. Mewinzha giiwenh gii-aakozi. Akina dash ogii-wanitoonan iniw wiinizisan. Oonh, gichi-aya'aawi a'aw akiwenzii.

[4]   Bi-maajaad iwidi Gabekanaansing gigizheb, mii amanj gaa-izhichigegwen, mii izhi-gwayak gaa-pi-izhaad. Maagizhaa gaye gaa-ozhitoogwen omiikanens, omaa dash neyaashiing gii-pi-izhaad. Ogosan imaa gii-taawan. Ogitab gii-izhinikaazowan. Gii-kagaanwaanikwe a'aw inini.

[5]   Miish iko imaa bi-nibaad a'aw akiwenzii. Mii miinawaa gigizheb goshkozigwen, mii miinawaa bi-maajaad, izhaad iwidi Gabekanaansing, dibishkoo sa go washki-giiwe. Mii i'iw ani-naadagoodood, miinawaa ani-naajiwanii'iged. Mii miinawaa onaagoshininig, iwidi dagoshing endaayaang.

Aazhawakiwenzhiinh

[1] We had a certain old man staying with us. He was the old lady's brother. His name was Aazhawakiwenzhiinh.

[2] We used to live far away at Portage Lake which was called Gabekanaansing 'At the End of the Trail'. The old man got up in the morning, put his moccasins on, tied up some tea, sugar, and a little bread, and packed it on his back.

[3] And a *misko-waabowayaan* 'red blanket'—that's what they called those big blankets long ago— that's what he wore. He never took off his hat. He was bald. It was said that he had been sick long ago. He lost all his hair. Oh, that old man was ancient.

[4] In the morning, when he left there at Portage Lake for here, I don't know how he did it, he came straight here. Maybe he made his own trail when he came here to the point. His son lived there. His name was Ogitab. That man had long hair.

[5] The old man slept there. And in the morning when he woke up, he left here to go there to Portage Lake, just like a round trip. He got his snares and traps on the way. In the evening he arrived back at our place.

[6]   Gaawiin gaye wiikaa nibaaganing gii-shingishinziin. Miinawaa
niibininig agwajiing wiigiwaaming gii-nibaa. Zagimewayaanan
ogii-aabaji'aan.

[7]   Noomaya-sh igo nawaj gii-nibo a'aw akiwenzii. Mii eta go
gaa-izhichiged, apane gii-izhaad iwidi Gabekanaansing
biibooninig, agoodood miinawaa wanii'iged.

[8]   Mii sa go minik.

[6]   He never lay down in a bed. In the summer he slept outside in a wigwam. He used a mosquito bar.

[7]   Not long after that the old man died. That's all he did, always going there to Portage Lake in the winter, snaring and trapping.

[8]   That's all.

Gegoo Gii-madwesing
Zaaga'iganiing

[1]   Gichi-mewinzha imaa ingii-noondam zaaga'igan
bezhig iwidi—amanj iidog ezhi-anishinaabewinikaadeg
ezhinikaadegwen zaaga'igan. Biiwaabikokaaning iwidi awas,
dagon i'iw zaaga'igan.

[2]   Bezhig giiwenh a'aw akiwenzii ezhi-maajaad, naadid mashkiki.
Miish giiwenh iwidi jiigibiig ezhi-namadabid giiwenh, ezhi-
nagamod manidoo-nagamonan, ingoji-sh igo niiwin, niiwin
nagamonan, iniw manidoo-nagamonan. Mii giiwenh ezhi-
maajijiwang i'iw zaaga'igaans. Miish giiwenh ingoding, ingoding
igo, mii imaa awiiya ezhi-mookiid. Onikaa miinawaa
oshtigwaani, akina sa go ezhi-naagozid igo anishinaabe, mii ezhi-
naagozid. Miish giiwenh ezhi-maajitaad manashkikiwed
onikaaning, maagizhaa gaye oshtigwaanining, akina go gegoo
miinawaa go imaa okaakiganaaning, miinawaa go okaadining.
Akina go, mii ezhi-bakwe'ang giiwenh, mii i'iw wegodogwen
dinowa.

[3]   Miish giiwenh giizhiitaad, mii ezhi-gaganoonaad, "Mii i'iw
minik waa-manashkikiwaaninaan," odinaan giiwenh. Mii
miinawaa ezhi-maajii-nagamod. Mii miinawaa ezhi-maajijiwang
zaaga'igaans. Miish giiwenh ezhi-gondaataad a'aw manidoo.

[4]   Ingoding-sh igo giiwenh apane go, gichi-mookomaanag imaa
nibaawaad, ezhi-noondamowaad i'iw medwesininig, ishkwaa-
aabitaa-dibikadinig. Mayagwewesinini. Miish igo gaa-izhi-
gotamowaad ingiw gichi-mookomaanag. Gaawiin imaa gii-
izhaasiiwag.

What Goes Clink in the Lake

[1]   A long time ago I heard about one lake over there—I don't know what the name of that lake is in Indian. That lake is on the other side of Ironton.

[2]   One old man went to get medicine. He sat right on the lake shore and sang spiritual songs there, about four of them. That lake started to whirl. Then somebody came up from the water. He had arms and a head and was just like what a human being looks like. Then the old man started making medicine off from the other one's arms, maybe his head, all over, even from his chest and legs. He started taking chunks from here and there of I don't know what.

[3]   When he got through, he told the other one, "That's all of the medicine I'll take from you," he said to him. Then he started singing again. The lake whirled again. Then the manitou went under.

[4]   One time some white people were sleeping there and after midnight they heard something clinking. It was a strange clinking sound. Those white people were afraid of it. They didn't go over there.

[5]   Miish ingoding ingii-nagadenimaanaan gichi-mookomaan
bezhig. Anooj gii-inaajimo, mii a'aw gichi-mookomaan. Miish
i'iw ekidod i'iw iwidi zaaga'igan gii-noondang gegoo
madwesininig, gii-noondamowaad. Miish giiwenh gaa-izhi-
gojichiged mii a'aw gichi-mookomaan gaa-o-izhi-nibaad iwidi.
Mii sa giiwenh eshkwaa-aabitaa-dibikadinig gaa-izhi-noondang
i'iw medwesininig imaa noondang i'iw medwesininig imaa. Mii
eta go minik gaa-izhi-noondamaan.

[6]   Miish geget gii-tebweyendamaan, miish imaa gii-noondawag
mii gaa-tibaajimotawid ikwe. Miish iwedi gaa-mikwendamaan mii
go naa i'iw zaaga'igan iidog gaa-tazhi-nagamod iko imaa
akiwenzii manashkikiwed.

[5]   Once we got to be friends with this one white man. He used to tell all sorts of stories, that white man. He said that he had heard something clinking over there at that lake, that they had heard it. That white man tried to go and sleep over there. After midnight he heard something clinking there. That's all I heard of it.

[6]   I believed what I heard that lady tell me. I remembered about that lake where the old man sang while getting medicine.

Waawaashkeshiwayaan

[1]   Miinawaa aabiding, mii iwidi ezhi-ozhiged
ayaangodinong agwajiing—aaniish naa gii-kichi-anishinaabe-
mindimooyenyiwi—imaa endaayaang wii-ozhi'aad anishinaabe-
bakwezhiganan, gegoo sa go wii-izhichiged, gegoo gaye wii-
panzang.

[2]   Dibi-sh iidog gaa-ondinaagwen iniw waawaashkeshiwayaanan.
Waa, enda-minwendam, gaa-izhi-dazhiikawaad gii-
chiishaakwa'waad. Gaawiin go michiigizisiin
gidagaakoonsiwayaan. Aaniish,[1] gaawiin igo, aanawi go
animoshag ingii-ayaawaanaanig iwidi. Miish boodawed ko imaa,
miish ko iwidi ishpiming iwidi giikanaamodenig mii iwidi gii-
asaad, gagwejimag aaniish i'iw ezhichiged. Miish[2] i'iw ekidod,
"Da-ayaa da-nookiigizi," ikido.

[3]   Biboonini. Ingoding-sh igo da-bi-dagoshinaan ishkwaa-
gikinoo'amaagooyaan, "Naawakamigook"—ganabaj makizinan
owii-ozhitoonan—"Naawakamigook daga o-ningiz a'aw goon.
Gizhaagamideg idash, agonjim a'aw ji-nookaabaawed. I'iw
inzhiishiibiigibinaanaan dibikak," indig.

[4]   Haa, izhi-maajaayaan enda-minwendam imaa wiigiwaaming
wii-o-namadabiyaan. Ningizo a'aw goon. Mii azhigwa go
ondemagak igo i'iw nibi,[3] gaa-izhi-biina'wag a'aw
waawaashkeshiwayaan; waa, gaa-izhi-gondaabiiginag imaa.
Gaawiin ingii-wiindamaagosiin, mii i'iw eta go gii-izhid ji-
ningizwag a'aw goon, ji-agonjimag a'aw waawaashkeshiwayaan.
Waa, mii azhigwa gegaa go ondeg nibi, miish imaa agonjimag.

A Deerhide

[1] Other times she [my grandmother] would build a lodge outside—well, after all she was a real old Indian woman—when she wanted to make some Indian bread there at our place, or do things like singeing.

[2] I don't know where she must have got the deerhide from. Oh, she's just happy working on it, scraping it. It was a not very big fawn hide. Well, we always had dogs there. She built a fire and hung it up above where it was smoky, so I asked her why she did that. She said, "It will get soft being there," she said.

[3] It was wintertime. After I came home from school, "Naawakamigook,"—maybe she was making moccasins—"Naawakamigook, go and melt the snow. After the water gets warm, soak it so it gets soft. We'll stretch it tonight," she told me.

[4] So I left, just glad to go and sit in that wigwam. The snow melted. Then when the water was boiling, I put the deerhide in, plunged it in there. She didn't tell me much about it; she just told me to melt the snow to soak the deerhide in it. The water was about to boil and I put it in to soak. It just shrank and shrank. It got real small.

Mii go naa ezhi-odaapishkaad, ezhi-odaapishkaad. Enda-
agaashiinyi. "Gaawiin wiikaa, aaniin naa izhiwebizid,"
indinendam. "Nimaamaanaan," indinaa, "mii go naa gaa-izhi-
odaapishkaad a'aw waawaashkeshiwayaan.

[5]   "Yay, yay, yay, yay," ikido, bazigonjised, "aaniin ezhi'ad?"

[6]   "Naan, ingii-onzaan i'iw nibi, miish imaa gaa-izhi-
gondaabiiginag," indinaa.

[7]   Mii sa gaa-izhi-banaaji'ag a'aw waawaashkeshiwayaan. Miish
gaawiin wiikaa ingii-anoonigosiin. Gego sa ingii-
kanawaabamaasiin ji-dazhiikawaad iniw waawaashkeshiwayaanan,
mewinzha. Mii gii-panaaji'imag iniw owaawaashkeshiwayaanan.

"Well, I never, what's happening to it," I thought.
"Grandma," I said to her, "the deerhide shrank."

[5]   "No, no, no, no," she said, getting up quick,
"what are you doing to it?"

[6]   "Gramma, I boiled the water and plunged it in
there," I told her.

[7]   So I ruined the deerhide. She had never had me
do it. I had never watched her working on a
deerhide, long ago. I ruined that deerhide of hers.

Gii-ningizowaad
Miskwaadesiwag

[1]   Miinawaa gii-wiijiiwag gaa-izhi-
agwaabiiga'amawid,[1] ingoji niishtana iniw miskwaadesiwan.
Aaniish[2] naa gaawiin mamaajiisiiwag, maagizhaa gaye
nebaawaagwen, gaa-izhi-okoshimagwaa imaa agwajiing, gaa-izhi-
zoogipog.

[2]   Ingoding-sh igo a'aw ninoshenh gaa-pi-izhi-izhaad. "Aaniish
apii Naawakamigook waa-amwadwaa ingiw gimiskwaadesiimag,"
indig.

[3]   "Oonh, wayiiba go," indinaa. Gaawiin gaye imaa biindig
imbagidinigoosiimin ji-giiziswangidwaa ji-maazhimaasowaad.
Gichi-mookomaanag imaa indayaawaanaanig.

[4]   Ingoding igo gii-izhi-zaaga'amaan akikoons gaa-izhi-mamag.
Nibi zaaga'iganiing iko ingii-onda'ibiimin. Gaawiin mashi ingii-
ayaanziimin imaa onda'ibaan, zaaga'amaan gaa-izhi-nibi-
naadiyaang, nibi imaa ji-ondemagak, naanan ingoji go naanan
ingiw miskwaadesiwag, imaa gaa-izhi-biina'wagwaa.
Mashkawaakwajiwag. Gaawiin mamaajiisiiwag, biina'wagwaa
miskwaadesiwag, mii imaa akikong. Mii go naa-sh mamaajiiwaad,
ganawaabamagwaa. "Aaniin ezhiwebiziwaad?" Ingoding
gizhaagamideg i'iw nibi, oo yay apagizowaad wiikwaji'owaad wii-
saagijiba'idiwaad imaa akikong. Oo, yay gichi-zegiziyaan ji-
zaagizibatooyaan. Miish iwidi, ninoshenh gashkigwaaso ganabaj
imaa, waabooyaan. "Mii akina gii-maajiiba'idiwaad ingiw
miskwaadesiwag, akina nengizowaad." Mii gaa-izhi-
zaagiziba'idiwaad[3] imaa akikong," indinaa, gichi-zegiziyaan.

When the Mud Turtles Thawed Out

[1]   And I was with my uncle when he took about twenty mud turtles off the lake for me. Well, they weren't moving, maybe they were asleep, so I piled them up outside and then it snowed.

[2]   My aunt came over one time. "Well, Naawakamigook, when are you going to eat your turtles?" she said to me.

[3]   "Oh, in a little while," I told her. We weren't allowed to cook them inside in case they would stink. We had white people around.

[4]   One day I went out taking a kettle along. We used to get our water from the lake. We didn't have a pump there yet, so I went outside and got water, water to boil in the kettle, and put five of the turtles in it. They were frozen. Those turtles weren't moving when I put them in the kettle. As I watched them, they started moving. "What's happening to them?" As the water got a little bit hotter, oh my, they were swimming against it trying to get out of the pail. I was really scared and I ran away. My aunt was there sewing, maybe on a quilt. "All the turtles ran away when they thawed out. They all got out of the kettle," I told her, really scared.

[5]   "Oo yay, gichi-baapinodawadwaa," indig.

[6]   Mii gaawiin miinawaa ingii-washki-giiwesiin. Gaawiin niwii-waabamaasiig.[4] Mii iidog imaa ningizowaad ingiw miskwaadesiwag, mii iidog imaa gaa-izhi-goshkoziwaad. Amanj iidog, gaawiin ingikendanziin amanj gaa-izhiwebiziwaagwen maagizhaa gaye gaa-maadoodewaagwen maagizhaa gaye gaa-nibaawaagwen miinawaa.

[7]   Mii sa go i'iw.

[5]   "Oh, my, you're being disrespectful and wasting them," she told me.

[6]   I didn't go back again. I didn't want to see them. When those turtles thawed out, they must have woken up. I don't know what must have happened to them, maybe they crawled away and went to sleep again.

[7]   That's it.

Giiwenigewin

[1]   Giishpin giiwenh awiiya nibod, inini, mii a'aw
iniw odayi'iiman akina ezhi-asiginigaadenig. Mii azhigwa wii-
ningwa'ond, mii ezhi-gashkibijigaadenig. Miish a'aw ogichidaa,
mii a'aw mayaajiidood. Mewinzha wiin gaye gaa-izhichigewaad.

[2]   Aapiji go niibowa gegoo ayaanzig, iniw okonaasan, miish
ingiw wayaanikejig, mii maajiinind, miish iwidi ezhi-miinindwaa
ingiw wayaanikejig, ininiwag. Mii mewinzha gaa-izhichigewaad.

[3]   Miinawaa niibowa gegoo ayaang, mii i'iw nibod,
bimiwanaanikaadenig iniw odayi'iiman, gashkibidenig, anooj igo
gegoo, baashkizigan, akina go gegoo, wanii'iganan, miinawaa go
iniw odayi'iiman, omakizinan, wegodogwen sa go ge-
dibendamogwen.

[4]   Miish a'aw ogichidaa ezhi-maajiidood. Miish iwidi ayaang iniw
odayi'iimini iniw nebonijin. Mii bebaa-izhi-izhiwinaad iniw
asemaan endaanid iniw anishinaaben. Mii ezhi-wiindamawaad
apii ge-niimi'idiwind. Miish ezhaawaad imaa ingiw anishinaabeg
niimi'idiing, niimi'idiwaad. Miish imaa miigiwewaad miinidiwaad
iniw odayi'iimini. Geget-sh wiin meshkwad miinaa a'aw ikwe
gegoo ge-aabajitood. Maagizhaa gaye waabooyaanan miinaa a'aw
ikwe, mii imaa niimi'idiwind.

Return Mourning

[1]   If anybody, a man, dies, everything he owned is gathered up. When he is to be buried, it's tied up in a bundle. The *ogichidaa* is the one who takes it away. That's what they did long ago.

[2]   If he doesn't have very many things, just blankets, the men who dig the grave are given them when he is buried. That's what they did long ago.

[3]   If he has a lot of things when he dies, then his belongings are put in a bundle and tied up, all sorts of things: the gun, everything, the traps, his clothes, his moccasins, whatever he owned.

[4]   The ogichidaa takes them away. He keeps the belongings of the one who died. He takes tobacco around to the Indian community. He tells them when the dance will be. Then the Indians go to the dance and dance. That's where they have a give-away and distribute his things. Of course the woman is given in exchange what she can use. Maybe the woman is given blankets there at the dance.

[5]   Giishpin-sh wiin ikwe nibod, mii a'aw ogichidaakwe, mii a'aw esiginang iniw ikwewan odayi'iimini, akina go gegoo. Mii go gaye dibishkoo ezhichigeng: niimi'idiing, miigiwewind iniw odayi'iiman.

[6]   Mii sa go i'iw.

[5]   If a woman dies, the *ogichidaakwe* picks up her
         things, everything. The same things are done;
         there's a dance and a distribution of her things.

[6]   That's it.

Gii-maajaa'ind A'aw Makwa

[1]   Mewinzha iwidi Gabekanaansing gii-taayaang, baanimaa go baanimaa awegwen iidog gaa-pi-dagoshinogwen.

[2]   "Wii-ayaamagad iwidi. Wii-sagaswe'idiwag,"[1] ikido a'aw nookomis. "Wii-maajaa'idim," ikido. Gaawiin ninisidotawaasiin amanj ekidogwen.

[3]   Miish gaawiin awiiya inini gii-ayaasiin. Inzhishenyiban wiin igo gii-ayaa. Gaawiin dash gii-mino-ayaasiin. Niin dash ingii-onapinaag bebezhigooganzhiig. Wii-pi-maajaa wewiib gigizheb, gaa-o-izhi-onapinagwaa bebezhigooganzhiig biboonodaabaanensing, gaa-pi-izhi-maajaayaang, maajidaabiiba'igoyaang, ginwenzh igo, amanj daso-diba'igan apii, ginwenzh igo bimiba'idiwaad ingiw bebezhigooganzhiig, de-onaagoshig, imaa dagoshinaang neyaashiing.

[4]   Bezhig-sh igo wiigiwaam, maagizhaa gaye wiigiwaam, maagizhaa gaye waakaa'igan, gaawiin sa go ingikendanziin, anishinaabeg iwidi biindigeyaawanidiwaad. Mii gaye niin ani-wiijiiwag a'aw nookomisiban. Niwenda-zegiz aaniin waa-izhichigewaad. Wegwaagi ani-biindigeyaang imaa, mii iidog a'aw bezhig a'aw inini mitig dakonang ezhi-ayinoo'amawaad iniw anishinaaben ji-namadabinid, imaa ishkwaandeming, ani-biindigeyaang inoo'amaagooyaang gaye niinawind iwidi ji-wawenabiyaang.

[5]   Iwidi inaabiyaan, inaabiyaan iwidi, ate ayi'iing imaa, miish imaa aya'aa, makoshtigwaan imaa gii-atemagad. Gii-wenda-

The Bear's Funeral

[1]   Long ago when we were living at Portage Lake, all of a sudden, somebody, I don't know who, came over.

[2]   "It's going to be over there. They are going to have a meeting over there," my grandmother said. "There's going to be a funeral," she said. I didn't understand what she was saying.

[3]   There wasn't any man around. Just my uncle was there. He wasn't well. I was the one who hitched up the horses. She wanted to leave early in the morning, so I went and hitched up the horses to the sleigh and we left for over here, driving for a long time, I don't know how many hours, with the horses running for a long time until late in the evening we arrived at the point.

[4]   There was one wigwam, either a wigwam or a house, I don't know which, where the Indians were going in. I started going along with my grandmother. I was scared about what they were going to do. Well, as we went in, there was a man holding a stick and pointing out where the people could sit, and as we went in the door, he pointed out where we too could sit.

[5]   Then I looked the other way and there it was, a bear's head. The bear was just huge and was all

mindido² a'aw makwa, zenibaansan akina gii-wawezhi'aawinden
a'aw makwa. Miish imaa onaaganan gichi-niibowa ezhi-ateg.
Miish imaa gaagiigidod a'aw akiwenzii, gaawiin dash
ingezikwendanziin aaniin gaa-ikidod. Mii dibishkoo go awiiya
nibod, maajaa'ind. Mii gaa-izhichigewaad, mewinzha.

decorated with ribbons. There were a lot of dishes around in there. An old man spoke, but I don't remember what he said. It was just like somebody died, a regular funeral. That's what they did long ago.

Zhemaagiwebiniganag

[1]   Mewinzha ingiw mindimooyenyag iko giiwenh gegabe-biboon, gaawiin gegoo izhichigesiiwag. Miish ingiw[1] zhemaagiwebiniganag izhinikaazowag ingiw ginebigoog— mazinikozowag, niiwin. Gaawiin-sh giiwenh gaye anishaa awiiya odaa-ayaawaasiin. Awiiya eta go obawaanaaganid, mii ezhi-ayaawaad. Miish i'iw gegabe-biboon ezhichigewaad ingiw mindimooyenyag; oonh, ikwewag igo, awegwen igo, zhemaagiwebinigewaad, ataadiwaad igo dibishkoo.[2]

[2]   Miish ingiw zhemaagiwebiniganag, mii go ginebigoog ezhi-naagoziwaad. Ingii-wiidookawaag[3] aabiding, ingii-kanawaabamaag. Miish gaa-izhi-achiged bezhig a'aw mindimooyenh bagiwayaan, gaa-izhi-maajitaayaan gaye niin— wegodogwen niin gaa-achigewaanen—maajitaayaan azhigwa, apaginagwaa ingiw ginebigoog. Mii[4] niizh gaa-izhi-aazhigijisewaad. Miinawaa niizh gii-animikosewag. Miish niizhing miinawaa gaa-izhi-apaginagwaa. Mii akina gaa-izhi-aazhigijisewaad, gaa-izhi-niiwenagwaa. Niswi gaye aazhigijisewaad, mii i'iw nising ayaang, miinawaa animikosewaad, mii go gaye dibishkoo, mii niizho-gabenaaged.[5]

[3]   Miish i'iw gaa-ikidowaad iko ingiw mindimooyenyag, gaawiin giiwenh awiiya ginwenzh odaa-odaminwaanaasiin iniw, miinawaa asemaan asaawaad azhigwa wii-ataadiwaad. Giishpin giiwenh anishaa awiiya izhichiged i'iw, niizhogon, maagizhaa gaye nisogon, maagizhaa gaye geginwenzh iko gii-ataadiwag, mii

The Snake Game Dice

[1] Long ago the women didn't have anything to do all winter long. Four snake game dice called *zhemaagiwebiniganag* are carved. No one should have any without a reason. Only someone who dreams of them can have them. That's what the old women did throughout the winter; oh, the ladies, whoever, played the snake game, just like they were gambling.

[2] Those dice look like snakes. I was helping them once and watched them. One old lady bet a piece of cloth, so I too started in—I don't know what I must have bet—I started in and cast those snakes. Two of them turned belly-side up. And two turned belly-side down. So I cast them two more times. All of them turned belly-side up so I beat everyone. If three turn belly-side up, the player gets three turns, and if they turn belly-side down, then it is as if it counts double.

[3] The old ladies used to say that no one should play with them for very long, and they put out tobacco when they wanted to play. If anyone did this without a reason, gambled for two or three days or longer, then when she went to sleep, she'd dream only of snakes. No one should play

giiwenh ani-nibaad, mii eta go ezhinang ginebigoon. Miish iidog i'iw, gaawiin ginwenzh awiiya odaa-odaminwaanaasiin miinawaa gaawiin anishaa awiiya odaa-ayaawaasiin, mii go genapii ginebigoon ezhi-waabamaad.

with them for very long and no one should just play with them for fun, or pretty soon she'll see snakes.

TEXTUAL NOTES

Material deleted, added, or changed in the redictation process is noted here. Material deleted is marked by angled brackets ‹ ›. Material inserted is marked by curly brackets { }. Other words not changed may be given to help locate the changes or to help understand the kind of change made. False starts which lead to accepted complete forms of the intended word of the false start are not noted.

GII-IKWEZENSIWIYAAN

1. ‹gii-ayaawaad› {gii-ayaag}
2. ‹wiigwaad... apakwayan› {wiigwaasabakwayan}
3. ‹gii-gikinoo... › gii-michaa-sh
4. ‹that time you know, I was watching her [laugh]› ganawaabamag
5. {i'iw ziinzibaakwadwaaboo}
6. ‹giizhikaandag› {zhingobaandag}
7. ‹miinawaa ogii-adaawaagenaawaa ko wewiibish ko maa gii-ayaa adaawewinini ko maa bi-izhiwidoowaad iniw› {miinawaa adaawewininiwan ogii-adaamigowaan ziiga'iganan}
8. ‹mii ezhi-... ingiiwemin... › mii ezhi-giiweyaang
9. ‹coffee› {makade-mashkikiwaaboo}

ISKIGAMIZIGANING

1. ‹iskigamiziganaatig› {iskigamiziganaak}
2. ‹miish i'iw, miish i'iw› miish ingiw
3. ‹miish... › oziikoobiiginaanaawaan

OMBIGAMIZIGEWIN

1. ‹gwaaba'amaan› {jekaagaminamaan}

2. ‹i'iw ayi'ii› i'iw ziinzibaakwad
3. ‹so... so... [laugh]› mii
4. ‹ezhi-biskitenang› {ezhi-bajiishkinang}
5. ‹gii-izhinikaade... › gii-izhinikaazowag
6. ‹ziibiiga'igan› giziibiiginakokwaanaaboo

INGII'IGOSHIM

1. ‹gaa-izhi... gaa-izhi-› gigizheb
2. ‹gaa-izhi... › naawakamigook
3. {eshkwaa-minikweyaan, agwajiing gaa-izhiwidood, gii-agoodood gii-peshibii'ang akakanzhe aabiding.}

ISHKODE-JIIMAAN

1. ‹aya'aa› {zhingwaakwag}
2. ‹zhingwaakwag› {zhingwaakwaandagoog}
3. ‹zhingwaakwag› {zhingwaakwaandagoog}
4. ‹that's about all›

GII-PAAGIJIGEWAAD ANIMIKIIG

1. ‹ezhin-... ezhi-ishk... ezhi-... › {ge-izhinikaadamowaambaanen}

GICHIGAMIIWASHKOON

1. ‹anaakanashkoon› {gichigamiiwashkoon}
2. ‹but... › ingii-kina'amaag-sh

JIIMAAN

1. ‹mii ezhi-biidaasagaa... biidaadagaaziiba'idiwaad and [laugh]› biidaadagaaziiba'idiwaad
2. [with extra vowel length: anooj]

GII-MAWINZOYAANG

1. ‹gaawiin go obima'aasiin› {ogii-kijinagizhiinaan}
2. ‹mii ezhi-ayaad› {indoodaabii'iwemin}
3. ingii-kitigaadaamin ‹miinawaa-sh ko ningwa'igeyaang›

MIKINAAKOONSAG

1. ‹cause... because... › ziinzibaakwadoons
2. ‹miish imaa, mii imaa apane› inzhaashaaginizide
3. ‹miish i'iw› imaa
4. ‹miish... › wewiib
5. ‹miish... › gaawiin
6. ‹miskwaadesiinsag› {mikinaakoonsag}
7. ‹miskwaadesiinsag› {mikinaakoonsag}
8. mii ingiw ‹miskwaadesiwag ikido. mii imaa... mikinaakoonsag ingiw, mikinaakoonsag, mii imaa obagidin," ikido› {mikinaakoonsag}
9. ‹miskwaades... › mikinaakwag

WESE'AN

1. ‹eni-gashkan... eni-anokiijig› {eni-gashkanokiijig}
2. ‹gaa-izhi-webaashin... › gaa-izhi-webaashiwaad

GII-O-BAPASHKOBIJIGEYAANG I'IW GITIGAAN

1. ‹ogii-madwe'waa... ogii-madweyaab... › ogii-madwe'waan

EGWANIGAAZOD ODAABAAN

1. ‹gii-izhaa... gii-izhaad... gii-i... gii-i... › {gii-izhaayaan}
2. ‹ikidowag... ikido... › ikido
3. ‹wenjibaawan... › wenjibaanid

MISKWAADESIWAG

1. ‹miish... › mii go
2. ‹gidaa... › aaniish naa

MINISIIWIKWE

1. ‹her spirit ayaa sa go, amanj iidog ge-ikidowaambaanen› mii
2. ‹that's all› {mii sa go i'iw}

IMBAGIDA'WAAMIN

1. ‹ninisidotanz... › ingezikwendanziin

NAAZHWASHKWAK BAASHKIZIGAN GII-MADWEZIGEYAAN
1. ‹mii imaa ayi'ii› mii

MIKINAAKWAG
1. ‹miish gaa-izhi... miish... › nookomis
2. ezhi-gaaskizwaawaad ‹ezhi-ayaa... ezhi-gaaskizwaawaad›
3. ‹what year› gikinoonowin

INDINIGAAZ, INDINIGAAZ MANIDOOMINENSAG
1. ‹around the fire› giiwitaashkode
2. ‹so... › gaa-izhi-agwazhe'id
3. [sung: indinigaaz, indinigaaz manidoominensag]
4. [sung: indinigaaz, indinigaaz manidoominensag]
5. ‹gegoo sa go, ziinzibaakwad, gegoo... › anishinaabe-
   ziinzibaakwad
6. ‹ogii-ayaanaawaa› wegodogwen

AWIIYA IMBIMINZHA'OG (VERSION 1)
1. ‹she gave me some tobacco and... › gaa-izhi-miizhid
2. ‹playing around› babaamibatooyaang
3. ‹akiwenzii› mindimooyenh
4. ‹he said go on› maajaan

AWIIYA IMBIMINIZHA'OG (VERSION 2)
Personal names in this text have been deleted or replaced by
grammatically appropriate nouns.
1. anishinaabeg ‹so much a pound›
2. ‹miish... › mii
3. waaj'-anokiimag ‹[name] inaa›
4. ‹[name]› {a'aw ikwe}
5. ‹[name] inaa› {niinimoshenh}

MANOOMINIKENG
1. ‹zaaga'iganiing gomaa go michaa› {manoominaganzhikaansing
   ezhaayaang}
2. ‹ezhi-ozhige... › ezhi-ozhigewaad

3. ‹ezhi-maajaawaad, eyaawaad [tape stopped]› ezhi-maajaawaad
4. ‹ziinzi . . . i'iw ayi'ii manoomin› i'iw manoomin

BIINDAAKWAAN

1. ‹mii ezhi- . . . › gii-niizhoonagiziwag
2. ‹minisin . . . no, not minisinaakwaang› miish
3. ‹miish . . . › niiyawen'enyiban-sh
4. ‹gaa-izhi-inoo . . . › gaa-izhi-ayaayaan
5. ‹maajida . . . › onapijigeg

MEMEGWESIWAG

1. ‹bimoseyaang› ani-bawa'amaang
2. ‹aazha . . . › ganabaj
3. gii-ikido {miish i'iw gaa-ikidod, gagiibwaweyiingwewag ingiw memegwesiwag}

GII-NAGISHKAWAG A'AW MOONIYAAWIKWE

1. ‹waabizheshiwag› {waabizheshiwan}
2. ‹gaawiin . . . › bagandiziwag

GEGO ONADINAAKEGON A'AW GOON

1. ‹o-biigwa'ok› {o-niigwa'ok}

WAAWAASHKESHIWAYAAN

1. ‹miish i'iw ekidod iwidi . . . › aaniish
2. ‹and she said [laugh]› miish
3. igo ‹azhigwa a'aw goon onzwag a'aw goon ondemagad azhigwa› {i'iw nibi}

GII-NINGIZOWAAD MISKWAADESIWAG

1. ‹gaa-izhini . . . › gaa-izhi-agwaabiiga'amawid
2. ‹miish iwidi gaa . . . › aaniish naa
3. ‹gaa-izhi-agwaabii . . . › gaa-izhi-zaagiziba'idiwaad
4. ‹ingi . . . › niwii-waabamaasiig

GLOSSARY

Using the Glossary

To aid students of the Ojibwe language in using these texts, each of the word stems appearing in them is presented in the Main Glossary, alphabetized according to the inflected citation form for each stem. A word class code and an English gloss are given for each main entry. Prefixes which occur in the texts are also listed in the Main Glossary.

As many Ojibwe words are inflected with suffixes, often combining into complex endings, these endings are listed in two differently arranged lists, the Forward List of Endings and the Inverse List of Endings. The first list contains endings alphabetized in the usual way, from left to right, and the second list contains endings alphabetized from right to left. Each entry in these lists has a word class code and information on the grammatical categories represented in the ending, but no further analysis into the separate suffixes.

An overview of the structure of Ojibwe words is presented below to help in using these tools.

OJIBWE WORD CLASSES

There are three basic classes of words in Ojibwe: two classes of inflected words, nouns and verbs, and a class of uninflected words, particles. Many subclasses can be set up within these, although only a few such distinctions are made here.

Nouns

Nouns contain a noun stem and may have one or more inflectional affixes, most of them suffixes. The basic suffix on a noun comes at the end of the word and indexes such grammatical categories as the gender of the noun (inherently animate or inanimate), the number of the noun (variably singular or plural), and, for animate nouns, a category of focus, obviation. The category of obviation distinguishes nouns and other third persons in close contact in discourse or a grammatical construction. A third person in focus is proximate (nonobviative) and may be inflected with the appropriate basic gender-number suffix. Other third persons in the close context of this third person are obviative. Obviative nouns which are animate in gender carry an obviative basic suffix, which does not distinguish number. Inanimate nouns are only covertly obviative in the same context; the usual basic gender-number suffix appears on them. In the proximate singular form of a noun, there is usually no overt basic suffix. The exceptions are a few very short stems.

The person of the possessor of a noun is shown on a possessed noun by a personal prefix (first, second, or third person). If the possessor is plural or obviative, a suffix indexing the categories of number or obviation appears on the possessed noun. The appropriate basic suffix comes at the end of the possessed noun. Certain noun stems, called dependent stems, are obligatorily inflected as possessed.

Nouns may also be inflected as preterit (most commonly on names and kin terms referring to someone deceased), pejorative, or vocative. A noun may also be converted to a particle by replacing the basic suffix with a locative suffix, the main use of which is to indicate spatial location.

In this glossary the singular form of a noun is given as the headword rather than an underlying stem. This form is followed by the plural ending or a full plural form. Knowledge of these forms is usually sufficient to create the underlying stem or to predict the forms the other affixes take when added to that noun. We do not analyze stems into any further components here. The endings are cited in the lists in the form they take when the singular is extracted. As a result, they may include some of the sound material that actually belongs to the underlying stem of the noun. Dependent nouns are listed twice, once under the underlying stem, cited between virgules, and once under a first person possessed form, if such a form is common.

Pronouns

Various types of noun substitutes are called pronouns. Interrogative, indefinite, and dubitative pronouns form a subclass of nouns and are similarly inflected except for person. Another nounlike pronoun serves as a pause word and a base for the construction of other nouns and particles. This base pronoun *aya'aa, ayi'ii* is generally inflected as a noun. These nominal pronouns have glossary entries similar to those for nouns.

The personal pronouns, which are animate in gender, reflect the categories of number and person. The demonstrative pronouns reflect the categories of gender, number, and obviation as well as different degrees of distance. Each of the demonstrative and personal pronouns that occur in the texts is given a separate entry in the glossary.

Verbs

A verb contains a verb stem around which inflectional affixes may appear. The categories (gender, number, obviation, and person) of the subject and/or object of a verb are indexed by these affixes on the verb. In a few forms, no overt affix occurs and the affix is treated as having a zero form or it has been deleted by phonological rules. These affixes occur in three distinct sets, each set marking an order of the verb having different grammatical functions. Generally, independent order verbs occur in main clauses, conjunct order verbs occur in subordinate clauses (but have a number of other uses) or as nominalizations called participles, and imperative order verbs occur in most commands and prohibitions. The verb stems, usually internally complex, are specialized for transitivity and, if intransitive, gender of the subject, or if transitive, for gender of the object.

In addition there may be suffixes indexing verbal categories such as mode, negation, and compassion. Prefixes for tense-aspect, location-direction and other adverbial categories may also appear in a verb. Two different processes can also alter the verb: in initial change, appearing only in some conjunct order verbs (including all participles), the first vowel in the verb can be altered; irregularly, a prefix is added. In reduplication a partial or full copy of the first part of a root can be prefixed to the stem, sometimes in altered form.

In the glossary, intransitive stems are cited in an inflected form that is generally the same as the abstract stem. Transitive verbs are cited in an imperative order form with a singular subject and a third person singular (inanimate or animate as the verb stem requires) object. An inanimate object is indicated by *s.t.* in the English gloss and an animate object is indicated by *s.o.*. Double object verbs which are inflected for an animate object but may occur with a second object of either gender, have the second object shown in the gloss with *something*. A few exceptions to this format are noted below.

For animate intransitive (VAI) stems, the citation form is the independent order third person singular form, a form identical to the abstract stem. The glosses, however, are given in the unmarked English form. For a few stems usually appearing only in the plural, the independent third person plural form is the citation form. The gloss in such an entry is given in the English third person plural form.

For inanimate intransitive (VII) stems, the citation form is the independent order singular form. This is the same as the stem except for a stem ending in *i* or *o*, which inserts an augment *n* in front of all endings other than those of the proximate conjunct forms.

For transitive inanimate stems, the citation form is an imperative form with a second person singular subject and a third person object. For verbs coded VTI the underlying stem, which is not a word, is found by dropping the inflectional ending *-an*. For verbs coded VTI2, the underlying stem is found by dropping the inflectional ending *-oon*. For verbs coded VTI3 and VTI4, the ending *-n* is dropped.

For transitive animate stems (VTA), the citation form is an imperative form with a second person singular subject and a third person singular object. In many cases this is the same as the underlying stem. Where it is not, the underlying stem is given between virgules. Stems ending in a consonant followed by /w/ have the citation forms ending in the consonant or *o*. Mutating stems whose last consonant varies depending on the following suffix are indicated with special symbols in the abstract stem. The symbol *N* indicates that the stem ends in *n* in some inflected forms and in *zh* in others. The symbol *S* indicates that the stem ends in *s* in some inflected forms and in *sh* in others. The symbol *nN* indicates that the stem ends in *n* in some inflected forms and *nzh* in others. In addition, the stem /iN-/ 'say so to s.o.', citation form *izhi*, drops completely in some inflected forms. While the main entry for such mutating stems is under the mutated imperative form, there is also a cross-reference entry under an incomplete unmutated form.

The verb endings given in the list are cited in the form taken when the underlying stem is removed. Endings that combine to some degree with the end of the stem are also cited in a second form. For example, transitive animate stems that end in /aw-/ show contraction of the /aw-/ to *aa* or *oo* before certain endings. These endings are cited once without the vowel and once with the contracted vowel. Similarly, transitive animate stems ending in /Cw-/ show vocalization of the /w/ to *o* before certain endings. These endings are cited once as consonant-initial and once as beginning with the *o*.

ANALYZING INFLECTED WORDS

To identify the full meaning of an Ojibwe inflected word, the stem, the prefixes, processes such as initial change and reduplication, and the inflectional ending must be identified. Identifying each of the components inside the stems and endings is difficult and requires a fuller grammatical treatment than can be presented here.

The following steps will help in the process of analysis:
(1) Consult the section Prefixes or the Main Glossary to identify the prefixes, if any.
(2) Look in the Main Glossary to locate the stem or main part of the word.
(3) Consult the Forward or Inverse List of Endings to identify the inflectional endings, if any.

PREFIXES

Prefixes on nouns are either personal prefixes or prenouns. The prefixes on verbs are personal prefixes, tense prefixes, direction prefixes, relative prefixes, or preverbs. Initial change alters the first syllable of the first part of a verb complex. Several tense prefixes may occur in a verb and there may be several preverbs, but generally only one of each of the other groups of prefixes may occur in a verb. The order in which these occur is given in the chart below:

VERB PREFIX ORDER CHART

1	2	3	4	5
(personal prefix) or (initial change)	(tense prefixes)	(direction prefix)	(relative prefix)	(preverbs)

In addition the process of reduplication adds a copy or partial copy of the first syllable to a verb stem, or occasionally one of the prefixes. The following steps will help in learning to peel off and identify prefixes.

1. Is there a personal prefix?

There are three personal prefixes, but each has a small number of variant forms. The personal prefix, if present, is the first part of the word. The following chart summarizes the forms of the personal prefixes as written in this book:

PERSONAL PREFIX CHART

	CONSONANT-INITIAL STEM			VOWEL INITIAL STEM	VOWEL-INITIAL DEP. NOUN STEM	
	b-	d-,j-,g-,z-,zh-	Other		-ii-	-oo-
1st	im	in	ni	ind	n	
2nd		gi		gid		g
3rd		o		od	w	(none)

A stem-initial *o* is lengthened to *oo* directly after a personal prefix.

2. Is there initial change?

If it has no personal prefix and has a conjunct ending, a verb might have initial change. This is a process that alters the first vowel sound (whether it is the first sound of the verb or comes after a consonant) in certain conjunct order verb forms. The nominalized verbs called participles (used, for example, in "who" and "what" questions) always have initial change. Initial change is also common in "when," "how," and some "where" questions, and in a number of other constructions. The first part of each changed form that occurs in the texts is given in the glossary with a cross-reference to the main entry. The regular pattern of initial change is given below. Not all words starting with such sequences (or having such sequences after an initial consonant) are changed forms.

INITIAL CHANGE CHART

UNCHANGED	CHANGED
a =	e =
aa =	ayaa =
e =	aye =
i =	e =
ii =	aa =
o =	we =
oo =	waa =

There are some stems with irregular initial change. These often begin with *dan=*, *das=*, *dazh=*, or *daa=* and make a changed form by prefixing *en=*. All examples occuring in the stories are given with a cross-reference to the main entry. For the changed form of the common prefixes see section 3.

3. Is there a verb prefix?

The following are the verb prefixes (other than the personal prefixes) that occur in the stories. They are always written with a trailing hyphen. The changed form, if known, is also given. All prefixes are also given in the glossary.

TENSE PREFIX CHART

UNCHANGED	CHANGED	
aano-		in vain
da-	ge-	(future)
daa-	ge-	(modal)
ga-	ge-	(future)
ji-	ge-	(future, modal)
gii-	gaa-	(past)
wii-	waa-	(desiderative)

DIRECTIONAL PREFIX CHART

UNCHANGED	CHANGED	
ani-	eni-	away; on the way
babaa-	bebaa-	about; around (extended)
baa-	—	about; around (local)
bi-	ba-	here; hither
bimi-	bemi-	by; along
o- (a'o- after a personal prefix)	we'o-	going over to

RELATIVE PREFIX CHART

UNCHANGED	CHANGED	
ako-	eko-	a certain length or extent
apiichi-	epiichi-	a certain exent; as much as
daso-	endaso-	so many; so much
dazhi-	endazhi-	there; in that place
izhi-	ezhi-	thus; so; there
onji-	wenji-	from; cause

4. Is there a preverb or prenoun?

Preverbs and prenouns are prefixes of fairly concrete meaning that may appear on word stems. They are listed in the glossary as PN if known primarily to occur on nouns, PV if on verbs, and PRE if on both, or on both and particles. More than one may occur in a word. They are usually written with a trailing hyphen. Since the first part of a verb stem often resembles or is identical to a preverb it may be difficult to be consistent in this practice. Some prenouns form uninflected particles with nouns. Some of the common prenouns and preverbs used are listed here:

PREVERBS AND PRENOUNS

PREFIX	TYPE	
agaji-	PN	on top
ashi-bezhigo-	PRE	eleven
aabita-	PRE	half
de-	PV	sufficient
enda- (wenda-)	PV	just; very
gabe-	PV	throughout; all of (a time)
gete-	PN	old
gichi-	PRE	very; great; big
giizhi-	PV	finish; complete
gwiinawi-	PV	unable to
ingo-	PRE	one
ishkwaa-	PV	after
jibwaa-	PV	before (ji- + bwaa-)
jiigi-	PN	near
madwe-	PV	audible at a distance
maji-	PN	bad
maajii-	PV	start; begin
maazhi-	PV	bad
michi-	PV	bare; just that
midaaso-	PRE	ten
mino-	PRE	good
misko-	PN	red
naano-	PRE	five
naawi-	PN	in the middle
niso-	PRE	three
niizho-	PRE	two
oshki-	PRE	new; young
wenda- (enda-)	PV	just; very
zhaangaso-	PRE	nine

5. Is there reduplication?

Reduplication is a process that affects the first syllable of verb stems, some prefixes, and a few particles. On many verbs it suggests extension or intermittency in time or space. On stative verbs it may indicate plurality. The full flavor of reduplication is not always fully reflected in the translations or glosses. Stems known to have reduplication are marked *Reduplicated form* in the Main Glossary. If the unreduplicate form is also in the texts, a cross-reference to it is given. No doubt there are stems in the glossary that have reduplication but are not so marked. Generally reduplication involves the prefixing of a syllable containing the same or a related consonant as the initial consonant of the un-reduplicated stem. The vowel of this prefixed syllable may differ from that of the unreduplicated stem. The original vowel and the original initial consonant may also change under reduplication. Vowel initial stems prefix *ay-* or *aay-* in most cases. There are some irregular patterns of reduplication.

CODES AND GRAMMATICAL TERMS

Verb Classes

VAI	animate intransitive verb—an intransitive verb with an animate subject.
VAI + O	VAI with object—a VAI stem inflected as a transitive verb.
VAI2	A VAI subclass—VTI-like stem inflected as intransitive.
VII	inanimate intransitive verb—an intransitive verb with an inanimate subject or an impersonal subject.
VTA	transitive animate verb—a transitive verb with an animate object. The stem is the same as the glossary headword unless given at the end of the entry.

VTI	transitive inanimate verb—transitive verb with an inanimate object. The stem is found by removing the imperative ending -*an* from the glossary headword; for example, *ganawendan* is an imperative form '(you) take care of it!' containing the stem /ganawend-/ and an imperative ending /-an/.
VTI2	a subclass of transitive inanimate verb. The stem is found by dropping the imperative ending /-oon/ from the imperative headword. Endings in the lists include the theme sign /oo/.
VTI3	another subclass of transitive inanimate verb. The only text examples are forms of *naadin* 'fetch s.t.' and *miijin* 'eat s.t.' The VAI + O verbs take the same suffixes as the VTI3 verbs.
VTI4	another subclass of transitive inanimate verbs. The only text example is *ayaan* 'have s.t.'.

Verb Category Codes

conjunct	conjunct order—the verb order generally used for subordinate clauses and in supplementary ("WH") questions.
conjunct particle	conjunct order participle (nominalized verb) in which the inflectional suffix complex differs from the usual conjunct suffix. Other participles also occur in the texts but if their suffix complex is the same as a regular conjunct one, then they are not distinguished from unchanged forms in the lists.
dubitative	dubitative mode
imperative	imperative order—used in commands.

imperative delayed	delayed imperative verb—used in requests to be executed in the future.
imperative prohibitive	prohibitive or negative imperative—prohibitions.
independent	independent order—generally used in main clauses.
negative	negative form
preterit	preterit mode
preterit dubitative	preterit dubitative mode

Person and Number Codes (subject and object)

If the ending is transitive, the person and number of the subject is given before the hyphen and the person and number of the object after the hyphen. The symbols used to show person and number are:

o	inanimate singular
op	inanimate plural
o(p)	inanimate singular or plural
o'	inanimate obviative singular
o'p	inanimate obviative plural
o'(p)	inanimate obviative singular or plural
1	first person singular
1p	first person plural exclusive (excluding the second person)
2	second person singular
21	first person plural inclusive (including the second person)

2p	second person plural
3	animate third person singular
3p	animate third person plural
3'	animate obviative
X	indefinite actor

Noun Class and Category Codes

N	noun of any gender
NA	animate noun
NAD	dependent animate noun—an animate noun which must occur with a personal prefix
NI	inanimate noun
NID	dependent inanimate noun—an inanimate noun which must occur with a personal prefix
locative	locative form of noun
pejorative	pejorative form of noun
vocative	vocative form of noun

Other Codes

e.o.	each other (marking reciprocal verbs)
o.s.	oneself (marking explicit reflexive verbs)
PC	particle (uninflected word)
PLACE	place name
PN	prenoun
PR	pronoun
PRE	prenoun, preverb, or preparticle

PV   preverb

s.o.   animate object of verb

s.t.   inanimate object of verb

Forward List of Endings

-ad	VTA conjunct 2-3
-adwaa	VTA conjunct 2-3p
-ag	N 3p
-ag	VTA conjunct 1-3
-agwaa	VTA conjunct 1-3p
-am	VAI2 independent 1,2,3
-amaambaan	VTI conjunct preterit 1-o,op
-amaan	VTI conjunct 1-o,op; VAI2 1
-amaang	VTI conjunct 1p-o,op; VAI2 conjunct 1p
-aminijin	VAI2 conjunct participle 3'
-amogwen	VTI conjunct dubitative 3-o,op
-amok	VTI imperative 2p-o,op
-amowaad	VTI conjunct 3p-o,op; VAI2 conjunct 3p
-amowaambaanen	VTI conjunct preterit dubitative 1-o
-amowaanen	VTI conjunct dubitative 1-o,op; VAI2 conjunct dubitative 1
-amoog	VAI2 independent 3p
-an	N op, 3'
-ang	VTA conjunct 21-3
-ang	VTI conjunct 3-o,op; VAI2 conjunct 3
-angen	VTI prohibitive 2-o,op; VAI2 prohibitive 2
-angid	VTA conjunct 1p-3
-angidwaa	VTA conjunct 1p-3p
-angig	VTI conjunct participle 3p-o,op; VAI2 conjunct participle 3p
-anzing	VTI conjunct negative X-o,op
-anziin	VTI independent negative 1,2,3-o; VAI2 independent negative 1,2,3

-anziinaawaa	VTI independent negative 2p,3p-o
-aa	VTA independent 1,2-3
-aa	VTA independent X-3
-aad	VTA conjunct 3-3'
-aadaanig	VTA imperative 21-3p
-aag	VTA independent 1,2-3p
-aag	VTA independent 3-1,2 (aw-)
-aagod	VTA conjunct 3'-3 (aw-)
-aagosiin	VTA independent negative 3-1 (aw-)
-aagowaad	VTA conjunct 3'-3p (aw-)
-aagoowaanen	VTA conjunct dubitative X-1 (aw-)
-aagooyaan	VTA conjunct X-1 (aw-)
-aagooyaang	VTA conjunct X-1p (aw-)
-aagwen	VTA conjunct dubitative 3-3'
-aajin	VTA conjunct participle 3-3'
-aakegon	VTA prohibitive 2p-3
-aamin	VTI independent 1p,21-o,op
-aan	VAI conjunct 1
-aan	VTA independent 3-3'
-aan	VTI independent 1,2,3-o
-aanan	VTI independent 1,2,3-op
-aanaan	VTA independent 1p,21-3
-aanaanig	VTA independent 1p,21-3p
-aanaawaa	VTI independent 2p,3p-o
-aanaawaan	VTI independent 2p,3p-op
-aang	N locative
-aang	VAI conjunct 1p
-aaning	N 3'-o locative
-aasigwaa	VTA conjunct negative 3p-3'
-aasiwag	VTA conjunct negative 1-3
-aasiwangid	VTA conjunct negative 1p-3
-aasiwaanaanig	VTA independent negative 1p,21-3p
-aasiwaawaan	VTA independent negative 3p-3'
-aasiig	VTA independent negative 1,2-3p
-aasiin	VTA independent negative 1,2-3, 3-3'

-aawag	VTA independent X-3p
-aawaad	VTA conjunct 3p-3'
-aawaagobanen	VTA conjunct preterit dubitative 3p-3'
-aawaan	VTA independent 3p-3'
-aawinden	VTA conjunct dubitative X-3
-ban	N preterit 3,o
-d	VAI conjunct 3; VAI + O 3-o,op; VTI3 conjunct 3-o,op
-d	VTA conjunct 3-1 (Cw-)
-daa	VAI imperative 21
-g	N 3p
-g	VAI conjunct 3
-g	VAI imperative 2p
-g	VII conjunct o,op
-g	VTA independent 3-1,2 (aw-) (Cw-)
-god	VTA conjunct 3'-3 (aw-)
-gosiin	VTA independent negative 3-1 (aw-)
-gowaad	VTA conjunct 3'-3p (aw-) (Cw-)
-goog	VTA independent 3p-1,2 (Cw-)
-goon	VTA independent 3'-3 (Cw-)
-goowaanen	VTA conjunct dubitative X-1 (aw-) (Cw-)
-gooyaan	VTA conjunct X-1 (aw-)
-gooyaang	VTA conjunct X-1p (aw-)
-gwen	VAI conjunct dubitative 3; VII conjunct dubitative o,op
-i	VTA imperative 2-3
-iban	N preterit 3,o
-id	VTA conjunct 3-1
-idog	N vocative plural
-ig	VTA independent 3-1,2
-igojin	VTA conjunct participle 3'-3
-igonaanig	VTA independent 3p-1p,21

-igosiimin	VTA independent negative 3-1p,21
-igosiin	VTA conjunct negative 3-1,2
-igowaa	VTA independent 3-2p
-igowaagwen	VTA conjunct dubitative 3'-3p
-igowaan	VTA independent 3'-3p
-igoo	VTA independent X-1,2
-igoog	VTA independent 3p-1,2
-igoomin	VTA independent X-1,2
-igoosiwaan	VTA conjunct negative X-1
-igoosiin	VTA independent negative X-1,2
-igoowaanen	VTA conjunct dubitative X-1
-igooyang	VTA independent X-21
-igooyaan	VTA conjunct X-1
-igooyaang	VTA conjunct X-1p
-igooyaanin	VTA conjunct participle X-1 (op as second object)
-ik	VTA imperative 2p-3
-im	N 1,2,3-0; 1,2-3
-imag	VTA conjunct 1-3'
-iman	N 3-3'
-iming	N 1,2,3-0 locative
-in	VTA independent 1-2
-inaan	VTA conjunct 1-2
-ind	VTA conjunct X-3
-indwaa	VTA conjunct X-3p
-ing	N locative
-ini	VII independent o'
-inid	VAI conjunct 3'
-inig	VII conjunct o',o'p
-ining	N 3'-o locative
-iniwan	VII independent op'
-ish	N pejorative 3,0
-ishig	VTA imperative 2p-1
-ishikegon	VTA prohibitive 2p-1
-ishin	VTA imperative 2-1
-isig	VTA conjunct negative 1-2
-isinooninim	VTA independent negative 1-2p
-iwaa	N 3p-0

-iwaad	VTA conjunct 3p-1
-iwaan	N 3p-op; 3p-3'
-iyan	VTA conjunct 2-1
-iyangid	VTA conjunct 3-1p
-iyangidwaa	VTA conjunct 3p-1p
-iyeg	VTA conjunct 2p-1
-iig	N 3p
-iimag	N 1,2-3p
-iin	N op, 3'
-iing	N locative
-iing	VAI conjunct X
-jig	VAI conjunct participle 3p
-k	VII conjunct o,op
-k	VTA imperative 2p-3 (Cw-)
-ken	VAI prohibitive 2; VTI3 prohibitive 2-o,op
-m	VAI independent X
-mag	N 1,2-3p
-man	N 1,2,3-op
-maan	VTI4 conjunct 1-o,op
-min	VAI independent 1p,21
-ming	N 1,2,3-o locative
-mini	N 3'-o,op
-mowaad	VTI4 conjunct 3p-o,op
-n	N op, 3'
-n	VAI imperative 2; VTI3 imperative 2-o,op
-n	VAI + O independent 1,2,3-o; VTI4 independent 1,2,3-o
-n	VTA independent 1-2 (aw-) (Cw-)
-nag	VAI + O independent 1,2-3p
-nan	VAI-O independent 1,2-3, 3-3'
-naan	N 1p,21-3
-naawaa	VTI4 independent 2p,3p-o

-naawaan	VAI-O independent 2p,3p-op
-nd	VTA conjunct X-3 (Cw-)
-ndwaa	VTA conjunct X-3p (Cw-)
-ng	N locative
-ng	VAI conjunct X; VAI4 conjunct X-o
-ni	VII independent o'
-nid	VAI conjunct 3'
-nig	VII conjunct o',o'p
-nigwen	VAI conjunct dubitative 3'; VII conjunct dubitative o',o'p
-nijin	VAI conjunct participle 3'
-nzig	VTI4 conjunct negative 3-o
-nziimin	VTI4 independent 1p,21-o,op
-od	VTA conjunct 3-1 (Cw-)
-og	VTA independent 3-1,2 (Cw-)
-ogowaad	VTA conjunct 3'-3p (Cw-)
-ogoog	VTA independent 3p-1,2 (Cw-)
-ogoon	VTA independent 3'-3 (Cw-)
-ogwen	VAI conjunct dubitative 3; VII conjunct dubitative o,op
-ok	VTA imperative 2p-3 (Cw-)
-on	VTA independent 1-2 (Cw-)
-ond	VTA conjunct X-3 (Cw-)
-ondwaa	VTA conjunct X-3p (Cw-)
-ong	N locative
-osinoon	VTA independent negative 1-2 (Cw-)
-owaad	VAI conjunct 3p
-owaan	N 3p-3'
-owaanen	VAI conjunct dubitative 1
-oyangid	VTA conjunct 3-1p (Cw-)
-ood	VTI2 conjunct 3-o,op
-oog	N 3p
-oog	VAI independent 3p
-oogwen	VTI2 conjunct dubitative 3-o,op
-oojin	VTI2 conjunct participle 3-op

-oomin	VTI2 independent 1p,21-0,0p
-oon	N op, 3'
-oon	VAI independent 3'
-oon	VII independent op
-oon	VTA independent 1-2 (aw-)
-oon	VTI2 independent 1,2,3-0
-oonan	VTI2 independent 1,2,3-op
-oonaawaa	VTI2 independent 2p,3p-0
-oonaawaan	VTI2 independent 2p,3p-op
-oong	VTI2 conjunct X-0,0p
-oonid	VTI2 conjunct 3'-0,0p
-oosiimin	VTI2 independent negative 1p,21-0,0p
-oosiinan	VTI2 independent negative 1,2,3-op
-oowag	VTI2 conjunct relative 1-3
-oowaad	VTI2 conjunct 3p-0,0p
-oowaagwen	VTI2 conjunct dubitative 3p-0,0p
-oowaajin	VTI2 conjunct participle 3p-op
-ooyan	VTI2 conjunct 2-0,0p
-ooyaan	VTI2 conjunct 1-0,0p
-ooyaang	VTI2 conjunct 1p-0,0p
-sig	VAI conjunct negative 3
-sigwaa	VAI conjunct negative 3p
-sinog	VII conjunct negative 0,0p
-sinoon	VII independent negative 0,0p
-sinoon	VTA independent negative 1-2 (Cw-)
-siwaan	VAI independent negative relative 1
-siim	VAI independent negative 2p
-siimin	VAI independent negative 1p,21
-siin	VAI independent negative 1,2,3; VTI3 independent negative 1,2,3-0
-siiwag	VAI independent negative 3p
-siiwan	VAI independent negative 3'
-wag	N 3p
-wag	VAI independent 3p
-wag	VAI conjunct relative 1

-wan	N op, 3'
-wan	VAI independent 3'
-wan	VII independent op
-waad	VAI conjunct 3p; VAI + O 3p-o,op; VTI3 conjunct 3p-o,op
-waagwen	VAI conjunct dubitative 3p
-waanen	VAI conjunct dubitative 1; VAI + O conjunct dubitative 1-o, op; VTI3 conjunct dubitative 1-o, op
-waangen	VAI conjunct dubitative 1p
-wind	VAI conjunct relative X
-wish	N pejorative 3,o
-yag	N 3p
-yan	N op, 3'
-yan	VAI conjunct 2
-yang	VAI conjunct 21
-yangid	VTA conjunct 3-1p (Cw-)
-yaambaan	VAI conjunct preterit 1
-yaan	VAI conjunct 1; VAI + O conjunct 1-o,op; VTI3 conjunct 1-o,op
-yaang	VAI conjunct 1p; VTI3 conjunct 1p-o,op
-yeg	VAI conjunct 2p
-yiban	N preterit 3,o
-yiman	N 3-3'
-zing	VAI conjunct negative X
-ziin	VAI independent negative 1,2,3
-ziiwag	VAI independent negative 3p

Inverse List of Endings

-aa	VTA independent 1,2-3
-aa	VTA independent X-3
-daa	VAI imperative 21
-naawaa	VTI4 independent 2p,3p-o
-aanaawaa	VTI independent 2p,3p-o
-anziinaawaa	VTI independent negative 2p,3p-o
-oonaawaa	VTI2 independent 2p,3p-o
-adwaa	VTA conjunct 2-3p
-angidwaa	VTA conjunct 1p-3p
-iyangidwaa	VTA conjunct 3p-1p
-ndwaa	VTA conjunct X-3p (Cw-)
-indwaa	VTA conjunct X-3p
-ondwaa	VTA conjunct X-3p (Cw-)
-agwaa	VTA conjunct 1-3p
-sigwaa	VAI conjunct negative 3p
-aasigwaa	VTA conjunct negative 3p-3'
-iwaa	N 3p-o
-igowaa	VTA independent 3-2p
-d	VTA conjunct 3-1 (Cw-)
-d	VAI conjunct 3; VAI + O 3-o,op; VTI3 conjunct 3-o,op
-ad	VTA conjunct 2-3
-aad	VTA conjunct 3-3'
-waad	VAI conjunct 3p; VAI + O 3p-o,op; VTI3 conjunct 3p-o,op
-aawaad	VTA conjunct 3p-3'

-iwaad	VTA conjunct 3p-1
-owaad	VAI conjunct 3p
-gowaad	VTA conjunct 3'-3p (aw-) (Cw-)
-aagowaad	VTA conjunct 3'-3p (aw-)
-ogowaad	VTA conjunct 3'-3p (Cw-)
-mowaad	VTI4 conjunct 3p-o,op
-amowaad	VTI conjunct 3p-o,op; VAI2 conjunct 3p
-oowaad	VTI2 conjunct 3p-o,op
-id	VTA conjunct 3-1
-angid	VTA conjunct 1p-3
-aasiwangid	VTA conjunct negative 1p-3
-yangid	VTA conjunct 3-1p (Cw-)
-iyangid	VTA conjunct 3-1p
-oyangid	VTA conjunct 3-1p (Cw-)
-nid	VAI conjunct 3'
-inid	VAI conjunct 3'
-oonid	VTI2 conjunct 3'-o,op
-nd	VTA conjunct X-3 (Cw-)
-ind	VTA conjunct X-3
-wind	VAI conjunct relative X
-ond	VTA conjunct X-3 (Cw-)
-od	VTA conjunct 3-1 (Cw-)
-god	VTA conjunct 3'-3 (aw-)
-aagod	VTA conjunct 3'-3 (aw-)
-ood	VTI2 conjunct 3-o,op
-g	VAI conjunct 3
-g	N 3p
-g	VTA independent 3-1,2 (aw-) (Cw-)
-g	VII conjunct o,op
-g	VAI imperative 2p
-ag	VTA conjunct 1-3
-ag	N 3p
-mag	N 1,2-3p
-imag	VTA conjunct 1-3'
-iimag	N 1,2-3p
-nag	VAI + O independent 1,2-3p

-wag	VAI conjunct relative 1
-wag	VAI independent 3p
-wag	N 3p
-aawag	VTA independent X-3p
-aasiwag	VTA conjunct negative 1-3
-siiwag	VAI independent negative 3p
-ziiwag	VAI independent negative 3p
-oowag	VTI2 conjunct relative 1-3
-yag	N 3p
-aag	VTA independent 3-1,2 (aw-)
-aag	VTA independent 1,2-3p
-yeg	VAI conjunct 2p
-iyeg	VTA conjunct 2p-1
-ig	VTA independent 3-1,2
-angig	VTI conjunct participle 3p-0,0p; VAI2 conjunct participle 3p
-ishig	VTA imperative 2p-1
-jig	VAI conjunct participle 3p
-nig	VII conjunct 0',0'p
-aadaanig	VTA imperative 21-3p
-aanaanig	VTA independent 1p,21-3p
-aasiwaanaanig	VTA independent negative 1p,21-3p
-igonaanig	VTA independent 3p-1p,21
-inig	VII conjunct 0',0'p
-sig	VAI conjunct negative 3
-isig	VTA conjunct negative 1-2
-nzig	VTI4 conjunct negative 3-0
-iig	N 3p
-aasiig	VTA independent negative 1,2-3p
-ng	VAI conjunct X; VAI4 conjunct X-0
-ng	N locative
-ang	VTA conjunct 21-3
-ang	VTI conjunct 3-0,0p; VAI2 conjunct 3
-yang	VAI conjunct 21
-igooyang	VTA independent X-21
-aang	N locative
-aang	VAI conjunct 1p

-amaang	VTI conjunct 1p-0,op; VAI2 conjunct 1p
-yaang	VAI conjunct 1p; VTI3 conjunct 1p-0,op
-ooyaang	VTI2 conjunct 1p-0,op
-gooyaang	VTA conjunct X-1p (aw-)
-aagooyaang	VTA conjunct X-1p (aw-)
-igooyaang	VTA conjunct X-1p
-ing	N locative
-ming	N 1,2,3-0 locative
-iming	N 1,2,3-0 locative
-aaning	N 3'-0 locative
-ining	N 3'-0 locative
-zing	VAI conjunct negative X
-anzing	VTI conjunct negative X-0,op
-iing	VAI conjunct X
-iing	N locative
-ong	N locative
-oong	VTI2 conjunct X-0,op
-og	VTA independent 3-1,2 (Cw-)
-idog	N vocative plural
-sinog	VII conjunct negative 0,op
-oog	N 3p
-oog	VAI independent 3p
-goog	VTA independent 3p-1,2 (Cw-)
-igoog	VTA independent 3p-1,2
-ogoog	VTA independent 3p-1,2 (Cw-)
-amoog	VAI2 independent 3p
-i	VTA imperative 2-3
-ni	VII independent o'
-ini	VII independent o'
-mini	N 3'-0,op
-k	VTA imperative 2p-3 (Cw-)
-k	VII conjunct 0,op
-ik	VTA imperative 2p-3
-ok	VTA imperative 2p-3 (Cw-)
-amok	VTI imperative 2p-0,op

-m	VAI independent X
-am	VAI2 independent 1,2,3
-im	N 1,2,3-0; 1,2-3
-isinooninim	VTA independent negative 1-2p
-siim	VAI independent negative 2p
-n	VTA independent 1-2 (aw-) (Cw-)
-n	N op, 3'
-n	VAI imperative 2; VTI3 imperative 2-0,op
-n	VAI + O independent 1,2,3-0; VTI4 independent 1,2,3-0
-an	N op, 3'
-ban	N preterit 3,0
-iban	N preterit 3,0
-yiban	N preterit 3,0
-man	N 1,2,3-op
-iman	N 3-3'
-yiman	N 3-3'
-nan	VAI-O independent 1,2-3, 3-3'
-aanan	VTI independent 1,2,3-op
-oosiinan	VTI2 independent negative 1,2,3-op
-oonan	VTI2 independent 1,2,3-op
-wan	VII independent op
-wan	VAI independent 3'
-wan	N op, 3'
-iniwan	VII independent op'
-siiwan	VAI independent negative 3'
-yan	VAI conjunct 2
-yan	N op, 3'
-iyan	VTA conjunct 2-1
-ooyan	VTI2 conjunct 2-0,op
-aan	VAI conjunct 1
-aan	VTA independent 3-3'
-aan	VTI independent 1,2,3-0
-amaambaan	VTI conjunct preterit 1-0,op
-yaambaan	VAI conjunct preterit 1
-maan	VTI4 conjunct 1-0,op

-amaan	VTI conjunct 1-0,op; VAI2 1
-naan	N 1p,21-3
-aanaan	VTA independent 1p,21-3
-inaan	VTA conjunct 1-2
-aawaan	VTA independent 3p-3'
-naawaan	VAI-O independent 2p,3p-op
-aanaawaan	VTI independent 2p,3p-op
-oonaawaan	VTI2 independent 2p,3p-op
-aasiwaawaan	VTA independent negative 3p-3'
-iwaan	N 3p-op; 3p-3'
-siwaan	VAI independent negative relative 1
-igoosiwaan	VTA conjunct negative X-1
-owaan	N 3p-3'
-igowaan	VTA independent 3'-3p
-yaan	VAI conjunct 1; VAI + O conjunct 1-0,op; VTI3 conjunct 1-0,op
-ooyaan	VTI2 conjunct 1-0,op
-gooyaan	VTA conjunct X-1 (aw-)
-aagooyaan	VTA conjunct X-1 (aw-)
-igooyaan	VTA conjunct X-1
-aawinden	VTA conjunct dubitative X-3
-angen	VTI prohibitive 2-0,op; VAI2 prohibitive 2
-waangen	VAI conjunct dubitative 1p
-ken	VAI prohibitive 2; VTI3 prohibitive 2-0,op
-aawaagobanen	VTA conjunct preterit dubitative 3p-3'
-amowaambaanen	VTI conjunct preterit dubitative 1-0
-waanen	VAI conjunct dubitative 1; VAI + O conjunct dubitative 1-0, op; VTI3 conjunct dubitative 1-0, op
-owaanen	VAI conjunct dubitative 1
-amowaanen	VTI conjunct dubitative 1-0,op; VAI2 conjunct dubitative 1
-goowaanen	VTA conjunct dubitative X-1 (aw-) (Cw-)
-aagoowaanen	VTA conjunct dubitative X-1 (aw-)
-igoowaanen	VTA conjunct dubitative X-1
-gwen	VAI conjunct dubitative 3; VII conjunct dubitative 0,op

-aagwen	VTA conjunct dubitative 3-3'
-waagwen	VAI conjunct dubitative 3p
-igowaagwen	VTA conjunct dubitative 3'-3p
-oowaagwen	VTI2 conjunct dubitative 3p-0,0p
-nigwen	VAI conjunct dubitative 3'; VII conjunct dubitative 0',0'p
-ogwen	VAI conjunct dubitative 3; VII conjunct dubitative 0,0p
-amogwen	VTI conjunct dubitative 3-0,0p
-oogwen	VTI2 conjunct dubitative 3-0,0p
-in	VTA independent 1-2
-ishin	VTA imperative 2-1
-aajin	VTA conjunct participle 3-3'
-oowaajin	VTI2 conjunct participle 3p-0p
-nijin	VAI conjunct participle 3'
-aminijin	VAI2 conjunct participle 3'
-igojin	VTA conjunct participle 3'-3
-oojin	VTI2 conjunct participle 3-0p
-min	VAI independent 1p,21
-aamin	VTI independent 1p,21-0,0p
-siimin	VAI independent negative 1p,21
-igosiimin	VTA independent negative 3-1p,21
-oosiimin	VTI2 independent negative 1p,21-0,0p
-nziimin	VTI4 independent 1p,21-0,0p
-oomin	VTI2 independent 1p,21-0,0p
-igoomin	VTA independent X-1,2
-igooyaanin	VTA conjunct participle X-1 (0p as second object)
-iin	N 0p, 3'
-siin	VAI independent negative 1,2,3; VTI3 independent negative 1,2,3-0
-aasiin	VTA independent negative 1,2-3, 3-3'
-gosiin	VTA independent negative 3-1 (aw-)
-aagosiin	VTA independent negative 3-1 (aw-)
-igosiin	VTA conjunct negative 3-1,2
-igoosiin	VTA independent negative X-1,2
-ziin	VAI independent negative 1,2,3

-anziin	VTI independent negative 1,2,3-0; VAI2 independent negative 1,2,3
-on	VTA independent 1-2 (Cw-)
-aakegon	VTA prohibitive 2p-3
-ishikegon	VTA prohibitive 2p-1
-oon	VII independent 0p
-oon	N 0p, 3'
-oon	VAI independent 3'
-oon	VTA independent 1-2 (aw-)
-oon	VTI2 independent 1,2,3-0
-goon	VTA independent 3'-3 (Cw-)
-ogoon	VTA independent 3'-3 (Cw-)
-sinoon	VTA independent negative 1-2 (Cw-)
-sinoon	VII independent negative 0,0p
-osinoon	VTA independent negative 1-2 (Cw-)
-igoo	VTA independent X-1,2
-ish	N pejorative 3,0
-wish	N pejorative 3,0

Main Glossary

abi (VAI) be in a certain place, sit in a certain place, be at home

abinoojiinh, abinoojiinyag (NA) child

abiwinikaade (VII) be made into a (single) room

abwe (VAI + O) roast (something)

achige (VAI) put things in a certain place, place a bet

adaam (VTA) buy something from s.o.

adaawange (VAI + O) rent (something)

adaawaage (VAI + O) sell (something)

adaawe (VAI + O) buy (something)

adaawewigamig, -oon (NI) store

adaawewinini, -wag (NA) storekeeper, trader

adaawewininiikwe, -g (NA) female storekeeper

adaawewininiikwewi (VAI) be a female storekeeper

adaawewininiiwi (VAI) be a male storekeeper

Adisinaake-manoominikaaning (PLACE) Dean Lake

agamiing (PC) on the shore

agawaateyaa (VII) be shade

agaamindesiing (PC) on the other side of the fire in a lodge

agaaming (PC) across the lake

agaasaa (VII) be small

agaashiinyi (VAI) be small

agaawaa (PC) hardly, barely

agidaaki (PC) on top of a hill

agidiskwam (PC) on top of the ice

agiji- (PRE) on top of

agiji-asin (PC) on top of a rock

aginzo (VAI) be counted, belong as a member

agokan = (VTA) *see:* **agokazh**

agokazh /agokaN-/ (VTA) stick s.o. on

agomo (VAI) float, be suspended in water

agonjichigaade (VII) be put in the water to soak

agonjim (VTA) put s.o. in the water to soak

agoodakikwaan, -an (NI) kettle hanger

agoode(magad) (VII) hang

agoodoo (VAI) set snares

agoodoon (VTI2) hang s.t.

agoojin (VAI) hang

agoon = (VTA) *see:* **agoozh**

agoozh /agooN-/ (VTA) hang s.o.

agwadaashiins, -ag (NA) sunfish

agwajiing (PC) outside

agwanem (VTA) put s.o. in one's mouth

agwanigaazo (VAI) be covered

agwazhe (VAI + O) cover oneself (with something),
wear a blanket

agwazhe' (VTA) cover s.o. with something

agwaabiiga'amaw (VTA) take something off the water
or the fire for s.o.

agwaabiigin (VTA) take s.o. off the water or the fire
by hand

agwaa'o (VAI) come in to shore with a boat, land

agwaa'oodoon (VTI2) take s.t. off the water

agwaashim (VTA) take s.o. in to shore, take s.o. off
the fire

agwaasidoon (VTI2) take s.t. in to shore, take s.t. off
the fire

agwaasijigaade (VII) be taken in to shore, be taken
off the fire

a'aw (PR) that *animate singular demonstrative*

ajidamoo, -g (NA) squirrel

ajina (PC) a little bit, a little

akakanzhe (NI) charcoal

akawe (PC) first (in time), first of all
akeyaa (PC) in the direction of
aki, akiin (NI) land, earth
akik, -oog (NA) pail, kettle
akikoons, -ag (NA) small pail, small kettle
akina (PC) all, every
akina gegoo (PR) everything
akiwenzii, -yag (NA) old man
ako- (PRE) as far as
akwaandawe (VAI) climb up
amadin (VTA) wake s.o.
amanj (PC) I don't know how, I wonder how
　dubitative adverb
ambe (PC) come on!
amo /amw-/ (VTA) eat s.o.
anama'e-giizhigad (VII) be a week
anang, -oog (NA) star
anaamayi'ii (PC) under something
ani- (PV) going away from, on the way, coming up to
　in time
animikii, -g (NA) thunderer
animikiikaa (VII) there is thunder
animikose (VAI) go upside down, turn belly-side
　down
animosh, -ag (NA) dog
animoshiwi (VAI) be a dog
aninaatigoons, -an (NI) maple twig
anishaa (PC) without reason, just for fun
Anishinaabe, -g (NA) Indian, Chippewa
Anishinaabe-bakwezhigan, -ag (NA) Indian bread
Anishinaabe-izhichigewin, -an (NI) Indian way
Anishinaabe-jiibegamig, -oon (NI) Indian grave
Anishinaabe-manoomin (NI) wild rice (especially
　traditionally processed rice)
Anishinaabe-mindimooyenyiwi (VAI) be an Indian
　old lady
Anishinaabewinikaade (VII) be called in Indian

Anishinaabe-ziinzibaakwad (NI) maple sugar
aniibiish, -an (NI) leaf, tea
aniibiishens, -an (NI) leaf-bud
aniibiishibag, -oon (NI) leaf
aniibiishike (VAI) make tea
anokii (VAI) work
anokiim (VTA) *see:* wiij'-anokiim
anokiitaazo (VAI) work for oneself
anooj (PC) various, all kinds
anooji-gegoo (PR) all sorts of things
anoon = (VTA) *see:* anoozh
anoozh /anooN-/ (VTA) hire s.o., commission s.o. to
    do something
anwaatin (VII) be calm
apagidaw (VTA) throw something to or for s.o.
apagin = (VTA) *see:* apagizh
apagizh /apagiN-/ (VTA) throw s.o. against
apagizo (VAI) throw oneself against, fall against,
    move against
apakwaadan (VTI) cover s.t. with mats, roof s.t.
apakwaan, -an (NI) wigwam covering mat
apakweshkway, -an (NI) cattail mat
apakweshkway, -ag (NA) cattail mat
apane (PC) always, continually
apatoo (VAI) run to a certain place
apegish (PC) I wish that...
apii (PC) when, at that time, a distance
apiichi- (PV) to a certain extent, as much as
apiichishin (VAI) lie to a certain depth
as = (VTA) *see:* ashi
asab, -iig (NA) net
asanjigoowigamig, -oon (NI) storage lodge
asemaa, -g (NA) tobacco
asham (VTA) feed s.o.
ashi- (PRE) and, ten and (in counting)
ashi /aS-/ (VTA) put s.o. in a certain place

ashi-aabita (PC) and one-half
ashi-bezhigo-biboonagizi (VAI) be eleven years old
ashi-ingodwaaswi (PC) sixteen
asiginan (VTI) put s.t. together, gather s.t. up
asiginigaade (VII) be gathered, be picked up
asin, -iig (NA) rock, stone
asiniins, -ag (NA) stone
ataadiwag /ataadi-/ (VAI) (they) gamble with e.o.
ate(magad) (VII) be in a certain place, be put in a
　certain place
atite(magad) (VII) be ripe
atoobaan, -an (NI) trough, tank
atoon (VTI2) put s.t. in a certain place
awas (PC) away, on the other side
awas-ayi'ii (PC) on the other side of something
awazo (VAI) warm oneself by the fire
awegwen, -ag (PR) I don't know who, I wonder who,
　whoever *dubitative animate*
awenen, -ag (PR) who *interrogative animate*
awiiya, -g (PR) someone, anyone *indefinite animate*
ayagwamo (VAI) float, be suspended in the water
　reduplicated form of: **agwamo**
aya'aa, -g (PR) person, being *animate base*
aya'aawi (VAI) be a being
ayamaniso (VAI) sense something *reduplicated form of:*
　amaniso
ayaa (VAI) be in certain condition, be in a certain
　place
ayaa(magad) (VII) be in a certain condition, be in a
　certain place
ayaabadizi = (VAI) *changed form of:* **aabadizi**
ayaabajitoo = (VTI2) *changed form of:* **aabajitoon**
ayaam = (VTI4) *see:* **ayaan**
ayaan (VTI4) have s.t.
ayaangodinong (PC) sometimes, occasionally
ayaaw (VTA) have s.o.

ayekozi (VAI) be tired

ayi'ii, -n (PR) that thing, it *inanimate base*: **ayi'ing,** **ayi'iing** *locative*

ayinagoojin (VAI) hang in a certain way or place *reduplicated form of*: **inagoojin**

ayina'o (VAI) paddle in certain directions *reduplicated form of*: **ina'o**

ayinaabi (VAI) look in certain directions *reduplicated form of*: **inaabi**

ayinaajimo (VAI) tell in a certain way *reduplicated form of*: **inaajimo**

ayinoo'amaw (VTA) point something out to s.o. *reduplicated form of*: **inoo'amaw**

ayizhaa (VAI) go various places *reduplicated form of*: **izhaa**

ayizhiwebizi (VAI) have happen in certain ways to one *reduplicated form of*: **izhiwebizi**

azheboye (VAI) row

azhegiiwe (VAI) return

azhetaa (VAI) go backwards, back up

azhigwa (PC) now, then, at that time, next

aa (PC) *exclamation*

aabadizi (VAI) be used

aaba' /aaba'w-/ (VTA) undo s.o., unhitch s.o.

aabaji' (VTA) use s.o.

aabajitoon (VTI2) use s.t.

aabanaabam (VTA) look back at s.o.

aabanaabi (VAI) look back

aabaakawad (VII) clear suddenly after a storm

aabiding (PC) once, at one time

aabita (PC) half

aabita- (PRE) half

aabita-niibin (VII) be halfway through the summer

aabita-zhooniyaans (NA) nickel (coin)

aabitaa-dibikad (VII) be midnight

aadizookaw (VTA) tell a legend to s.o.

aagawewetaa (VAI) go behind something

aagaweweyaakotaa (VAI) go behind trees

aagim, -ag (NA) snowshoe

aakozi (VAI) be sick

aakoziiwigamig, -oon (NI) hospital

aanawi (PC) anyway, nevertheless

aandi (PC) where *interrogative locative*

aangodinong (PC) sometimes, occasionally

aanikegamaa (VII) be a chain of lakes

aanind (PC) some

aanish (PC) well, well then, of course, you see

aaniin (PC) how *interrogative adverb*

aaniiin apii (PC) when?

aaniin dash (PC) why?

aaniin nanda (PC) why not?

aaniish (PC) well, well then, of course, you see

aaniish (PC) how?, why? *interrogative adverb*

aaniish apii (PC) when?

aano- (PV) in vain

aapiji (PC) very

aatebin = (VTA) *see:* **aatebizh**

aatebizh /aatebiN-/ (VTA) beat out a fire on s.o.

aawi (VAI) be someone, be something

aayaabita (PC) half each *reduplicated form of:* aabita

aayaazhikwe (VAI) scream

aazhawagaaziibatoo (VAI) run across wading

Aazhawakiwenzhiinh (NAME) Maude Kegg's great
uncle

aazhawaabiigin (VTA) string s.o. (as a net) across

aazhawaakoshin (VAI) lie across (of something
sticklike)

aazhawaakosidoon (VTI2) lay s.t. across (of
something sticklike)

aazhawaakosin (VII) lie across (of something
sticklike)

aazhawigwaashkwani (VAI) jump across
aazhigidaabikinan (VTI) draw s.t. (of metal or stone) back
aazhigijise (VAI) go on one's back, turn belly-side up
aazhigijishim (VTA) place s.o. over on back
aazhoge (VAI) cross, go across
aazhogewin = (VTA) *see:* **aazhogewizh**
aazhogewizh /aazhogewiN-/ (VTA) carry s.o. across, take s.o. across
aazhooshkaa (VAI) go across

ba- (PRE) *changed form of:* **bi-**
babagamaanimad (VII) wind blows in *reduplicated form of:* **bagamaanimad**
babagiwayaanegamig, -oon (NI) tent
babaa- (PV) about, around, in no definite direction
babaamenim (VTA) bother s.o.
babaamibatoo (VAI) run about
babaamishkaa (VAI) paddle about
babaamoode (VAI) crawl about
babima'adoo (VAI) travel about (on a road or trail) *reduplicated form of:* **bima'adoo**
babimose (VAI) walk about *reduplicated form of:* **bimose**
babiichii (VAI) put on footwear
badagwana' /badagwana'w-/ (VTA) cover s.o.
badakibidoon (VTI2) pull upright s.t. fixed in
badakinan (VTI) put upright s.t. fixed in
bagamiba'iwewag /bagamiba'iwe/ (VAI) (they) arrive running in a group
bagamibatoo (VAI) arrive running
bagamibide (VII) arrive with speed, arrive (of mail)
bagamidaabii'iwe (VAI) arrive driving
bagamishkaa (VAI) arrive paddling
bagandizi (VAI) be ignorant and lazy
bagida'waa (VAI) set a net
bagidin (VTA) put s.o. down, release s.o., allow s.o.

bagidinan (VTI) put s.t. down, plant s.t. (a garden)

bagidinige (VAI) put things down, put in a garden

bagijwebinan (VTI) release s.t. quickly, drop s.t.

bagiwayaan, -an (NI) piece of cloth

bagiwayaanegamig, -oon (NI) tent

bagiwayaanegamigoons, -an (NI) small tent

bagizo (VAI) swim

bajiishkiga'an (VTI) hew s.t. pointed

bajiishkinan (VTI) make s.t pointed

bakade (VAI) be hungry

bakaan (PC) different

bakebatoo (VAI) run off to side

bakite' /bakite'w-/ (VTA) hit s.o., strike s.o.

bakobiiyaashi (VAI) be blown into the water

bakwajibidoon (VTI2) pull s.t. up, pluck s.t.

bakwe'an (VTI) take off a piece of s.t. with a tool

bakwem (VTA) bite off a piece of s.o.

bakwene(magad) (VII) smoke

bakwezhigan, -ag (NA) flour, bread

bakwezhiganike (VAI) make bread

bakwezhigaans, -ag (NA) pastry, cookie

bami' (VTA) take care of s.o., tame s.o. (of an animal)

banaaji' (VTA) spoil s.o.

bangan (VII) be quiet, be calm

bangii (PC) a little, a little bit

banzan (VTI) singe s.t.

banzo (VAI) be singed

banzo /banzw-/ (VTA) singe s.o.

bapajiishkikon = (VTA) *see:* **bapajiishkikozh**

bapajiishkikozh /bapajiishkikoN-/ (VTA) cut s.t. pointed *reduplicated form of:* **bajiishkikozh**

bapakite' /bapakite'w-/ (VTA) keep hitting s.o. *reduplicated form of:* **bakite'**

bapakite'igaazo (VAI) get a licking *reduplicated form of:* **bakite'igaazo**

bapakite'ige (VAI) strike things, hit things *reduplicated form of:* **bakite'ige**

bapashanzhe' /bapashanzhe'w-/ (VTA) whip s.o., strike s.o. *reduplicated form*

bapashkobijige (VAI) pluck things, pull weeds *reduplicated form of:* **bashkobijige**

Bapashkwaaminisensing (PLACE) name of a stream of the west shore of Mille Lacs Lake between Vineland and Garrison

bapazhiba' /bapazhiba'w-/ (VTA) spear s.o. repeatedly *reduplicated form of:* **bazhiba'**

basangwaabi (VAI) shut one's eyes

bashkobin = (VTA) *see:* **bashkobizh**

bashkobizh /bashkobiN-/ (VTA) pluck s.o.

bashkwashkibidaw (VTA) weed something for s.o.

bashkwashkibidoon (VTI2) weed s.t.

bashkwashkibijige (VAI) pull weeds

basikawaan = (VTA) *see:* **basikawaazh**

basikawaazh /basikawaaN-/ (VTA) kick s.o.

bawa'am (VAI2) harvest wild rice, knock rice

bawa'iganaak, -oog (NA) rice knockers (sticks for harvesting wild rice)

bawinan (VTI) shake s.t. off

bazhiba'amaw (VTA) spear something for s.o.

bazhizikaw (VTA) go over s.o.

bazigonjise (VAI) stand up in a hurry

bazigwii (VAI) stand up

baa- (PV) around a place, locally distributed

/-baabaay-/ (NAD) someone's father: **imbaabaa** my father

baabiibaagi (VAI) call, shout *reduplicated form of:* **biibaagi**

baabiibaagim (VTA) keep calling to s.o., keep shouting to s.o. *reduplicated form of:* **biibaagim**

baabiichishim (VTA) put s.o. to fit *reduplicated form*

baabii' (VTA) wait for s.o. *reduplicated form of:* **bii'**

baabiijibatoo (VAI) run here *reduplicated form of:* **biijibatoo**

baagijige (VAI) make a lightning strike

baajise (VII) come off, be ejected
baakibii'an (VII) be open water
baamendan (VTI) bother s.t.
baamishkaa (VAI) paddle around in a place
baandige = (VAI) *changed form of:* biindige
baanimaa (PC) later, after a while.
baapi (VAI) laugh
baapinodaw (VTA) mock s.o., waste s.o., show
    disrespect for s.o.
baasan (VTI) dry s.t., parch s.t.
baasaa = (VII) *changed form of:* biisaa(magad)
baashkakwa'am (VAI2) make a thunder-clap
baashkaawe'o (VAI) hatch
baashkiz /baashkizw-/ (VTA) shoot s.o.
baashkizigan, -an (NI) gun
baasinigo (VAI) be bloated
baaso (VAI) be dry
baatayiinadoon /baatayiinad-/ (VII) (they) are many
baatayiinowag /baatayiino-/ (VAI) (they) are many
baate (VII) be dry
bebaa- (PV) *changed form of:* babaa-
bebezhig (PC) one-by-one *reduplicated form of:* bezhig
bebezhigooganzhii, -g (NA) horse
bekaa (PC) wait!
bemezhisin = (VII) *changed form of:* bimezhisin
bemiwin = (VTA) *changed form of:* bimiwizh
bemose = (VAI) *changed form of:* bimose
benga = (VII) *changed form of:* bangan
beshibii'an (VTI) put a stripe or mark on s.t.
besho (PC) near
bewa' = (VAI) *changed form of:* bawa'am
bezhig (PC) one
bezhigo (VAI) be single, be the only one
bezhigo- (PRE) one
bezhigoopijige (VAI) hitch up one horse
bi- (PV) here, hither
biboon (VII) be winter

biboonagizi (VAI) *see:* **ashi-bezhigo-biboonagizi**
biboonodaabaanens, -ag (NA) little sleigh
bigiw (NA) pitch
bigiwizigan, -an (NI) maple sugar taffy
bijiinag (PC) recently, after a while, just then
bimamon /bimamo-/ (VII) go by or along (as a road or trail)
bimaadagaazii (VAI) wade along
bimaadizi (VAI) live
bimaanimad (VII) blow along as wind
bimaawadaasowag /bimaawadaaso-/ (VAI) (they) haul along, trail along as a school or flock
bimezhisin (VII) leave a trail or track going along
bimi- (PV) along, by, on the way
bimi-ayaa (VAI) come by, go along
bimiba'idiwag /bimiba'idi-/ (VAI) (they) run along in a group
bimibatoo (VAI) run along
bimibide(magad) (VII) drive along, speed along
bimidaabiiba'igo (VAI) drive along in a wagon or sleigh
bimidaabii'iwe (VAI) drive along
bimide (NI) lard
bimikawe (VAI) leave tracks going along
biminizha' /biminizha'w-/ (VTA) chase along after s.o.
biminizha'ige (VAI) chase along after things
bimishkaa (VAI) paddle along
bimitigweyaa (VII) flow along (as a river)
bimiwanaanikaade (VII) be made into a pack
bimiwidoon (VTI2) carry s.t. along
bimiwin = (VTA) *see:* **bimiwizh**
bimiwizh /bimiwiN-/ (VTA) carry s.o. along
bimose (VAI) walk along
bimoode (VAI) crawl along
bimoom (VTA) pack s.o. along on back

bimoondan (VTI) pack s.t. along on back

bimweweshin (VAI) make noise going along stepping or falling

bina' /bina'w-/ (VTA) take s.o. down, take s.o. off

bina'an (VTI) take s.t. down, take s.t. off

binaakwii (VAI) fall (as a leaf)

binda'am (VAI2) be caught in a net

bineshiinh, bineshiinyag (NA) bird

binesi, -wag (NA) Thunderbird

bingwi (NI) sand

bishagikodan (VTI) peel s.t.

bishigiishkibikaakweyaa (VII) be dark forest along a shore

bishigon (VTA) let s.o. slip out of one's grip

biskitenaagan, -an (NI) folded birchbark bucket

bizhiki, -wag (NA) cow, ox, bison

bizhishigwaa (VII) be empty

bizindaw (VTA) listen to s.o.

biidaadagaaziiba'idiwag /biidaadagaaziiba'idi-/ (VAI) (they) run into water in a group

biidaanakwad (VII) clouds approach

biidaasamose (VAI) walk here

biidoon (VTI2) bring s.t.

biidweweshin (VAI) be heard stepping here, be heard coming with a striking noise

biidwewidam (VAI2) approach with noise (as thunder)

biigwawe (VAI) be bushy

biigwaasin (VII) be blown to pieces

biijiba'idiwag /biijiba'idi-/ (VAI) (they) run here in a group

biijibatoo (VAI) run here

biijibizo (VAI) fly here, speed here

biijidaabii'iwe (VAI) drive here

biina' /biina'w-/ (VTA) put s.o. in

biina'an (VTI) put s.t. in

biindaakoon = (VTA) *see:* **biindaakoozh**

biindaakoozh /biindaakooN-/ (VTA) make an offering of something (especially tobacco) to s.o.

biindaakwaan, -ag (NA) snuff

biindaakwaani-makakoons, -an (NI) small snuff box

biindaakwe (VAI) take a pinch of snuff

biindig (PC) inside

biindige (VAI) enter, go inside, come inside

biindigeba'idiwag /biindigeba'idi-/ (VAI) (they) enter running in a group

biindigeyaawanidiwag /biindigeyaawanidi-/ (VAI) (they) enter as a group

biingeyendam (VAI2) be puzzled, reflect on events

biini' (VTA) clean s.o.

biinitoon (VTI2) clean s.t.

biisaa(magad) (VII) be fine, be in particles

Biiswejiwang (NAME) name of an old man

Biiwaabikokaaning (PLACE) Crosby-Ironton, Minnesota

biizikaw (VTA) wear s.o.

booch (PC) necessarily, certainly

boodawaade (VII) be a fire

boodawe (VAI) build a fire

bookobidoon (VTI2) break s.t. (in half)

bookogaadeshin (VAI) fall and break one's leg

bootaagan, -ag (NA) board-lined pit for dehusking rice, mill

bootaaganike (VAI) make a mill

bootaaganikewin (NI) making a mill

bootaagaadan (VTI) mill or tread to dehusk s.t.

bootaage (VAI) mill or tread things

boozi (VAI) get on, embark

boozitoon (VTI2) load s.t.

/-bwaamens-/ (NID) little thigh: **obwaamens** gun hammer

bwaan, -ag (NA) Dakota (Sioux) Indian

bwaanawi' (VTA) be unable to get s.o. (to do), be unable to manage s.o.

bwaanawitoon (VTI2) be unable to do s.t.

da (PC) *see:* **daga**

da- (PV) will *future prefix on independent verbs with no personal prefix*

dadaakwaakoga'an (VTI) hew s.t. (sticklike) short *reduplicated form of:* **dakwaakoga'an**

dadibaajimotaw (VTA) tell something repeatedly or in different places *reduplicated form of:* **dibaajimotaw**

daga (PC) please! do this! come on!

dagon /**dago-**/ (VII) be in a certain place

dagoshim (VTA) arrive with s.o., get s.o. to destination

dagoshin (VAI) arrive

dagozo (VAI) be cooked in with something

dagwaagin /**dagwaagi-**/ (VII) be fall

dakamide(magad) (VII) boil in a certain place

daki-ayaamagad (VII) be cool, be cold

dakobidoon (VTI2) tie s.t. well

dakon (VTA) hold s.o., carry s.o.

dakonan (VTI) hold s.t., carry s.t.

dananjige (VAI) eat things in a certain place

danenim (VTA) think s.o. to be in a certain place

danoo (VAI + O) keep (something) in a certain place

dapaabam (VTA) look through an opening or window at s.o.

dapaabi (VAI) look through an opening or window

dash (PC) and, but

dashiwag /**dashi-**/ (VAI) (they) are in a certain number

daso- (PRE) a certain number, so many, every

daso-diba'igan (PC) a certain number of miles

daso-diba'iganed (VII) be a certain number of miles

dasogamigiziwag /**dasogamigizi-**/ (VAI) (they) are in a certain number of lodges dasoon = (VTA) *see:* **dasoozh**

dasoozh /dasooN-/ (VTA) trap s.o.

daswi (PC) a certain number

datakobidoon (VTI2) tie s.t. up *reduplicated form of:* **dakobidoon**

/-(d)ay-/ (NAD) someone's dog, someone's horse: **inday** my dog, my horse

dazhi- (PV) there, in a certain place

dazhim (VTA) talk about s.o.

dazhitaa (VAI) play, be occupied in a certain place

dazhiikan (VTI) work on s.t., be occupied with s.t.

dazhiikaw (VTA) work on s.o.

dazhiike (VAI) occupy a certain place

daa- (PV) would, could, can, ought *modal prefix*

daa (VAI) live in a certain place

/-daan-/ (NAD) someone's daughter: **odaanan** his/her daughter(s)

daangandan (VTI) taste (a sample of) s.t.

daangin (VTA) touch s.o.

/-daanis-/ (NAD) someone's daughter: **indaanis** my daughter

daashkiboojigan, -ag (NA) sawmill

daashkikwadin (VII) there is a crack in the ice

de- (PV) sufficently, completely

debashkine (VAI) have sufficient room, fit in well

debashkine(magad) (VII) have sufficient room, fit in well

debibidaw (VTA) catch something for s.o.

debibin = (VTA) *see:* **debibizh**

debibizh /debibiN-/ (VTA) catch s.o., seize s.o.

debika = (VII) *changed form of:* **dibikad**

debiseyendam (VAI2) think there is enough, think something is sufficient

debisinii (VAI) be full from eating

debwewesin (VII) be heard striking at a distance

debweyendam (VAI2) believe

degoshin = (VAI) *changed form of:* **dagoshin**

desa'onike (VAI) make a platform in lodge

/di-/ (VAI) *see:* endiyan

diba'amaw (VTA) pay something to s.o.

diba'igiiziswaan, -ag (NA) clock

dibaabandan (VTI) look to check the extent of s.t.,
  survey s.t.

dibaajimo (VAI) tell

dibaajimotaw (VTA) tell something to s.o.

dibendan (VTI) own s.t.

dibi (PC) I don't know where, I wonder where
  dubitative locative

dibikad (VII) be night

dibikaabaminaagwad (VII) be dark

dibiki-ayaa (VAI) be dark

dibishkoo (PC) just like, as if

dimii (VII) be deep water

dino (PR) sort, kind *also:* dinowa: dinowag *animate
  plural*, dinong *locative*

dipaabaawadoon (VII) make s.t. swell up by
  moistening

ditibasikaw (VTA) knock and roll s.o.

ditibaashin (VAI) roll over (as in an accident)

ditibidaabaan, -ag (NA) wagon

doodan (VTI) do something to s.t.

/-(d)oodem-/ (NAD) someone's totem (clan):
  indoodem my totem

Dookisin (NAME) Maude Kegg's maternal aunt

ebi= (VAI) *changed form of:* abi

egoo= (VTA) *changed form of:* izhi *stem deleted before
  inverse theme sign*

egwanigaazo= (VAI) *changed form of:* agwanigaazo

egwazhe= (VAI) *changed form of:* agwazhe

ekido= (VAI) *changed form of:* ikido

eko- (PRE) *changed form of:* ako-

en= (VTA) *changed form of:* izhi

enadog (PC) evidently (?)

enagoojin = (VAI) *changed form of:* **inagoojin**
ena'o = (VAI) *changed form of:* **ina'o**
enamo = (VII) *changed form of:* **inamon**
enanokii = (VAI) *changed form of:* **inanokii**
enaasamabi = (VAI) *changed form of:* **inaasamabi**
enda- (PRE) very, just *initial form of:* **wenda-**
enda-besho (PC) real close
enda-gichi-niibowa (PC) a whole lot
endago = (VII) *changed form of:* **dagon**
endakamide = (VII) *changed form of:*
  dakamide(magad)
enda-niibowa (PC) a lot
endanoo = (VAI + O) *changed form of:* **danoo**
endaso- (PRE) every *changed form of:* **daso-**
endaso- (PV) *changed form of:* **daso-**
endaso-giizhig (PC) every day
endazhi- (PV) *changed form of:* **dazhi-**
endazhiikaw = (VTA) *changed form of:* **dazhiikaw**
endazhiike = (VAI) *changed form of:* **dazhiike**
endazhiitaa = (VAI) *changed form of:* **dazhiitaa**
endaa = (VAI) *changed form of:* **daa**
endiyan /di-/ (VAI) have something the matter with
  you *conjunct 2 of* /di-/ *a stem used in conjunct only*
enendaagwa = (VII) *changed form of:* **inendaagwad**
eni- (PV) *changed form of:* **ani-**
enigaa' = (VTA) *changed form of:* **inigaa'**
enigini = (VAI) *changed form of:* **inigini**
enigok (PC) with effort, harder
enigokwadeyaa = (VII) *changed form of:*
  inigokwadeyaa
enigokwadeyezhisin = (VII) *changed form of:*
  inigokwadeyezhisin
enigokwaa = (VII) *changed form of:* **inigokwaa**
eniwek (PC) more intense, harder
enyan' (PC) yes
eshkwaa- (PV) *changed form of:* **ishkwaa-**
Eshkwegamaag (PLACE) Lake Onamia

eshkwegoojin = (VAI) *changed form of:* ishkwegoojin
eshkwesin = (VII) *changed form of:* ishkwesin
esigin = (VTI) *changed form of:* asiginan
et = (VTI2) *changed form of:* atoon
eta (PC) only
eyaa = (VAI) *changed form of:* ayaa
eyinagoojin = (VAI) *changed form of:* ayinagoojin
eyishkwe-ayi'ii (PC) at the end(s)
eyiidawayi'ii (PC) on both sides of something
ezh = (VTA) *changed from of:* izhi
ezhaa = (VAI) *changed form of:* izhaa
ezhi- (PV) *changed form of:* izhi-
ezhi = (VTA) *changed form of:* izhi
ezhichige = (VAI) *changed form of:* izhichige
ezhi' = (VTA) *changed form of:* izhi'
ezhin = (VAI2) *changed form of:* izhinam
ezhinikaad = (VTI) *changed form of:* izhinikaadan
ezhinikaade = (VII) *changed form of:* izhinikaade
ezhinikaan = (VTA) *changed form of:* izhinikaazh
ezhinikaazo = (VAI) *changed form of:* izhinikaazo
ezhiweba = (VII) *changed form of:* izhiwebad
ezhiwebizi = (VAI) *changed form of:* izhiwebizi

ga- (PV) will *future independent verb prefix when a personal prefix is used*
gabaashim (VTA) cook s.o. by boiling
gabe- (PRE) throughout, all (of a time)
gabe-dibik (PC) all night
gabe-giizhig (PC) all day
Gabekanaansing (PLACE) Portage Lake
gabenaage (VAI) score in a game
gabe-niibin (PC) all summer
gabeshi (VAI) camp
gaganoon = (VTA) *see:* gaganoozh
gaganoozh /gaganooN-/ (VTA) converse with s.o.
    reduplicated form of: ganoozh

gagaanoondewan /gagaanoonde-/ (VII) (they) are long dwellings *reduplicated form of:* **ginoonde**

gagaanwaawan /gagaanwaa-/ (VII) (they) are long *reduplicated form of:* **ginwaa**

gagaanwaakwadoon /gagaanwaakwad-/ (VII) (they) are long (of something sticklike) *reduplicated form of:* **ginwaakwad**

gagaanwaakwawe (VAI) have long fur *reduplicated form*

gagaanwaanikwe (VAI) have long hair *reduplicated form*

gagaanwegadoon /gagaanwegad-/ (VII) (they) are long (of something sheetlike) *reduplicated form of:* **ginwegad**

gagaawinaweyendaagozi (VAI) be stubborn

gagiibaadizi (VAI) be foolish

gagiibwaweyiingwe (VAI) be hairy-faced

gagwejichige (VAI) try things

gagwejim (VTA) ask s.o.

Gakaabikaang (PLACE) Minneapolis

gakiiwe (VAI) portage

gakiiwewidoon (VTI2) portage s.t.

ganabaj (PC) perhaps, maybe

ganage (PC) *see:* **gaawiin ganage, gego ganage**

ganakinan (VTI) snatch a handful of s.t.

ganawaabam (VTA) look at s.o.

ganawaabandan (VTI) look at s.t.

ganawaabi (VAI) take a look

ganawendan (VTI) take care of s.t.

ganawenim (VTA) take care of s.o.

gashkadin (VII) be freeze-up, lake freezes up

gashkanokii (VAI) be able to work

gashkibide (VII) be tied up in a bundle

gashkibidoon (VTI2) tie s.t. up in a bundle

gashkibijigaade (VII) be tied up in a bundle

gashki-dibiki-ayaa (VII) be pitch dark

gashkigwaaso (VAI) sew

gashki' (VTA) manage s.o., be able to get s.o. to do something

gawishimo (VAI) lie down

gayaagiimaabam = (VTA) *changed form of:* **gaagiimaabam**

gaye (PC) and, also; as for

gaa- (PV) *changed form of:* **gii-**

gaa (PC) no, not

gaa wiikaa (PC) never

gaabige (PC) right away

gaagiigido (VAI) speak, make a speech *reduplicated form*

gaagiimaabam (VTA) secretly look at s.o. for a time *reduplicated form of:* **giimaabam**

gaanizi = (VAI) *changed form of:* **giinizi**

gaaskiz /gaaskizw-/ (VTA) smoke s.o.

gaawashkwebii = (VAI) *changed form of:* **giiwashkwebii**

gaawiin (PC) no, not

gaawiin awiiya (PR) nobody, no one

gaawiin ganage (PC) not in the least

gaawiin gegoo (PR) nothing, none

gaawiin mashi (PC) not yet

gaawiin wiikaa (PC) never

gaazhagens, -ag (NA) domestic cat

gaazo (VAI) hide

ge- (PV) will, would, could, might, can *changed form of:* **ga-, da-, ji-, daa-**

Gebe-giizhig (PC) Maude Kegg's male parallel cousin

gegabe- (PN) all of (a season) *reduplicated form of:* **gabe-**

gegabe-biboon (PC) all winter

gegaa (PC) nearly, almost

geget (PC) certainly, for sure

geginwezh (PC) for a very long time

gegizhebaawaga = (VII) *changed form of:* **gigizhebaawagad**

gego (PC) don't
gego ganage (PC) don't in any way
gego wiikaa (PC) don't ever
gegoo (PR) something, anything *indefinite inanimate*
gekend= (VTI) *changed form of:* **gikendan**
genapii (PC) after a while, now and then
genoozi= (VAI) *changed form of:* **ginoozi**
gete- (PN) very old, ancient
geyaabi (PC) still, yet
gezikwendam (VAI2) barely remember
gezikwendan (VTI) barely remember s.t.
gi= (PRE) *second person prefix before a consonant*
gibaakobidoon (VTI2) can s.t.
gibaakwa'igan (NI) dam
Gibaakwa'iganing, -an (PLACE) Onamia, Minnesota
gibichiitaa (VAI) take a break
giboodiyegwaazhonenzhish, -ag (NA) little no-good
    pants
giboogwaan= (VTA) *see:* **giboogwaazh**
giboogwaazh /**giboogwaaN-**/ (VTA) sew s.o. shut
gibwanaabaawe (VAI) drown
gichi- (PRE) great, big, very
gichi-anang (NA) North Star
gichi-aya'aa, -g (NA) elder
gichi-aya'aawi (VAI) be very old
Gichi-aakogwan (NAME) Maude Kegg's maternal
    aunt
gichigamiiwashk, -oon (NI) bulrushes
gichi-gigizheb (PC) very early in the morning
Gichi-jaagigaabaw (NAME) name of an old man
Gichi-miskogiizhig (NAME) George Pine, Maude
    Kegg's uncle
Gichi-mookomaan, -ag (NA) whiteman
Gichi-mookomaani-ayaa (VAI) be a whiteman
Gichi-ziibi (PLACE) Mississippi River: **Gichi-ziibiing**
    locative

gid = (PRE) *second person prefix before a vowel in a verb stem or a nondependent noun stem*

gidagaakoonsiwayaan, -ag (NA) fawn hide

gidasan (VTI) parch s.t. (especially of wild rice)

gidasige (VAI) parch things (especially of wild rice)

gidoode (VAI) crawl out

gigizheb (PC) in the morning

gigizhebaawagad (VII) be morning

gijinagizhiin (VTA) take guts out of s.o.

gijiigibin = (VTA) *see:* **gijiigibizh**

gijiigibizh /gijiigibiN-/ (VTA) pull the skin off s.o.

gijiipizi, -yag (NA) gypsy

gikendan (VTI) know s.t., remember s.t.

gikenim (VTA) know s.o.

gikinoo'amaw (VTA) teach s.o.

gikinoonowin (NI) year

gimiwan (VII) rain

gimoodi (VAI + O) steal (something)

gimoodim (VTA) steal something from s.o.

ginagaapi (VAI) giggle

gina'amaw (VTA) forbid s.o.

gina'amaadim /gina'amaadi-/ (VAI) there is a prohibition

ginebig, -oog (NA) snake

ginigawisin (VII) be mixed

ginjiba' (VTA) run away from s.o.

ginjiba'iwe (VAI) flee, run away

ginjida'an (VTI) tap s.t. in, pound s.t. in

ginoozi (VAI) be long, be tall

ginwaakozi (VAI) be tall (of a person); be long, be tall (of something sticklike)

ginwegambizo (VAI) wear a long skirt

ginwenzh (PC) long (in time), for a long time

ginzhizhawizi (VAI) be a hard worker

gisinaa (VII) be cold

gitigaadan (VTI) plant s.t.

gitigaan (NA) child intended for marriage
gitigaan, -an (NI) garden, vegetable
gitige (VAI) plant, garden, farm
gitimi (VAI) be lazy
gizhaagamide (VII) be hot (of a liquid)
gizhaate (VII) be hot (atmosphere)
gizhibaabizo (VAI) spin around, rotate
gizhigaa (VII) run hard (as sap in spring)
gizhiikaabatoo (VAI) run fast
giziibiigin (VTA) wash s.o.
giziibiiginakokwaanaaboo (NI) kettle-washing liquid
giziibiiginan (VTI) wash s.t.
giziibiiginigaade (VII) be washed
gii- (PV) *past prefix*
giichigobin = (VTA) *see:* **giichigobizh**
giichigobizh /giichigobiN-/ (VTA) detach s.o. by
    pulling
giichigon (VTA) detach s.o.
giichiwakwaane (VAI) take off headwear
giigoonh, giigoonyag (NA) fish
giigoonh-adaawewinini, -wag (NA) fish trader
Giigoonh-kiwenzhiinh (NAME) name of a fish trader
giigoozens, -ag (NA) minnow
gii'igoshimo (VAI) fast
giikaji (VAI) be cold (of a person)
giikanaamode (VII) be smoky in a dwelling
giikaam (VTA) quarrel with s.o.
giikiibingwashi (VAI) be sleepy
giimaabam (VTA) secretly look at s.o.
giin (PR) you *second person singular*
giinizi (VAI) be sharp-edged
giishka'aakwewigamig, -oon (NI) lumber camp
giishkiboodoon (VTI2) saw s.t. off
giishkiboojigan, -an (NI) saw
giishkizh /giishkizhw-/ (VTA) cut s.o. off
giishkizhan (VTI) cut s.t. off
giishpin (PC) if

giiwanimo (VAI) tell a lie

giiwashkwe (VAI) be dizzy

giiwashkwebii (VAI) be drunk

/giiwashkweshkaw-/ (VTA) make s.o. dizzy (especially of a substance consumed)

giiwe (VAI) go home, return

giiwebatoo (VAI) run home

giiwe-biboon (VII) the winter turns toward spring

giiwe'o (VAI) go home by boat

giiwenh (PC) so the story goes, as it is said

giiwenige (VAI) have a give-away, give presents in an exchange

giiwenigewin (NI) give-away, property exchange as a mourning custom

giiwitaashim (VTA) lay s.o. down in a circle

giiwitaashkode (PC) around the fire

giizhakidoon (VTI2) finish setting s.t. up

giizhaa (PC) beforehand

giizhaajimo (VAI) tell all, finish telling

giizhi- (PV) finish, complete

giizhibagaa (VII) be all out in leaves

giizhide (VII) get done cooking

giizhigamide (VII) finish boiling

giizhigamizige (VAI) be done boiling something

giizhige (VAI) finish building

giizhigi (VAI) be fully grown

giizhigin (VII) be fully grown

giizhi' (VTA) finish making s.o.

giizhik, -ag (NA) cedar tree

giizhikaandag, -oog (NA) cedar bough

giizhikon = (VTA) *see:* giizhikozh

giizhikozh /giizhikoN-/ (VTA) finishing carving s.o.

giizhishim (VTA) finish putting s.o.

giizhitoon (VTI2) finish making s.t.

giizhiikan (VTI) finish s.t.

giizhiitaa (VAI) finish

giizis, -oog (NA) sun, moon

giizis /giizisw-/ (VTA) cook s.o.

go (PC) *emphatic particle*

godotaagan, -an (NI) bell

godotaagaans, -an (NI) small bell

gojichige (VAI) try things out

gomaa (PC) some amount, some extent, some degree

gomaapii (PC) after a while, by and by, at or to a
    middling distance

gondaabiigin (VTA) put s.o. in water, dip s.o.

gondaataa (VAI) go under the surface, sink

gopiibatoo (VAI) run inland

/-gos-/ (NAD) someone's son: **ogosan** his/her son(s)

gos = (VTA) *see:* **goshi**

gosha (PC) *emphatic*

goshi /goS-/ (VTA) fear s.o.

goshkom (VTA) surprise s.o. verbally

goshkozi (VAI) wake

gotan (VTI) fear s.t.

gotaaji (VAI) be scared

gozi (VAI) move camp or residence

gozigwan (VII) be heavy

gozigwani (VAI) be heavy

/-goodaas-/ (NID) someone's skirt, someone's dress:
    ingoodaas my skirt; **ingoodaazhish** my no-good
    skirt

/-goodaasens-/ (NID) someone's little skirt:
    ingoodaazhenzhish my no-good little skirt

gookooko'oo, -g (NA) owl

gookoosh, -ag (NA) pig, pork

goon (NA) snow

goonikaa (VII) be a lot of snow

gwayak (PC) correct, straight, right

gwayakoboodoon (VTI2) saw s.t. straight

gwaaba'an (VTI) scoop s.t.

gwaashkwani (VAI) jump

gwekibagizo (VAI) turn over, right oneself

gwekwekiwebin (VTA) turn s.o. over, fling s.o. over
reduplicated form of: gwekiwebinan
gweshkozi = (VAI) *changed form of:* goshkozi
gwiinawaabam (VTA) be unable to see s.o.
gwiinawi- (PV) unable to
gwiiwizens, -ag (NA) boy: gwiiwizhenzhish *pejorative*
Gwiiwizensiwi-ziibiing (PLACE) Boy River,
Minnesota

haa (PC) *exclamation,* so! well! *also:* ha, haw, haaw

idash (PC) and, but
igaye (PC) and, also, as for
igo (PC) *emphatic*
igoo (VTA) *see:* izhi
i'iw (PR) that *inanimate singular demonstrative*
ikido (VAI) say something, say in a certain way
iko (PC) used to, usually
ikogabaa (VAI) get off
ikwe, -wag (NA) woman, lady
ikwezens, -ag (NA) girl
ikwezensiwi (VAI) be a girl
ikwezhenzhishiwi (VAI) be a naughty girl
im = (PRE) *first person prefix before b-*
imaa (PC) there
imbaabaa, -yag /-baabaay-/ (NAD) my father
in = (PR) *first person prefix before d-, g-, j-, z-, zh-*
in = (VTA) *see:* izhi
ina (PC) *yes-no question marker*
inagoojin (VAI) hang in a certain way or place
ina'o (VAI) go to a certain place by boat
inamon /inamo-/ (VII) go in a certain way or
direction (as a road or trail)
inanokii (VAI) work in a certain way or a certain
place
inanoon = (VTA) *see:* inanoozh

inanoozh /inanooN-/ (VTA) hire s.o. to go to a
certain place

inawem (VTA) be related to s.o.

inawendiwag /inawendi-/ (VAI) (they) are related to
e.o.

inaabi (VAI) take a look, peek

inaajimo (VAI) tell something, tell in a certain way

inaajimotaw (VTA) tell s.o. something, tell s.o. in a
certain way

inaandawe (VAI) climb to a certain place

inaanzo (VAI) be colored a certain way

ind = (PRE) *first person prefix before a vowel in a verb
stem or a nondependent noun stem*

inday, -ag /-(d)ay-/ (NAD) my dog, my horse

indaanis, -ag /-daanis-/ (NAD) my daughter

indig (VTA) *see:* **izhi**

indigo (PC) it is as if, just like, looks like

indoodem, -ag /-(d)oodem-/ (NAD) my totem (clan)

inendam (VAI2) think something, think in a certain
way

inendan (VTI) think something of s.t., think in a
certain way about s.t.

inendaagwad (VII) be thought of in a certain way

ingiw (PR) those *animate plural demonstrative*

ingiwedig (PR) those over there *animate plural
demonstrative*

ingo- (PRE) one, single

ingo-anama'e-giizhigad (PC) one week

ingo-diba'igan (PC) one mile

ingo-dibaabiishkoojigan (PC) one pound

ingoding (PC) once, one time

ingodobaneninj (PC) one handful

ingodogamig (PC) one house or household

ingodozid (PC) one foot (measurement)

ingodwaaswi (PC) six

ingo-giizis (PC) one month

ingoji (PC) somewhere, anywhere, approximately
    indefinite locative
ingoodaas /-goodaas-/ (NID) my dress
ingoodaasens, -an /-goodaasens-/ (NID) my little
    dress:
ingoodaazhenzhish *pejorative*
ini- (PV) *see:* **ani-**
inigaa' (VTA) do an injustice to s.o., make s.o. feel
    bad, be mean to s.o.
inigaazi (VAI) be in a poor state, mourn
inigini (VAI) be a certain size
inigokwadeyaa (VII) be a certain width
inigokwadeyezhisin (VII) be a track of a certain width
inigokwaa (VII) be a certain size
inikaa (VAI) disappear
inikoozo (VAI) be shot in a certain place or way
ininaatig, -oog (NA) maple tree
inini, -wag (NA) man
ininishib, -ag (NA) mallard
initam (VAI) hear a certain noise
iniw (PR) those *inanimate plural demonstrative*; that,
    those *animate obviative demonstrative*
inoo'amaw (VTA) point to a certain place for s.o.,
    point to something for s.o.
inzhishenh, inzhishenyag /-zhisheny-/ (NAD) my
    (cross-) uncle (mother's brother)
inzid, -an /-zid(aa)-/ (NID) my foot
ipide(magad) (VII) drive to a certain place
isa (PC) *emphatic*
ishkode (NI) fire
ishkode-jiimaan, -an (NI) steamboat
ishkodewan (VII) be a fire, be afire
ishkwaa- (PV) after
ishkwaagamizige (VAI) finish sap-boiling
ishkwaagaa (VII) be the last run of the sap
ishkwaa-naawakwe (VII) be afternoon

ishkwaandem, -an (NI) door, doorway
ishkwaataa (VAI) finish an activity
ishkwe-ayi'ii (PC) at the far end
ishkwege (VAI) live in last house
ishkwegoojin (VAI) hang last in a row
ishkwesin (VII) lie in last place
ishkweyaang (PC) behind
ishpate (VII) there is high snow
ishpiming (PC) up above, in the sky
ishpimisagokaade (VII) have an upper story
ishwaaswi (PC) eight
iskigamizan (VTI) boil s.t. down
iskigamizigan (NI) sap-boiling place, sugar camp
iskigamiziganaak, -oon (NI) sap-boiling frame
iskigamiziganaatig, -oon (NI) sap-boiling pole
iskigamizige (VAI) boil sap
iskigamizigewigamig, -oon (NI) sap-boiling lodge
iwedi (PR) that over there *inanimate singular demonstrative*
iwidi (PC) over there
izh = ((VTA)) *see:* **izhi**
izhaa (VAI) go to a certain place
izhaamagad (VII) go to a certain place
izhi- (PRE) in a certain way, in or to a certain place, so, thus
izhi /iN-/ (VTA) say something to s.o., say in a certain way to s.o., call s.o. a certain way
izhichige (VAI) do in a certain way, do a certain thing
izhichigewin, -an (NI) way of doing something
izhidaabiiba'igo (VAI) drive a horse to a certain place
izhidaabii'iwe (VAI) drive to a certain place
izhi-gwayak (PC) straight to a certain place
izhi' (VTA) cause s.o. to do something, make s.o. in a certain way
izhinam (VAI) have a certain dream or vision
izhinikaadan (VTI) name s.t. a certain way

izhinikaade (VII) be named a certain way, have such a
name
izhinikaan = (VTA) *see:* **izhinikaazh**
izhinikaazh /izhinikaaN-/ (VTA) name s.o. a certain
way
izhinikaazo (VAI) be named a certain way, have a
certain name
izhisin (VII) be a certain date
izhitoon (VTI2) make s.t. in a certain way
izhiwebad (VII) happen a certain way
izhiwebizi (VAI) behave a certain way, have
something happen to one
izhiwidoon (VTI2) carry s.t. to a certain place, take
s.t. to a certain place
izhiwijigaade (VII) be carried to a certain place, be
taken to a certain place
izhiwin = (VTA) *see:* **izhiwizh**
izhiwizh /izhiwiN-/ (VTA) carry s.o. to a certain
place, take s.o. to a certain place

iidog (PC) maybe, must be *dubitative particle*
/-iinimosheny-/ (NAD) cross-cousin of opposite sex,
sweetheart: **niinimoshenh** my cross-cousin, my
sweetheart
/-iinizis-/ (NID) someone's (single) hair: **niinizisan** my
hair (plural)
/-iiw-/ (NAD) someone's wife: **wiiwan** his wife
/-iiyawen'eny-/ (NAD) someone's namesake,
(reciprocal relationship of a name-giver and a
namee): **niiyawen'enh** my namesake

jaagizo (VAI) burn
jekaagaminan (VTI) dip s.t. in a liquid
ji- (PV) will, could, should, might, can, so that, that
conjunct future and modal
jibwaa- (PV) before

jiibaakwaan = (VTA) *see:* **jiibaakwaazh**

jiibaakwaazh /jiibaakwaaN-/ (VTA) cook s.o.

jiibaakwe (VAI) cook

jiibegamigoons, -n (NI) small grave

jiibiseny, -ag (NA) gypsy

jiichiigawiganebin = (VTA) *see:* **jiichiigawiganebizh**

jiichiigawiganebizh /jiichiigawiganebiN-/ (VTA) scratch s.o.'s back *reduplicated form*

jiigayi'ii (PC) by something, near something

jiigaatig (PC) by a tree

jiigi- (PN) by, near

jiigibiig (PC) by the water, on the shore

jiigishkode (PC) by the fire

jiigi-zaaga'igan (PC) by a lake

jiimaan, -an (NI) canoe, boat

Jiipaawenh (NAME) girl's name

jiishaakwa' /jiishaakwa'w-/ (VTA) scrape s.o. with a stick to remove hair (as a hide)

ka (PC) no!

/-kaad-/ (NID) someone's leg: **nikaad** my leg

/-kaakigan-/ (NID) someone's chest: **nikaakigan** my chest

ko (PC) used to, usually

/-konaas-/ (NID) someone's blanket (especially as a garment): **nikonaas** my blanket

/-kwegan(aa)-/ (NID) someone's neck: **nikwegan** my neck

madaabii (VAI) go down to the shore

madaabiibatoo (VAI) run down to the shore

madaabii-gozi (VAI) move camp down to the lake

madwe- (PV) audible

madwe' /madwe'w-/ (VTA) pound on s.o. (as on a drum)

madwesin (VII) ring, clink

madwewe (VII) make a noise, go bang

madwezige (VAI) shoot off a gun

ma'iingan, -ag (NA) wolf

maji- (PN) bad

maji-aya'aawish, -ag (NA) evil being or spirit

makade-mashkikiwaaboo (NI) coffee

makadewaa (VII) be black

makadewiminagad (VII) be black (of a berry or grain)

makadewizi (VAI) be black

makak, -oon (NI) box

makakosag, -oon (NI) tub, barrel

makakoons, -an (NI) small box

makam (VTA) take something away from s.o.

makizin, -an (NI) moccasin

makoshtigwaan, -an (NI) bear's head

Makoons (NAME) Little Bear

makwa, -g (NA) bear

makwasaagimens, -ag (NA) little bear-paw snowshoe

mam = (VTA) *see:* mami

mamaadaajimo (VAI) start to tell *reduplicated form of:* maadaajimo

mamaajide'eshkaa (VAI) have a heart attack

mamaajii (VAI) move, stir

mamaajiikwazhiwe (VAI) paddle off *reduplicated form of:* maajiikwazhiwe

mamaandidowag /mamaandido-/ (VAI) (they) are big *reduplicated form of:* mindido

mamaangizide (VAI) have big feet *reduplicated form of:* mangizide

mamaashkawapidoon (VTI2) tie s.t. tightly *reduplicated form of:* mashkawapidoon

mami /mam-/ (VTA) take s.o.

mamoon (VTI2) take s.t.

manashkikiwaan = (VTA) *see:* manashkikiwaazh

manashkikiwaazh /mashkikiwaaN-/ (VTA) gather medicine from s.o.

manashkikiwe (VAI) gather medicine

manezi (VAI + O) need (something), be short of (something)

mangaanibaadan (VTI) shovel s.t. out

mangaanibaajigan, -an (NI) snow shovel

mangaanibaajige (VAI) shovel out

manidoo, -g (NA) manitou

manidoominens, -ag (NA) bead

manidoo-nagamon, -an (NI) spiritual song

manisaadan (VTI) cut s.t. for firewood

manise (VAI) cut wood

manoomin (NI) wild rice

Manoominaganzhikaansing (PLACE) Little Rice Lake

manoominike (VAI) harvest wild rice, rice

mashi (PC) *see:* **gaa mashi**

mashkawaakwaji (VAI) be frozen solid

mashkawi-ayaa (VII) harden

mashkawizii (VAI) be powerful, be strong

mashkiki, -wan (NI) medicine

mashkikiwaaboo (NI) liquid medicine

mashkikiiwinini, -wag (NA) doctor

mashkodesimin, -ag (NA) bean

mashkosiw, -an (NI) plant, blade of grass; *plural* grass, meadow

mashkosiins, -an (NI) (blade of) grass

mawadis = (VTA) *see:* **mawadish**

mawadish /mawadiS-/ (VTA) visit s.o.

mawadishiwe (VAI) visit people

mawi (VAI) cry

mawim (VTA) cry for s.o.

mawinzo (VAI) pick berries

mayagenim (VTA) think s.o. strange, wonder about s.o. unfamiliar

mayagwesin (VII) make a strange ringing or clinking sound

mayaajiidoo = (VTI2) *changed form of:* **maajiidoon**

mazaan (NA) broken rice and chaff

mazaanens (NI) fine broken rice
Mazhii'iganing (PLACE) Garrison, Minnesota
mazinadin (VTA) make an image of s.o.
mazina'igan, -an (NI) book, paper
mazina'iganiiwinini, -wag (NA) mailman
mazinaakizo (VAI) be pictured
mazinigwaaso (VAI) do beadwork embroidery
mazinikozo (VAI) be carved
maada'adoo (VAI) follow a trail or track
maadaajimo (VAI) start to tell
maadaajimotaw (VTA) start to tell something to s.o.
maadaanimizi (VAI) start to get scared
maadaawanidiwag /maadaawanidi-/ (VAI) (they)
    start off in a group
maadoode (VAI) crawl off
maadoom (VTA) carry off s.o. on one's back
maagizhaa (PC) perhaps, maybe
maagobidoon (VTI2) squeeze s.t., press s.t.
maajaa (VAI) leave, go away
maajaa' (VTA) give s.o. a funeral, bury s.o.
maajaa'idim /maajaa'idi-/ (VAI) there is a funeral
maajidaabiiba'igo (VAI) drive off (as in a wagon or
    sleigh)
maajidaabii'iwe (VAI) start to drive off
maajijiwan (VII) start to flow as a current
maajinaazha' /maajinaazha'w-/ (VTA) send s.o. off
maajitaa (VAI) start an activity
maajitigweyaa (VII) start to flow (as a river)
maajii- (PV) start, begin
maajiiba'idiwag /maajiiba'idi-/ (VAI) (they) run off in
    a group
maajiiba'igo (VAI) ride off on a horse
maajiibatoo (VAI) run off, start running
maajiidoon (VTI2) take s.t. along or away
maajiin = (VTA) *see:* maajiizh
maajiizh /maajiiN-/ (VTA) take s.o. along or away
/-maamaay-/ (NAD) someone's mother: nimaamaa

my mother, **nimaamaanaan** grandmother (our (1p) mother)

maamaajikwazhiwe (VAI) paddle off *reduplicated form*

maamigin (VTA) pick up s.o., gather s.o.

maaminonendam (VAI2) think, consider

maamiijin (VTI3) eat s.t. *reduplicated form of:* **miijin**

maanaadad (VII) be bad, be ugly

maanendam (VAI2) feel bad

maanoo (PC) anyway

maawandoonan (VTI) gather s.t.

maawandoopidoon (VTI2) tie s.t. together

maawanji'idiwag /maawanji'idi-/ (VAI) (they) get together, meet

maazhi- (PV) bad

maazhi-ayaa (VAI) feel bad, feel sick

maazhimaaso (VAI) stink cooking or burning

medaabiibatoo = (VAI) *changed form of:* **madaabiibatoo**

medwesin = (VII) *changed form of:* **madwesin**

megwayaak (PC) in the woods

megwaa (PC) while, during

megwejiishkiwag (PC) in the mud

megwe-mashkosiw (PC) in midst of the grass, in a meadow

memegwesi, -wag (NA) hairy-faced bank-dwelling dwarf spirit

menezi = (VAI) *changed form of:* **manezi**

meshkwad (PC) in turn, in exchange

metasin (VTA) miss s.o.

mewinzha (PC) long ago, a long time ago

meziwezi = (VAI) *changed form of:* **miziwezi**

michayi'ii (PC) at the ground

michaa(magad) (VII) be big

michi- (PV) bare, just that

michiigizi (VAI) be big (of something sheetlike)

midaaso- (PRE) ten

midaaso-diba'igan (PC) ten miles

midaasogon (PC) ten days
midewi (VAI) go through the Midewiwin, be a
member of the Midewiwin
migizi, -wag (NA) bald eagle
mikaw (VTA) find s.o.
mikigaade (VII) be found
mikinaak, -wag (NA) snapping turtle
mikinaakoons, -ag (NA) little snapping turtles
mikwam, -iig (NA) ice
mikwendam (VAI2) remember, consider, think of
something
mikwendan (VTI) remember s.t., consider s.t., think
of s.t.
mikwenim (VTA) remember s.o., consider s.o., think
of s.o.
mimigoshkam (VAI2) jig wild rice
mina' (VTA) give s.o. a drink
mindido (VAI) be big
mindimooyenh, mindimooyenyag (NA) old lady
mindimooyenyiwi (VAI) be an old lady
minik (PC) much, many, amount
minikwe (VAI + O) drink (something)
minisaabik, -oon (NI) rock island
minisaabikowan (VII) be a rock island
minisiiwan (VII) be an island
Minisiiwikwe (NAME) Lady of the Island
Minisiiwinini (NAME) name of storekeeper
minjikanaakobijigan, -an (NI) fence
minjiminamaw (VTA) hold something in place for
s.o.
minjiminan (VTI) hold s.t. in place
minjiminigemagad (VII) hold things in place
minjimishkaw (VTA) hold s.o. in place with foot or
body
minjimishkoodoon (VTI2) hold s.t. in place with a
weight
mino- (PRE) good

mino-ayaa (VAI) feel good

mino'o (VAI) be well-dressed

minopogwad (VII) taste good

/minopw-/ (VTA) like the taste of s.o.: niminopwaa I
like the taste of it (animate)

minoshin (VAI) lie comfortably, fit well

minwanjige (VAI) eat well

minwaabam (VTA) be happy to see s.o., like the look
of s.o.

minwaabandan (VTI) like the look of s.t.

minwaagamin /minwaagami-/ (VII) be good (of
something liquid)

minwendam (VAI2) be glad, be happy

minwenim (VTA) like s.o.

/-misad(aa)-/ (NID) someone's belly: nimisad my
belly

misajidamoo, -g (NA) grey squirrel

misan/miS-/ (NI) firewood *plural form of:* mishi

misawenim (VTA) desire s.o. badly

mishi, misan /miS-/ (NI) firewood

mishiikenh, -yag (NA) painted turtle

Misi-zaaga'igan (PLACE) Mille Lacs Lake: Misi-
zaaga'iganiing *locative*

misko- (PRE) red

miskwaadesi, -wag (NA) mud turtle *possibly local name
for map turtle*

miskwiiwi (VAI) bleed

mitakamig (PC) on bare ground

mitaawangaa (VII) be a sandy place

mitig, -oog (NA) tree

mitig, -oon (NI) stick, wood

mitigo-jiimaan, -an (NI) wooden boat

mitigokaa (VII) be a lot of trees

mitigomin, -an (NI) acorn

mitigo-waakaa'igaans (NI) small shack

mitigoogamigoons, -oon (NI) small shack

mitigoons, -an (NI) stick

mitigwemikwaan, -an (NI) wooden spoon or ladle
mizhakwad (VII) there is a clear sky
miziwezi (VAI) be whole
mii (PC) it is thus, it is so, then
mii dash (PC) and then
miigiwe (VAI) give things away
miijin (VTI3) eat s.t.
miikana, -n (NI) road, trail
miikanens, -an (NI) trail
miikaans, -an (NI) trail
miin = (VTA) *see:* miizh
miinan /miin-/ (NI) blueberries
miinawaa (PC) and, also, again
miinidiwag /miinidi-/ (VAI) (they) give something to
    e.o., mutually or reciprocally distribute something
miish (PC) and then
miizh /miiN-/ (VTA) give something to s.o.
moshwe, -g (NA) shawl
mooka'am (VII) be sunrise: wenji-mooka'ang east
mookawaakii (VAI) cry to go along
mookii (VAI) emerge from surface
mookomaan, -an (NI) knife
moonikaan, -an (NI) cellar
Mooniyaawikwe, -g (NA) Canadian woman
Mooniyaawinini, -wag (NA) Canadian
mooshkinebii (VII) be full of liquid
moozhag (PC) always, all the time

n = (PRE) *first person prefix before ii- or oo- in a*
    dependent noun stem
na (PC) *yes-no question marker*
nabagisag, -oog (NA) board, plank
naboob, -iin (NI) soup
nagadenim (VTA) be acquainted with s.o., be friends
    with s.o.
nagadenindiwag /nagadenindi-/ (VAI) (they) are
    acquainted with e.o., are friends with e.o.

nagamo (VAI) sing

nagamon, -an (NI) song

nagan = (VTA) *see:* **nagazh**

nagazh /nagaN-/ (VTA) abandon s.o., leave s.o. behind

nagishkaw (VTA) meet s.o.

na'inan (VTI) store s.t. away

namadabi (VAI) sit down

nanaa'itoon (VTI2) fix s.t. up, repair s.t.

nanaa'ii (VAI) be specially dressed and made up

nanaamadabi (VAI) sit for a while *reduplicated form of:* **namadabi**

nanaandawi'iwe (VAI) heal people

nandawaabam (VTA) look for s.o., search for s.o.

nandawaabandan (VTI) look for s.t., search for s.t.

nandawisimwe (VAI) look for horses

nandodamaage (VAI) beg someone for something

nandom (VTA) call s.o. over, summon s.o.

naseyaawangwaan, -an (NI) sugaring trough

naseyaawangwe (VAI) granulate sugar

nashke (PC) behold

nawadin (VTA) grab s.o., take s.o. by the hand

nawadinan (VTI) grab s.t.

nawaj (PC) more than

nawapo (VAI) take a lunch along

nawapwaanike (VAI) make a lunch to take along

naweshkosin (VII) lie bent over as grass

nayaawakwe = (VII) *changed form of:* **naawakwe**

nazikwe'o (VAI) comb one's own hair, have combed hair

naa (PC) *emphatic*

/-naabem-/ (NAD) someone's husband: **ninaabem** my husband

naadagoodoo (VAI) go after snares

naadin (VTI3) get s.t., fetch s.t., go after s.t.

naadoobii (VAI) go after water, go after sap

naagaj (PC) after a little while, right now

naagozi (VAI) appear
naagwad (VII) appear
naajinizha'an (VTI) send for s.t.
naajiwanii'ige (VAI) go after traps
naan (NAD) gramma! *vocative of:* nimaamaanaan
   grandmother
naan= (VTA) *see:* naazh
naanan (PC) fire
naanaagadawaabam (VTA) watch s.t. carefully
   reduplicated form
naanaazikan (VTI) approach s.t. one after another
   reduplicated from of: naazikan
naaniibawi (VAI) stand *reduplicated form of:* niibawi
naano- (PRE) five
naano-diba'igan (PC) five miles
naawagaam (PC) middle of the lake
Naawakamigookwe (NAME) Maude Kegg:
   Naawakamigook *vocative*
naawakwe (VII) be noon
naawayi'ii (PC) in the middle of something
naawi- (PN) in middle of
naawi-gitigaan (PC) in the middle of the garden
naawij (PC) in the middle of the lake
naazh /naaN-/ (VTA) get s.o., fetch s.o.
naazhibide (VII) fly down, speed down
naazhwashka= (VII) *changed form of:* niizhwashkad
naazikaw (VTA) approach s.o.
nebaa= (VAI) *changed form of:* nibaa
nebo= (VAI) *changed form of:* nibo
negwaabam (VTA) look out of corner of one's eye at
   s.o.
negwaakwaan, -an (NI) tap for tree
ne'in= (VTI) *changed form of:* na'inan
nenaandawi'iwe= (VAI) *changed form of:*
   nanaandawi'iwe
nenaandawi'iwed (NA) Indian doctor *changed form of:*
   nanaandawi'iwe

nengizo = (VAI) *changed form of:* **ningizo**
neningodoonag (PC) in single boat-loads
neniibowa (PC) a whole lot *reduplicated form*
nesoogoojin = (VAI) *changed form of:* **nisoogoojin**
neyakokwaanens, -an (NI) little stirring paddle
neyaashi (NI) point of land: **neyaashiing, neyaashing**
  locative
Neyaashiwanishinaabe, -g (NA) resident of Vineland
  settlement on the west shore of Mille Lacs Lake
neyaashiiwan (VII) be a point of land
ni = (PRE) *first person prefix before consonants other than*
  b-, d-, g-, j-, z-, zh-
nibaa (VAI) sleep
nibaagan, -an (NI) bed
nibi (NI) water
nibinaadin (VTI3) get water
nibinaadookana (NI) water-carrying trail
nibiikaa (VII) there is a lot of water
nibiikaang (PC) in a wet or marshy place
nibiiwakamigaa (VII) be wet ground
nibo (VAI) die, be dead
nichiiwad (VII) be a storm
nikanisidoon (VTI2) leave s.t. undisturbed for a day
/-nik(aa)-/ (NID) arm: **ninik** my arm
nikaad, -an /-kaad-/ (NID) my leg
nikaakigan, -an /-kaakigan-/ (NID) my chest
nikonaas, -an /-konaas-/ (NID) my blanket (especially
  as a garment)
nikwegan, -an /-kwegan(aa)-/ (NID) my neck
nimaamaa, -yag /-maamaay-/ (NAD) my mother
nimaamaanaan (NAD) grandmother *1p possessed form*
  of: **/-maamaay-/** mother
nimisad, -an /-misad(aa)-/ (NID) my belly
ninaabem, -ag /-naabem-/ (NAD) my husband
ningide (VII) melt, thaw
ningiz /ningizw-/ (VTA) melt s.o., thaw s.o.
ningizo (VAI) melt, thaw

ningwa' /ningwa'w-/ (VTA) bury s.o.

ningwaja' /ningwaja'w-/ (VTA) hoe s.o.

ningwaja'ige (VAI) hoe things

ningwakamigin (VTA) put s.o. under the ground

/-ningwiigan(aa)-/ (NID) someone's wing:
   niningwiigan my wing

ninik, -an /nik(aa)-/ (NID) my arm

niningwiigan, -an /-ningwiigwan(aa)-/ (NID) my
   wing

nininj, -iin /-ninjy-/ (NID) my hand

niniijaanis, -ag /-niijaanis-/ (NAD) my child

/-ninjy-/ (NID) someone's hand: nininj my hand

ninoshenh, -yag /-nosheny-/ (NAD) my (parallel-)
   aunt (mother's sister)

nis = (VTA) _see:_ nishi

nisaabaawe (VA/II) be wet

nishi /niS-/ (VTA) kill s.o.

nishiime, -yag /-shiimey-/ (NAD) my younger sibling
   or parallel cousin

nishkaadizi (VAI) be mad, be angry

nishkaadiziitaw (VTA) get mad at s.o.

nishtigwaan, -an /-shtigwaan-/ (NID) my head

nisiwag /nisi-/ (VAI) (they) are three

nisidawinan (VTI) recognize s.t.

nisidawinaw (VTA) recognize s.o.

nisidotaw (VTA) understand s.o.

nisimidana (PC) thirty

nising (PC) three times

niso- (PRE) three

niso-diba'igan (PC) three miles

nisogamaawan /nisogamaa-/ (VII) (they) are three
   lakes together

nisogamigiziwag /nisogamigizi-/ (VAI) (they) are in
   three lodges

nisogon (PC) three days

nisoogoojinoog /nisoogoojin-/ (VAI) (they) hang
   three in a row

niswi (PC) three
nitawag, -an /-tawag-/ (NID) my ear
nitaawigi (VAI) grow up
nitaawigi' (VTA) raise s.o. (as a child)
niibawi (VAI) stand
niibaa-dibik (PC) late at night
niibin (VII) be summer
niibowa (PC) much, a lot, many
niigaan (PC) in front, leading
niigaan-agoojin (VAI) hang in front
niigoshkan (VTI) break s.t.
niigoshkaa (VII) break up
niigwa' /niigwa'w-/ (VTA) break up s.o.
niigwa'an (VTI) break up s.t.
niigwa'igaade (VII) be broken up
/-niijaanis-/ (NAD) someone's child: **niniijaanis** my
    child
niimi'idiwag /niimi'idi-/ (VAI) (they) have a dance
niimi'idiiwigamig, -oon (NI) dance hall
niin (PR) I, me *first person singular*
niinawind (PR) we, us *first person exclusive*
niineta (PR) only me *first person singular*
niinimoshenh, -yag /-iinimosheny-/ (NAD) my cross-
    cousin of the opposite sex, my sweetheart
niinizis, -an /-iinizis-/ (NID) my (single) hair
niisaakiiwe (VAI) go downhill
niisaakiiwebatoo (VAI) run downhill
niishtana (PC) twenty
niiwana' /niiwana'w-/ (VTA) kill s.o., slaughter s.o.
niiwen = (VTA) *see:* **niiwezh**
niiwezh /niiweN-/ (VTA) beat s.o. at game
niiwin (PC) four
niiyawen'enh, -yag /-iiyawen'eny-/ (NAD) my
    namesake: **niiyawen'** *vocative*
niizh (PC) two
niizhinoon /niizhin-/ (VII) (they) are two, are double

niizhing (PC) twice
niizho- (PRE) two
niizho-diba'igan (PC) two miles
niizhogon (PC) two days
niizhozid (PC) two feet
niizhoonagizi (VAI) have two canoes
niizhwashkad (VII) be double-barrelled
 /-nosheny-/ (NAD) someone's (parallel-) aunt
 (mother's sister):
ninoshenh my aunt
noodin (VII) be windy
noogibatoo (VAI) stop running
noogishkaa (VAI) stop paddling
nooji' (VTA) catch s.o.
nookaabaawe (VAI) soften by soaking
nookiigizi (VAI) be soft (of something sheetlike)
nookomis, -ag /-ookomis-/ (NAD) my grandmother
noomaya (PC) recently, not long ago, after not too
 long a time
noondam (VAI2) hear
noondan (VTI) hear s.t.
noondaw (VTA) hear s.o.
noondaagozi (VAI) make noise, shout and yell, make
 thunder
noongom (PC) now, today
noos, -ag /-oos-/ (NAD) my father
nooshkaachigaade (VII) be winnowed
nooshkaatoon (VTI2) winnow s.t.
noozhishenh, -yag /-oozhisheny-/ (NAD) my
 grandchild: **noozis** *vocative*
noozis (NAD) *see:* **noozhishenh**
nwaandaagozi = (VTA) *changed form of:* **noondaagozi**

o- (PV) go over to
o = (PRE) *third person prefix before a consonant*
obawaanaagani (VAI) have dreams

obwaamens, -an /-bwaamens-/ (NI) gun hammer

od = (PRE) *third person prefix before a vowel in verb stems and nondependent noun stems*

odaminwaan = (VTA) *see:* **odaminwaazh**

odaminwaazh /odaminwaaN-/ (VTA) play with s.o. (as a plaything)

odawemaawi (VAI + O) have (someone as) a sibling or parallel cousin of the opposite sex

odawemaawikaawi (VAI + O) have (someone like) a sibling or parallel cousin of the opposite sex

odayi (VAI + O) have (someone as) a dog or horse

odaabaan, -ag (NA) wagon, car

odaabaanens, -ag (NA) small wagon: **odaabaanenzhish** *pejorative*

odaabaanikana (NI) railroad track, wagon road

odaabii' (VTA) drive s.o.

odaabii'iwe (VAI) drive a team of horses, go by horse and wagon

Odaadawa'amoog /odaadawa'am-/ (NA) Orion's Belt

odaan = (NAD) *see:* **/-daan-/**

odaapishkaa (VA/II) shrink

ode'imini-giizis (NA) June (strawberry moon)

odewe'igani (VAI) have drum(s)

odoodemi (VAI + O) have (something as) a totem

odoodemindiwag /odoodemindi-/ (VAI) (they) share a totem (clan) with e.o.

odoonibiins, -ag (NA) tullibe

ogaa, -wag (NA) walleye pike

ogichidaa, -g (NA) ritual attendant in a ceremony

ogichidaakwe, -g (NA) wife of ogichidaa

Ogitab (NAME) son of Aazhawakiwenzhiinh

ogiin (NAD) his/her mother: **inga** my mother

ogos = (NAD) *see:* **/-gos-/**

o'o (PR) this *inanimate singular demonstrative*

ojibinigo (VAI) have a convulsion

ojiibikaawan (VII) have roots

okaadakik, -oog (NA) cauldron, treaty kettle
okoge (VAI) build dwellings together
okoshim (VTA) pile s.o. up
okoshin (VAI) lie in a pile
okosidoon (VTI2) pile s.t. up
okwapide (VII) be tied in a bundle
omaa (PC) here
ombaangeni (VAI) raise up wings
ombibide (VII) fly up, speed up
ombigamizan (VTI) sugar s.t. off
ombigamizigan, -an (NI) boiled sugar
ombigamizige (VAI) sugar off
ombigamizigewin (NI) sap-boiling
ombijiishkaa (VAI) have a swollen stomach
onadin (VTA) form an image out of s.o. (as of snow)
onakidoon (VTI2) set s.t. up
onakin = (VTA) _see:_ **onakizh**
onakizh /onakiN-/ (VTA) set s.o. up
onapidoon (VTI2) tie s.t. up
onapijige (VAI) harness up
onapin = (VTA) _see:_ **onapizh**
onapizh /onapiN-/ (VTA) harness s.o.
onashkinade (VII) be loaded
onashkina' (VTA) load s.o. (as a pipe)
onaabiigin (VTA) string s.o. in place
onaagan, -an (NI) dish
onaagaans, -an (NI) cup, small dish
onaagoshin /onaagoshi-/ (VII) be evening
onda'ibaan, -an (NI) pump
onda'ibii (VAI) get water from a certain place
onde(magad) (VII) boil
ondendam (VAI2) strongly desire
ondin (VTA) get s.o. from a certain place
ongo (PR) these _animate plural demonstrative_
onigamiins, -an (NI) small bay
Onigamiinsing (PLACE) Vineland Bay on west shore
    of Mille Lacs Lake

Onigamiiwanishinaabe, -g (NA) resident of the Cove settlement on the south shore of Mille Lacs Lake

onikaa (VAI) have arms

onikon = (VTA) *see:* **onikozh**

onikozh /onikoN-/ (VTA) cut s.o. to fit

onishkaa (VAI) get up (from sleep)

onizhishi (VAI) be nice, be good

onizhishin (VII) be nice, be good

onji- (PV) from a certain place, for a certain reason

onjibaa (VAI) come from a certain place

onjigaa (VII) run (of a liquid)

onzan (VTI) boil s.t.

onzaam (PC) too (much)

onzaamaapi' (VTA) laugh excessively at s.o.

onzikaa(magad) (VII) come from a certain place

onzo /onzw-/ (VTA) boil s.o.

opime-ayi'ii (PC) off to one side

opin, -iig (NA) potato

opwaagan, -ag (NA) pipe (for smoking)

oshkaabewis, -ag (NA) officer, ritual official

oshk'-aya'aa, -g (NA) young person

oshki- (PRE) new, young, for the first time

oshkiniigikwe, -g (NA) young lady

Oshki-oodenaang (PLACE) Brainerd

oshtigwaani (VAI) have a head

owa (PC) *exclamation of surprise*

owaazisii, -g (NA) bullhead

owaazisiins, -ag (NA) small bullhead

owiiyawen'enyi (VAI + O) have (someone) as a namesake

ozaawizi (VAI) be yellow, be brown

ozhaawashko- (PC) green, blue

Ozhaawashkobiikwe (NAME) Maude Kegg's maternal aunt

ozhaawashko-manoomin (NI) green rice

ozhaawashkwaa (VII) be blue, be green

ozhiga'ige (VAI) tap trees

ozhige (VAI) build
ozhi' (VTA) make s.o.
ozhitaw (VTA) make something for s.o.
ozhitoon (VTI2) make s.t.
ozhiitaa (VAI) get ready
ozide-miikana, -n (NI) footpath
ozide-miikanens, -an (NI) footpath
oziisigobimizhiins, -an (NI) willow strip
ozosodamwaapine (VAI) have tuberculosis

oo (PC) oh!
oodena, -wan (NI) town: **oodenaang** *locative*
/-ookomis-/ (NAD) someone's grandmother:
   nookomis my grandmother
oonh (PC) oh!
/-oos-/ (NAD) someone's father: **noos** my father
/-oozhisheny-/ (NAD) someone's grandchild:
   noozhishenh my grandchild

sa (PC) *emphatic*
-sh (PC) and, but
/-shiimey-/ (NAD) someone's younger sibling or
   parallel cousin: **nishiime** my younger sibling or
   parallel cousin
/-shtigwaan-/ (NID) someone's head: **nishtigwaan** my
   head

/-tawag-/ (NID) someone's ear: **nitawag** my ear

w= (PRE) *third person prefix before ii- or oo- in*
   dependent noun stems
wa'aw (PR) this *animate singular demonstrative*
wanako-neyaashi (PC) at end of the point
wanendan (VTI) forget s.t.
wani' (VTA) lose s.o.
wanishin (VAI) be lost
wanitoon (VTI2) lose s.t.

wanii'igan, -an (NI) trap
wanii'ige (VAI) trap
wanoode (VAI) crawl all over
wapaa' (VTA) disturb s.o. in sleep
washki-giiwe (VAI) turn and go back, return home
washkitigweyaa (VII) flow back (as in a river bend)
wawaawiyeziwag /wawaawiyezi-/ (VAI) (they) are
   round *reduplicated form of:* **waawiyezi**
wawenabi (VAI) be seated *reduplicated form of:* **onabi**
wawenabibagizo (VAI) sit and swing *reduplicated form*
wawezhi' (VTA) decorate s.o.
wawijiim (VTA) kiss s.o. repeatedly *reduplicated form*
   of: **ojiim**
wawikwapizo (VAI) be in bundles *reduplicated form of:*
   okwapizo
wawiyadendaagozi (VAI) be thought cute
wawiinge (PC) carefully
way (PC) *exclamation*
wayaaban = (VII) *changed form of:* **waaban**
wayaanike = (VAI) *changed form of:* **waanike**
wayaawiyeyaa = (VII) *changed form of:* **waawiyeyaa**
wayiiba (PC) in a little while
wazhashk, -wag (NA) muskrat
wazhashkwiish, -an (NI) muskrat lodge
waa (PC) *exclamation*
waa- (PV) *changed form of:* **wii-**
waabam (VTA) see s.o.
waaban (VII) be dawn, be tomorrow
waabandan (VTI) see s.t.
waabashkiki (NI) swamp
waabishkawedoon (VAI) have white whiskers
waabishkizi (VAI) be white
waabizhagindibe (VAI) be bald
waabizheshi, -wag (NA) marten
waabowayaan, -an (NI) blanket
waabooyaan, -an (NI) blanket
waaginogaan, -an (NI) domed lodge

waaginogaanens, -an (NI) small domed lodge

waaj'-anokiim = (VTA) _changed form of:_ **wiij'-anokiim**

waakaabiwag /waakaabi-/ (VAI) (they) sit around in a circle

waakaa'igan, -an (NI) house

waakaa'igaans, -an (NI) small house

waanashkaa (VII) be a pool of water in a meadow

waanashkobiiyaa (VII) be a pool of water (as in a bog)

waandamaw = (VTA) _changed form of:_ **wiindamaw**

Waandane (NAME) name of a local storekeeper

waanikaan, -an (NI) excavation, pit, cellar

waanike (VAI) dig a hole, dig a grave

waaninigamiiyaa (VII) be a bay between points

waaninishkaa (VAI) circle around

waasa (PC) far, a long way

waasechigan, -an (NI) window

waawaashkeshi, -wag (NA) deer

waawaashkeshiwayaan, -ag (NA) deer hide

Waawaashkeshiwi-zaaga'iganiing (PLACE) Deer River, Minnesota

waawiyaaginan (VTI) form s.t. into circle by hand

waawiyeyaa (VII) be circular

waawiyezi (VAI) be circular

waawiin = (VTA) _see:_ **waawiinzh**

waawiindamaw (VTA) tell s.o. about something, tell s.o. to do something _reduplicated form of:_ **wiindamaw**

waawiinzh /waawiinN-/ (VTA) name s.o. _reduplicated form of:_ **wiinzh**

webaashi (VAI) be blown away

wedayi = (VAI + O) _changed form of:_ **odayi**

wedaabii' = (VTA) _changed form of:_ **odaabii'**

wedoodemi = (VAI + O) _changed form of:_ **odoodemi**

wegodogwen, -an (PR) I don't know what, I wonder what, whatever _inanimate dubitative_

wegonen, -an (PR) what? *inanimate interrogative*

wegwaagi (PC) behold

wenaagoshi = (VII) *changed form of:* **onaagoshin**

wenda- (PV) very, just *noninitial form of:* **enda-**

wenikon = (VTA) *changed form of:* **onikozh**

wenji- (PV) *changed form of:* **onji-:** **wenji-mooka'ang** east

wenjibaa = (VAI) *changed form of:* **onjibaa**

wese'an (VII) be a tornado

Wese'an (NA) Tornado

wewebanaabii (VAI) fish (with a line)

wewebikwetaw (VTA) shake one's head at s.o.

wewebizo (VAI) swing

wewebizon, -an (NI) swing

weweni (PC) properly, carefully

wewiib (PC) hurry, quick(ly)

wewiibishkaa (VAI) hurry

wewiibitaa (VAI) hurry in an activity

wii- (PV) will, want to *desiderative future*

wiidige (VAI) marry, be married

wiidigem (VTA) marry s.o.

wiidigendiwag /wiidigendi-/ (VAI) (they) marry e.o., are married to e.o.

wiidookaw (VTA) help s.o.

wiigiwaam, -an (NI) wigwam, lodge

wiigiwaamaak, -oon (NI) wigwam frame

wiigiwaamige (VAI) live in a wigwam

wiigiwaamike (VAI) make wigwams

wiigob, -iin (NI) inner bark of basswood, bast

wiigwaas, -an (NI) birch bark

wiigwaasabakway, -an (NI) birch bark roll

wiigwaasi-jiimaan, -an (NI) birch bark canoe

wiigwaasi-makak, -oon (NI) birch bark box

wiigwaasi-makakoons, -oon (NI) small birch bark box

wiij'-anokiim (VTA) work with s.o.

wiij'-ayaam (VTA) stay with s.o.

wiiji- (PV) with
wiiji' (VTA) play with s.o.
wiiji'iwe (VAI) go along with people, accompany
  people
wiijiiw (VTA) go with s.o., accompany s.o.
wiikaa (PC) ever, for a long time
wiikobin= (VTA) *see:* **wiikobizh**
wiikobizh /wiikobiN-/ (VTA) pull in s.o.
wiikwaji'o (VAI) try (to get out)
wiin (PC) *contrastive particle*
wiin= (VTA) *see:* **wiinzh**
wiinawaa (PR) they, them *third person plural*
wiindamaw (VTA) tell s.o. about something, tell s.o.
  to do something
wiindan (VTI) name s.o.
wiinde(magad) (VII) be named
wiindigoowi (VAI) be a windigo (cannibal)
wiinzh /wiinN-/ (VTA) name s.o., mention s.o.'s
  name
wiishkoban (VII) be sweet
wiishkobaagamin /wiishkobaagami-/ (VII) be sweet
  (of a liquid)
wiisini (VAI) eat
wiisiniwin, -an (NI) food
/-wiiw-/ (NAD) someone's wife: **giwiiw** your wife; *see
  also:* **/-iiw/ wiiwan** his wife
wiiwegin (VTA) wrap s.o.

yay (PC) *exclamation*

zagaswaa (VAI) smoke (tobacco)
zagaswe'idiwag /zagaswe'idi-/ (VAI) (they) have a
  ceremonial meeting, have a feast
zagaswe'iwe (VAI) have or give a feast
zagimewayaan, -ag (NA) mosquito net
zaka' /zaka'w-/ (VTA) light s.o.
zakide (VII) burn down

zayaagewe = (VAI) *changed form of:* zaagewe
zayaagewebide = (VII) *changed form of:* zaagewebide
zaziiko (VAI) spit *reduplicated form of:* ziko
zaaga'am (VAI2) go outside
zaaga'igan, -iin (NI) lake: zaaga'iganiing *locative*
zaaga'igaans, -an (NI) small lake
zaagewe (VAI) come into view, appear
zaagewebide (VII) speed into view, suddenly appear
zaagido (VAI) beg ritually
zaagigin (VII) sprout up, grow up
zaagijiba'idiwag /zaagijiba'idi-/ (VAI) (they) run out
   in a group
zaagikweni (VAI) stick out one's head
zaagiziba'idiwag /zaagiziba'idi-/ (VAI) (they) run out
   in a group
zaagizibatoo (VAI) run out
Zaagiing (PLACE) Vineland
zaasakokwaan, -ag (NA) fry bread
zaasakokwaan = (VTA) *see:* zaasakokwaazh
zaasakokwaazh /zaasakokwaaN-/ (VTA) fry s.o.
zaasitam (VAI2) hear a sizzling noise
zegi' (VTA) scare s.o.
zegim (VTA) scare s.o. verbally
zeginaagwad (VII) look scary
zegizi (VAI) be scared
zegwewe(magad) (VII) rumble
zenibaans, -ag (NA) ribbon
zesegizi (VAI) be scared *reduplicated form of:* zegizi
Zezabegamaag (PLACE) Bay Lake
zhazhiibitam (VAI2) be stubborn, not obey
zhazhiishigagowe (VAI) keep vomiting *reduplicated
   form of:* zhishigagowe
zhaaganaashiimo (VAI) speak English
zhaagwenimo (VAI) be hesitant, be timid
zhaangaso- (PRE) nine
zhaangaso-diba'igan (PC) nine miles
zhaashaaginizide (VII) be barefoot

zhaashaagwandan (VTI) chew on s.t.
zhemaagiwebinigan, -ag (NA) stick die for snake
    game
zhemaagiwebinige (VAI) play the snake game
zhingadenan (VTI) spread s.t. out
zhingishin (VAI) lie down
zhingobaandag, -oog (NA) fir bough
zhingwaak, -wag (NA) white pine tree
Zhingwaakwakiwenzhiinh (NAME) John Pine
    (Maude Kegg's grandfather)
zhingwaakwaandag, -oog (NA) pine needle, bough
/-zhisheny-/ (NAD) someone's (cross-) uncle (mother's
    brother): **inzhishenh** my uncle
zhishigagowe (VAI) vomit
zhiingendamaw (VTA) dislike s.o. (for something)
zhiishiib, -ag (NA) duck
zhiishiibiigibin = (VTA) *see:* zhiishiibiigibizh
zhiishiibiigibizh /zhiishiibiigibiN-/ (VTA) stretch s.o.
    (of something sheetlike)
zhiishiigwaans, -ag (NA) sugar cone
zhiiwaagamide (VII) thicken into syrup
zhiiwaagamizigan (NI) syrup
zhiiwaagamiziganike (VAI) make syrup
zhooniyaans, -ag (NA) dime
zhooshkonan (VTI) slide s.t.
zhooshkwaakonan (VTI) slide s.t. (of something
    sticklike)
/-zid(aa)-/ (NID) someone's foot: **inzid** my foot
zinigonan (VTI) rub s.t. with something
zinigwiingwenidizo (VAI) rub one's face with
    something
ziibi, -wan (NI) river
ziibiins, -an (NI) stream, creek
ziiga'igan, -an (NI) sugar cake
ziiga'iganike (VAI) make sugar cakes
ziiga'igaans, -an (NI) small sugar cake
ziiga'ige (VAI) mold sugar cakes

ziigigamide (VII) boil over
ziiginan (VTI) pour s.t., spill s.t.
ziigwan (VII) be spring
ziigwebinan (VTI) spill s.t., spill s.t. out
ziikoobiiginan (VTI) strain s.t.
ziinzibaakwad (NI) sugar, maple sugar
ziinzibaakwadoons, -an (NI) candy
ziinzibaakwadwaaboo (NI) maple sap
zoogipon /**zoogipo-**/ (VII) snow
zoongide'e (VAI) be brave